THE I TATTI
RENAISSANCE LIBRARY

James Hankins, General Editor

POLIZIANO

LETTERS

VOLUME I

ITRL 21

ANGELO POLIZIANO
✦ ✦ ✦
LETTERS
VOLUME I ✦ BOOKS I–IV

EDITED AND TRANSLATED BY

SHANE BUTLER

THE I TATTI RENAISSANCE LIBRARY
HARVARD UNIVERSITY PRESS
CAMBRIDGE, MASSACHUSETTS
LONDON, ENGLAND
2006

Series design by Dean Bornstein

Library of Congress Cataloging-in-Publication Data

Poliziano, Angelo, 1454–1494.
[Correspondence. English & Latin]
Letters / Angelo Poliziano ; edited and translated by Shane Butler.
p. cm. — (The I Tatti Renaissance Library ; 21)
Contents: v. 1. Books I–IV
ISBN: 0-674-02196-7 (cloth : alk. paper)
1. Poliziano, Angelo, 1454–1494—Correspondence.
I. Butler, Shane, 1970–   II. Title.   III. Series.
PA8565 .P65 2006
871′.04—dc22
2005056705

Contents

ॐ॥१॥ॐ

Introduction

꩜

Angelo Poliziano himself needs no introduction to students of Renaissance humanism or to historians of Lorenzo de' Medici's Florence. Nor is he a stranger to musicologists (by whom his *Orfeo* is given a pivotal role in the prehistory of opera) or to historians of classical scholarship (for whom he anticipates philological methods codified only centuries later). It will suffice to rehearse the basic biographical facts. Born Agnolo Ambrogini to moderately prosperous parents in Montepulciano in 1454, and sent to Florence at some point after his father's brutal murder by a rival family in 1464, Angelo (as he preferred) Poliziano (after *Mons Politianus*) caught the attention of Lorenzo de' Medici, in whose unofficial court he would soon become the leading man of letters, and under whose sponsorship he would become an arbiter of all things philological throughout humanist Italy. He used his influence above all to advocate an eclectic range of ancient models for humanist Latin, a position which brought him into conflict with those who were, instead, in Poliziano's famous (though not wholly original) formulation, "apes" of Cicero.[1]

Poliziano is that rare figure whose importance is perhaps best measured by the dyspepsia of his detractors, both Renaissance and more recent. Nevertheless, even the reader inclined to acknowledge Poliziano's genius detects something of smoke and mirrors behind the construction of his almost impossibly erudite and authoritative persona. A few of his surviving manuscripts (one thinks especially of his never-finished second *Miscellanea*) reveal the painstaking efforts behind his seemingly effortless displays of learning. But perhaps even more revealing are the narcissistic reflections and obfuscations of his correspondence, the Latin tradi-

tion's leading technology, as Poliziano well knew, of self-invention and self-presentation.

Hundreds of Poliziano's letters, both in the vernacular and in Latin, survive. Many may properly be called private. Many more, however, were written to be read by more than just the addressee. Often this was because they were, in one way or another, letters of recommendation; these often depended on Poliziano's access to the ear of his powerful patron. Others, however, rested solely on Poliziano's own authority, providing the addressee with the satisfaction and honor of a letter from the great Florentine scholar and poet — or, alternatively, asserting Poliziano's shared rank with the other illustrious humanists among his correspondents. Many of these more public letters, often written in a Latin dense with echoes of classical literature, themselves provided concrete evidence of Poliziano's erudition and eloquence. In large part, his reputation beyond Florence was built on such letters, arguably even more so than on his literary and scholarly works. At this broader level, Poliziano's letters, including not only those he wrote but also those he received, join his publications to comprise the social fabric of the *literatorum res publica*[2] in which he participated — and over which he was glad to be seen as presiding.

On May 23, 1494, Poliziano wrote to his former student, Piero de' Medici, who, two years after the death of his father Lorenzo, was still struggling to fill the Magnificent's shoes. The letter closes with this news: "I have finished the book of Letters . . . I have also produced a letter to you specifically for the preface to the entire book. I shall await your return before having them printed."[3] This (along with the promised prefatory letter, on which more anon) is all we know from Poliziano himself about the planned edition of his correspondence. Four months later, the great humanist was dead (undone by love for a boy, later detractors would claim), and his work on the edition passed, we assume, along with

others of his papers, to his student Pietro Crinito (Del Riccio Baldi).

Then, in July 1498, the Venetian press of Aldo Manuzio produced an edition of Poliziano's collected Latin and Greek works, which begins with 251 letters (by Poliziano, to Poliziano, and between his correspondents) divided into twelve "books" (*libri*). Despite unmistakable signs of re-managing by Poliziano's executors and editors, the Aldine *Epistolarum libri* must in the main preserve the corpus assembled by Poliziano himself shortly before his death. (For fuller discussion, see the Note on the Text.)

The collection opens, as promised, with a dedicatory letter to Piero de' Medici, which itself begins with echoes of Cicero's *De amicitia*.[4] As a boy, Piero, along with his younger brothers Giovanni and Giuliano, had been given to Poliziano to educate. (The boys are depicted in their teacher's train in Ghirlandaio's famous fresco in the Church of Santa Trinita in Florence.) Upon his father's death, Piero, barely in his twenties, had assumed Lorenzo's unofficial position at the helm of the Florentine republic. His fall from grace was rapid, and his inept handling of the cataclysms that attended the century's end brought exile for the entire Medici family (on November 9, 1494) and the scorn of subsequent historians. In fairness, however, it must be said that he was not dealt an enviable hand, from Savonarola in Florence to Charles VIII looming on the northern horizon.

Piero's predicament was scarcely accidental to Poliziano's decision to frame his collection in his name and to include therein several letters that sing his praises, nowhere more pointedly than in the famous letter on the death of Lorenzo (Letter 4.2), whose own opinion of his eldest son's talents Poliziano represents as glowing. Poliziano, of course, whose entire career had been built around his relationship to his patron Lorenzo, badly wanted Piero to succeed. The dedication is, in fact, more than simple flattery of the Medici

heir, for Poliziano doubtless thought, however naively, that he had something concrete to offer his former student: public demonstration of the young Medici's new position, not merely at the head of Florentine politics, but also at the front and center of the Italian cultural and intellectual scene.[5]

Nevertheless, though Poliziano's collection in this regard looks forward (albeit to a future very different from the one which fate had in store), it simultaneously looks back over a golden age to which — Poliziano himself surely knew — there could be no real return. Indeed, in the final analysis, it is tempting to regard Piero as merely the cover for Poliziano's true goal: that of putting together a kind of history of late *quattrocento* humanism, one which would document for all time (and before it was too late) Poliziano's own preeminent role. It is in this regard that the collection is best understood, for Piero and politics remain fairly peripheral to the more conspicuous assembly of vignettes of Poliziano and his humanist friends, hard at work on the revival of learning. Not surprisingly, the selection and arrangement of these were deliberate, with Poliziano's closest friends and allies predominating, and with no shortage of letters praising Poliziano himself, although, to his credit, Poliziano does not entirely exclude his critics.

The style of the letters in the collection, however, may have been just as important to Poliziano as their substance. This too began with the determination of which letters to publish and was punctuated by the dedicatory letter to Piero, in which Poliziano playfully rehearses the ancient authors to whose imitation critical readers might be tempted to attribute his epistolary style. Preparation of the present edition, however, has illuminated an intermediate phase. Several manuscript collections of Poliziano's correspondence contain letters also found in the Aldine corpus; where they overlap, comparison regularly reveals differences; in aggregate, these differences make it clear that what we find in the Aldine is often a revised version of the original letter it purports to repro-

duce. Some glaring differences have already been noticed by scholars who have blamed them on Poliziano's editors, but many or most of the changes must in fact be Poliziano's own. While it is not surprising that Poliziano would have reviewed and corrected the letters before publication, the extent of his revisions is remarkable. These range from the suppression of tedious or politically awkward passages to almost countless adjustments of stylistic details too minor to yield a change in sense but scarcely inconsequential to Poliziano's obsessive perfectionism. What is perhaps most impressive about these *pentimenti* is their widespread presence in letters written by others but included in the collection, with Poliziano lavishing improvements, for example, on the prose of his friend Pico della Mirandola. More than any other factor, these revisions make it clear that Poliziano saw the collection not as a documentary archive but as a polished and somewhat unified literary work, not unlike, in this last regard, his *Miscellanea*.

It was as literature — not, certainly, as Medici apologetics — that the *Epistolarum libri* exerted widespread influence from the moment of their publication, attracting numerous editions subsequent to (and based on) the Aldine, both with and without Poliziano's other Latin works, as well as a commentary by the French humanist François Du Bois (influential professor of and writer on rhetoric, also known for his commentaries on classical texts), first published in 1517, largely concerned with identifying Poliziano's references and allusions to ancient authors. Perhaps most notable among Poliziano's early readers was Erasmus of Rotterdam, who mined the letters for material for his own *Adagia* (published in a series of ever-expanding editions beginning in 1500). The letters had their last edition in 1644 (though facsimiles of the Aldine and of the 1553 edition of Nicolaus Episcopius were produced in the last century). By the eighteenth century, the letters were chiefly read by historians and biographers, among them William Roscoe, whose *Life of Lorenzo de' Medici, Called the Magnificent* (first pub-

lished in 1796 and often reprinted) includes what remains the best general introduction to Poliziano in English.

The publication of the *Epistolarum libri* in the I Tatti Renaissance Library represents their first modern edition and the first translation of the entire corpus into any modern language. Editorial criteria for the Latin text (which seeks to offer a readable text of the published corpus, not a reconstruction of the original letters, though some information about the latter has been provided) are explained in the Note on the Text at the end of this volume. Regarding the translation, it should perhaps be noted that some idiosyncratic expressions and technical terms often have been rendered literally to avoid confusion; thus, for example, the ubiquitous *humanitas* is generally translated "humanity" even when it seems to have little more than its normal meaning of "kindness," since, in Letter 3.11.2, Poliziano takes pains to defend the broader reach of the word that would, in later historiography, give the "humanists" their name. Finally, the Notes to the Translation aim to identify most explicit citations of classical literature but not all echoes or allusions; references by name to ancient people and places often have not been encumbered with notes when information may easily be found in the *Oxford Classical Dictionary*, which the reader is encouraged to keep handy.

I would like to extend my thanks to the following for their invaluable assistance: Stephen Campbell, Gian Mario Cao, Emma Dillon, Nelda Ferace, Anthony Grafton, Alan Grieco, Sandra Grieco, Margaret Haines, Andrew Hopkins, Sean Keilen, Nicola Marletta, Pedro Memelsdorff, Roberta Morosini, John Pollock, Michael Rocke, Peter Stallybrass, Daniel Traister, Carmela Vircillo Franklin, an anonymous reader of this book in typescript, and all of my former colleagues in the Department of Classical Studies at the University of Pennsylvania. Special thanks to James Thacker. Much of the work on this edition was carried out while I

was fortunate to be Ahmanson Fellow at the Villa I Tatti, the Harvard University Center for Italian Renaissance Studies in Florence. Additional support was provided by the Loeb Classical Library Foundation. The following libraries generously placed their manuscripts at my disposal: the Biblioteca Apostolica Vaticana; in Florence, the Biblioteca Medicea Laurenziana and the Biblioteca Riccardiana; in Philadelphia, the Rare Book and Manuscript Library of the University of Pennsylvania. Thanks as well to the Library of the American Academy in Rome. Finally, I would like to thank James Hankins, editor of this series, for his enduring enthusiasm and patience, to say nothing of his numerous suggestions and improvements.

Florence, December 2004

NOTES

1. Letter 8.16.2.

2. Angelo Poliziano, *Commento inedito alle selve di Stazio,* ed. Lucia Cesarini Martinelli (Florence, 1978), p. 20, ll. 10–11.

3. Isidoro Del Lungo, ed., *Prose volgari inedite e poesie latine e greche edite e inedite di Angelo Ambrogini Poliziano* (Florence, 1867), p. 85.

4. "You frequently have endeavored to persuade me . . . to collect my letters and edit them for publication in a single volume" (*Egisti mecum saepenumero . . . ut colligerem meas epistolas et in volumen redactas publicarem*). Cf. Cicero, *De amicitia* 4: "While you often were endeavoring to convince me to write something on friendship . . ." (*Cum enim saepe mecum ageres ut de amicitia scriberem aliquid . . .*).

5. Whether Piero was able or even willing to play such a role would, in the end, never be tested: after years of exile, he was drowned while retreating with French troops toward Gaeta in December 1503.

LETTERS

LIBER PRIMUS

Angelus Politianus Petro Medici suo s. d.

1 Egisti mecum saepenumero, magnanime Petre Medices, ut colligerem meas epistolas et in volumen redactas publicarem. Collegi, ne non in omnibus obsequerer tibi, quo sunt in uno spes omnes opesque meae sitae. Neque collegi tamen universas; id enim laboriosius quam Sibyllae folia. Non scripseram videlicet ad hoc, ut in unum corpus referrentur, sed ad usum praesentem duntaxat, oblatis argumentis, non quaesitis. Ita nec exempla mihi retinui, nisi quarundam (puto) minus felicium, quae diu iam cum blattis et tineis rixabantur. Veruntamen, ut instar voluminis efficerem, nonnullas etiam missas ad me, sed a doctis duntaxat, inserui, quae marcentem quasi stomachum lectoris excitarent.

2 Est autem omnino stilus epistolarum mearum ipse sibi dispar, quo nomine multum quoque, scio, reprehendar. Nam nec eadem mihi semper voluntas, nec idem cuique vel personae vel materiae congruebat. Non deerunt ergo qui dicant, ubi tam varias epistolas legerint (si qui modo legerint), iterum me miscellanea, non epistolas composuisse. Sed inter diversas opiniones et praecipientium de epistolis et epistolas scribentium, speravi fore profecto necubi

BOOK I

: I :

Angelo Poliziano to his dear Piero de' Medici

You frequently have endeavored to persuade me, nobly generous 1
Piero de' Medici, to collect my letters and edit them for publication in a single volume. I have collected them, so as not neglect, in
any respect, the wishes of one in whom are placed all my hopes
and means. Nevertheless, I have not collected every last one, since
doing so would be harder work than collecting the Sibyl's leaves.[1]
Needless to say, I had not written them with an eye to their eventual redaction into a single corpus, but simply for the purpose
then at hand. The subject matters were those the occasion presented, not ones for which I had gone looking. Thus I did not
keep copies for myself, except of a few, and these I regard as less
fortunate, since for a long time now they have been fighting it out
with the bookworms and moths. In any case, in order to come up
with something book-sized, I have inserted a number of letters
written also to me (though only by learned persons), so that these
can pique the reader's fading appetite.

The style of my letters is utterly inconsistent, on which score I 2
know that I will be greatly criticized. My intention was not always
the same, nor was the same thing suitable for every single person
or subject-matter. There will be no lack of people who, when they
read such varied letters (assuming anyone reads them at all), will
say that, rather than my correspondence, I have put together, once
again, a miscellany.[2] But among the various opinions both of those
who give instructions about letters and of those who write them, I
really did expect that at no point would I fail to have someone to
defend me. Perhaps someone will come along inclined to say that

mihi patrocinium deesset. Occurret aliquis forsan qui Cicero-
nianas esse neget: huic ego dicam (nec sine auctore tamen) in epis-
tolari stilo silendum prorsus esse de Cicerone. Rursus alius hoc ipsum culpabit, quod aemuler Ciceronem: sed respondebo nihil
mihi esse magis in votis quam ut vel umbram Ciceronis assequar.
Optaret alius ut oratorem Plinium saperem, quod huius et matu-
ritas et disciplina laudatur: ego contra totum illud aspernari me
dicam Plinii saeculum. Sed etsi Plinium cuique redolebo, tuebor
ita me, quod Sidonius Apollinaris, non omnino pessimus auctor,
palmam Plinio tribuit in epistolis. Symmachum si cui referre vide-
bor, non pudebit, ut cuius et brevitas celebretur et rotunditas.
Abesse rursus a Symmacho si cui credar, negabo mihi siccitatem
placere. Longiores quaedam dicentur epistolae: tales Plato scripsit,
Aristotles, Thucydides, Cicero. Dicentur aliae contra nimis bre-
ves: obiciam tunc ego Dionem, Brutum, Apollonium, Marcum,
Philostratum, Alciphronem, Iulianum, Lybanium, Symmachum,
sed et Lucianum, quem falso Phalarim vulgo putant. Damnabit
alius me quod argumenta non sint hic epistolaria: damnari me patiar, sed cum Seneca. Nolet aliquis in epistolis sententias: provo-
cabo rursus ad Senecam. Poscet alius rursum sententias: huic ergo
pro me Dionysius resistet ac pertinere sententias ad epistolam ne-
gabit. Stilus esse nimium dicetur apertus: hunc tamen laudat Philostratus. Dicetur obscurus: at est ad Atticum talis M. Tullii. Ne-
glegens erit: at epistolis neglegentia est ipsa pro cultu. Rursus erit
idem diligens: convenit maxime, quoniam pro munere mittuntur
epistolae. Si concinnitas ibi sit, asseretur a Dionysio. Si desit, ab
Artemone. Tum quoniam Romani quoque sunt Atticismi quidam,

these letters are not Ciceronian.[3] To him I shall say (not, mind you, without precedent) that, regarding epistolary style, we really need to stop talking about Cicero. Another, by contrast, will fault the very fact that I emulate Cicero. But I shall answer that nothing is more in my prayers than to catch up with even the shadow of Cicero. Someone else would have preferred me to have the flavor of Pliny the orator,[4] since his mature style and learning win praise. I shall answer back that I reject Pliny's whole era. At the same time, if to anyone's nose I am redolent of Pliny, I shall defend myself as follows: Sidonius Apollinaris, not exactly an authority of the lowest level, gave Pliny the prize in letter-writing.[5] If to someone I appear to resemble Symmachus, I shall not be sorry, given that his concision and smoothness are celebrated. On the other hand, if I strike someone else as being far away from Symmachus, I shall say that I do not like his dry style. Some of the letters will be said to be rather long: such were written by Plato, Aristotle, Thucydides, Cicero. Others, by contrast, will be said to be too short; by way of objection I shall then cite Dio, Brutus, Apollonius, Marcus, Philostratus, Alciphron, Julian, Libanius, Symmachus—and even Lucian, who commonly (and wrongly) is thought to be called Phalaris. Someone else will condemn me because, he says, my subjects are not epistolary. I shall allow myself to be condemned—but along with Seneca. Someone will not want maxims in letters: once again, I shall appeal to Seneca. Another in turn will ask for maxims: Dionysius will stand up to him on my behalf and will deny that maxims belong in a letter. My style will be said to be too open: Philostratus, however, praises this. It will be said to be obscure: but so is that of Marcus Tullius, writing to Atticus. The style will be "negligent": but in letters, neglect takes the very place of polish. Alternatively, it will be "scrupulous": always a good idea, since the sending of letters corresponds to an exchange of gifts. Should they be a home to harmony, Dionysius will take up the cause. If not, Artemon. Then, given the presence of

si non erit Attica, decebit hoc ipsum; nam quo alio damnatur Herodes quam quod Atticus homo nimis Atticisset? Sin contra nimis
Attica, Theophrastus hic proferetur, in hoc notatus ab anicula, licet homo non Atticus. Non erit festiva: me vero severitas delectat.
Non erit severa: sed ego deliciis capior. Figuras habebit: hos ergo
ipsos quasi gestus amat epistola sermoni propior. Carebit figuris:
at hoc ipsum carere figuris figurat epistolam. Promet indolem scribentis: id quoque praecipitur. Non promet: non scilicet quaesivit,
ut quae carere ambitione debet. Circulo claudetur: hoc et Graeci
faciunt. Aberit circulus: nec hoc Philostratus improbat. Soluta erit
et incomposita: non displicet Aquilae. Pedes habebit et iuncturam:
non displicet Quintiliano. Non aget: non est enim dialogus. Aget:
est affinis dialogo. 'Communiter dicis,' inquit alius, 'quae communia, nove quae nova': cum stilo res igitur congruit. Immo autem,
'Communiter nova dicis, nove communia': nempe quoniam memor sum praecepti veteris, τὰ μὲν κοινὰ καινῶς, τὰ δὲ καινὰ
κοινῶς.

3   Ad hunc igitur modum posse usquequaque spero tergiversari.
Sed tamen ipsi viderint. Tibi vero, mi Petre suavissime, certo satis-
faciam vel in epistolis, si bonae fuerint, vel in obsequio, si non
bonae.

    Vale.

certain Roman Atticisms, should a letter not actually be "Attic,"
then this very fact will give it grace. For of what other crime
was Herodes found guilty than that of Atticizing to excess even
though he was a man from Attica? But if instead a letter will be
"too Attic," Theophrastus will here be called to testify, for he was
cited for the same by a little old lady, though he was not from
Attica.[6] A letter will not be "lively": but I enjoy seriousness. Not
"serious": but I love to have fun. It will contain figures of speech: a
letter, being closer to spoken language, loves these very gestures
(pardon the metaphor). It will lack figures: but the very fact of
lacking figures gives a letter a figure. It will place the writer's natural talent on display: this too is recommended. It will not: this, of
course, was not its aim, given that a letter should do without vain
display. It will close by coming back to where it started: the Greeks
do this too. Such a structure will be lacking: no objections from
Philostratus! It will be disjointed and irregular: that's fine by
Aquila. It will contain metrical combinations: that's fine by Quintilian. It will not try to persuade: after all, it's not a dialogue. It
will try to persuade: it's closely related to dialogue. Someone says,
"You express familiar things in a familiar way, new things in a new
way": thus does my style agree with my substance. Alternatively,
"You express new things in a familiar way, familiar things in a new
way": of course! For I am mindful of that ancient advice, "Do the
usual unusually, and the unusual usually."[7]

In such a manner I hope to be able to wriggle my way out of 3
whatever comes my way. In any case, let them make up their own
minds. But you I certainly shall make happy, Piero my sweet, either with my letters, if they turn out to be good, or with my loyalty, if they do not.

Farewell.

: II :

Angelus Politianus Petro Medici suo s. d.

1 Cum saepe ex nobis audisses Florentiam, qua tu in urbe principem locum sicuti diu maiores tui merito tenes, aliam prorsus habuisse originem quam quae ab historiae nostrae scriptoribus prodatur, rogasti humanissime, quod semper soles, ut quicquid ea de re comperti haberem literis mandarem. Fore enim aiebas ut mihi civitas omnis iure deberet quod parentes ei suos demonstrassem, praesertim qui tales extitissent ut, si sumendi ex quacunque historia[1] fuissent, praestantiores omnino deligi non potuerint. Ego igitur, mi Petre, cum ut civitati gratum faciam quae me benigne semper humaneque tractavit, tum ut tibi honesta postulanti, quo nihil mihi gratius in terris vivit, obtemperem, breviter hac epistola complectar quid in literarum monimentis de urbis huius[2] auctoribus invenerim; tum de nomine ipso pauca subnectam, quoniamque satis constat etiam Faesulanos in partem civitatis fuisse acceptos, unde appellatas quoque crediderim Faesulas exponam.

2 Deduxere igitur Florentiam coloniam triumviri Caius Caesar qui deinde Augustus, Marcus Antonius, et Marcus Lepidus, etiam pontifex maximus. Coloni autem deducti: Caesariani milites, quibus assignata ducenta iugera per cardines et decumanos, quod ego apud Iulium Frontinum reperio celeberrimum scriptorem, qui Nervae aetate floruit, in libro de agrorum mensuris, quem tu librum domi habes, Petre Medices, vetustissimum. Ita, quod nulli

: II :

Angelo Poliziano to his dear Piero de' Medici

Since you often have heard me say that Florence, the city in which   1
you rightly occupy the place of preeminence that your family has
long held, had a beginning that was entirely different from the one
which is handed down by historians of our past, you have asked
me, with your customary exceeding kindness, to set down in writing whatever information I have uncovered on this subject. You go
so far as to say that the entire citizen body would be indebted to
me for revealing its progenitors, especially since these were of such
a stature that, if men were to be selected[1] from any history whatsoever, none more impressive could possibly be found. As a result,
my dear Piero, in order that I may render agreeable service to the
city that always has treated me with kindness and generosity and,
at the same time, oblige you in your honorable request (for nothing dearer to me than you lives on the face of the earth), I shall
briefly cover in this letter what I have come across in the literary
record regarding the founders of this city. To this I shall add a
thing or two about the city's name, and since it is fairly clear that
the Fiesolani were considered part of the citizen body, I shall also
explain what I believe to be the origin of the name Fiesole.

The triumvirs Gaius Caesar (later called Augustus), Marcus   2
Antonius, and Marcus Lepidus, who was also high priest, established the colony of Florentia.[2] The colonists who were settled
there were soldiers from Caesar's armies to whom two-hundred
iugera of land was allotted,[3] arranged along north-south and east-
west axes. (My source for this is Julius Frontinus, the illustrious
writer from the time of Nerva, in his book on land-surveying,
which you, Piero de' Medici, have at home in an extremely old
copy.[4]) Florentia thus owed its beginning to three generals, one of

unquam contigit, a tribus imperatoribus, quorum unus omnium summus, alter etiam pontifex maximus, orta est Florentia. Cives autem primi Florentini viri illi fuerunt quorum virtuti nulla nec arma nec munimenta nec robora restiterunt.

3   Explorata origine causam quoque nominis indagemus. Triplex Romae urbi fuisse nomen proditur, unum hoc quod diximus pervulgatum, alterum quod arcanum fuit, unde Amaryllida suam, quae amorem proprie significat, in Bucolicon carmen poeta detorsit, tertium sacrificiis debitum, de quo vocabulum Floralibus impositum, quod Anthusam Graece Philadelphus interpretatur homo doctus, a quo haec accepimus. Hoc tu Latine vel Florentem vertas vel aptius Floram fortasse aut Florentiam. Scimus autem populi Romani colonias quasi effigies parvas eius et simulachra fuisse; constat etiam Florentiam conditam ad Romae imaginem quod (ut alia praeteream) nomen quoque adhuc Capitolii et regionum quarundam testificatur. Idem autem fuisse Anthusae vocabulum Constantini urbi positum, quae nova Roma diceretur, tam Philadelphus idem quam etiam doctissimus Eustathius[3] tradiderunt. Inde igitur productum nomen unde urbs quoque ipsa producta. Nam apud Plinium vel corrupta voce Fluentinos legi pro Florentinis vel ita veteres olim populos qui profluentis Arni ripas incolerent appellatos crediderim, qui tamen deinde in Florentinos condita urbe deductaque colonia commigraverint, ut edictum quoque Desiderii Langobardorum regis Fluentinos appellantis ad utramvis redigi causam facile possit. Ptolemaeus certe, ut quidem vetusti fatentur codices, Florentiam dixit, idemque libro Historiae naturalis quartodecimo Plinius, quanquam vulgatis codicibus mendosissimus omnino sit locus. Meminit et Paulinus Ambrosii

whom was the greatest of all, another of whom was also high priest—something which has happened in the case of no other city. The first Florentine citizens were those men of old whose valor no arms or armor or might could withstand.

Having examined the city's origin, let us now investigate the reason for its name. History relates that Rome had a three-fold name: the one just given which everyone uses, a second one which was kept secret, out of which the poet fashioned for his Bucolic the name of his "Amaryllis,"[5] which properly means "love," and a third which was required for sacrificial rites. Philadelphus, our learned source for all of this, translates this last, from which the festival of Flora really takes its name, into Greek as *Anthusa*,[6] which you would translate back into Latin as *Florens* (Flowering), or perhaps better as *Flora* or *Florentia*. We know that colonies of the Roman people were something like miniature replicas of Rome; even leaving aside other evidence, it is clear from the name of the Capitol and the names of certain districts that Florentia too was first laid out in Rome's likeness. Again it is Philadelphus who relates (as does the extremely learned Eustathius) that the same epithet, *Anthusa*, had been given to the city of Constantine, inasmuch as it was said to be the new Rome.[7] The derivation of the name thus corresponds to the derivation of the city itself. For two explanations seem plausible to me: either *Fluentini* appears in Pliny in place of *Florentini* as the result of textual corruption, or this is in fact what the ancient communities that inhabited the banks of the "flowing" Arno were called, before their eventual relocation among the *Florentini* once the city had been founded and the colony settled.[8] An edict of Desiderius, king of the Lombards, calling on the *Fluentini* can easily be accommodated to either theory as well. Ptolemy certainly (as old copies testify) said *Florentia*, as does Pliny in the fourteenth book of his *Natural History*, although in the most commonly available copies the passage is utterly corrupt.[9] Paulinus, the student of Ambrose who also provides the richest

discipulus Florentiae, qui nostro[4] etiam praesuli Zenobio locuple-
tissimum sanctitatis testimonium perhibet. Indicat etiam Procopius quam etiam tum valida haec urbs et praepotens fuerit, quae
tentata saepius a Gotthis expugnari non potuit.

4   Unum antiquitatis in ea vestigium pulcherrimum[5] extat adhuc:
templum hoc mirifica structura olim Martis, nunc Praecursoris ti-
tulum gerens. Etenim Martem Romani originis auctorem Caesariani potissimum colebant milites, orbis terrarum victores, et
praecipue[6] vestrae urbis conditor Augustus, ut cui Romae quoque
medio foro cognomento Ultori posuit templum. Quominus mirandum Florentinam iuventutem, quamvis patrio more abstineat
armis, ludicris tamen adhuc certaminibus etiam inter milites exer-
citatissimos excellere. Nam de te, Petre, nihil hoc loco mihi dicendum, qui tot palmas nuper paucis diebus totiens victor abstuleris,
ne forte nostra hac epistola tui laudandi captasse occasionem cuiquam videar.

5   Faesulae restant, quas ab Atlante illo caelifero conditas et vetus
fama fert et homo ut illis temporibus doctissimus Ioannes Boc-
cacius confirmat, quae ne diutius tamen vacillet auctoritas, Hesio-
dum citare possum vetustissimum poetam, qui Faesulam fuisse
unam sed et primam nympharum declarat a quibus Hyadum, seu
Latine Sucularum, sidus exprimitur, quarum scilicet positum luna
repraesentat, quae[7] adhuc insigne Faesulanis est, nisi potius ob id
lunam gestant, quod ultima Erraticarum verticem ipsum Atlantis
caelum fulcientis potissimum premit. Sed audi iam versus Hesio-
dios, quos ex libro ipsius cui titulus Astraea, partim gravis auctor
Theon, partim Zezes ille grammaticus repetit in epistolarum sua-

testimony to the holiness of our patron Zenobius, likewise makes
mention of Florentia. And Procopius enables us to see how strong
and powerful this city was even then, when, though attacked repeatedly by the Goths, it could not be defeated.[10]

In the city a single, though very beautiful, trace of antiquity re-   4
mains visible: the temple, with its extraordinary design, which
once bore a dedication to Mars and now bears one to the Forerunner.[11] As the moving force behind Rome's origin, Mars was wor-
shipped especially by Caesar's legionnaires, but first and foremost
by Augustus, who erected a temple to him in the middle of the forum, with the epithet "Avenger." This makes it rather less surprising that the young men of Florence, although in the tradition of
their fathers they refrain from armed conflict, nevertheless continue to excel in sporting contests, even when matched with the
best-trained soldiers. In this context I should keep quiet about
you, Piero, who recently over the course of a few days again and
again carried away so many prizes, since otherwise someone might
think that in the guise of this my letter I had schemed for an opportunity to praise you.

This leaves Fiesole, which longstanding tradition holds was   5
founded by Atlas (the sky-bearer); this is confirmed by Giovanni
Boccaccio, who was as learned as one could be in his day. But in
order to prevent the authoritativeness of this view from remaining
in doubt in the future, I can cite that most ancient poet Hesiod,
who reveals that Faesula was not only one but indeed the first of
the nymphs out of whom the constellation of the Hyades (Suculae
in Latin) is formed. This remains even to this day the emblem of
the Fiesolani, for it is evident that the moon represents the arrangement of the nymphs, unless alternatively they wear the moon
because, as the last of the planets, it more than any other presses
down on the very head of Atlas as he holds up the sky. But listen
now to Hesiod's verses, which, from his book entitled Astronomy,
are repeated in part by that weighty authority Theon, in part by

rum commentariis, incomparabilis memoriae vir atque infinitae pene lectionis.

Νύμφαι Χαρίτεσσιν ὁμοῖαι,
Φαισύλη, ἠδὲ Κορωνὶς, ἐυστέφανός τε Κλέεια,
Φαιώ θ᾽ ἱμερόεσσα, καὶ Ἐυδώρη τανύπεπλος,
νύμφαι ἅς Ὑάδας καλέουσι φῦλ᾽ ἀνθρώπων.

Vides ut, Faesulam nominat Hesiodus inter Hyades potissimam, quod apud Eustathium quoque reperias, quamvis in eo mendosis codicibus Aesula sit. Sed et Ammonius grammaticus Faesulae meminit ut unius e Bacchi nutricibus. Hyades autem fuisse Atlantis filias et easdem Bacchi nutrices nullus credo paulo humanior ignorat. In ea vero civitate fulminum claros interpretes vetere Ethrusca[8] disciplina fuisse docet ita Silius: 'Affuit et sacris interpres fulminis alis Faesula.' Cui quoniam semper ego nescio quo pacto plus caeteris favi, tacere illud non possum totius etiam Italiae salutem referri acceptam Faesulanis oportere, videlicet in quorum iugo Radagasius olim Gothorum rex immanissimus cum ducentis hominum milibus orbem terrarum vastantibus, divinitus conclusus, exceptus, trucidatusque fuerit.

6   Haec sunt, mi Petre, quae de Florentia et Faesulis intacta nostris[9] annalibus apud reconditos quidem sed idoneos tamen auctores invenerim, quae nisi fallor civibus nostris tibique[10] gratissima esse debent. Ego certe nihil hoc maius, homo studiis deditus literarum, praestare vobis potui, qui me in civitatem asciveritis,[11] quam ut labore industriaque mea parentes aliquando vestros, tam

Tzetzes, a man of peerless memory and nearly infinite reading, in his commentaries on his own letters:

> Nymphs like the Graces:
> Phaisule and Koronis and well-crowned Kleeia
> and comely Phaio and Eudora of the flowing robes,
> nymphs whom tribes on Earth call Hyades.[12]

As you see, Hesiod places Faesula at the top of his list of Hyades. The same thing may be found in Eustathius, although there corrupt copies have *Aesula*. The grammarian Ammonius adds a mention of Faesula as one of the nursemaids of Bacchus. I am sure, however, that no one with even a slight acquaintance with literature is unaware that the daughters of Atlas and the nursemaids of Bacchus are one and the same. We learn from Silius that Fiesole was home to renowned interpreters of lightning by the ancient Etruscan methods: "Also present was Faesula, interpreter of lightning with its sacred wings."[13] And since in one way or another I have always been partial to Fiesole over other cities, I cannot pass over in silence the fact that it ought to be recorded that the preservation of all Italy was a gift of the Fiesolani, since it was on their ridge that Radagasius, who once upon a time was the utterly monstrous king of the Goths, was, by divine strategy, surrounded, captured, and killed, along with 200,000 of his troops, who were then laying waste to the whole world.

Here you have, my dear Piero, everything which, though untouched by our own history books, I have been able to discover about Florence and Fiesole in the works of authors who are, to be sure, obscure, but right for the job — discoveries which, unless I am mistaken, should be most welcome to our citizens and to you. As one devoted to literary studies, I surely was capable of offering all of you, in return for having adopted me into your city,[14] nothing greater than for you, by my energy and effort, to come to know

6

multis adhuc saeculis ignoratos, celebres illustresque viros agnosceretis.

Vale.

: III :

Ioannes Picus Mirandula Angelo Politiano s. d.

1 Cum Musas tenues meas, quibus, dum per aetatem licuit, de amoribus meis iocatus sum, in libellos quinque digesserim, mitto ad te illorum primum, missurus et alios[1] si in hoc uno amicum experiar te, non assentatorem. Ea enim lege ad te veniunt, ut castigentur, ut vapulent, ut erratorum poenas et ungue et obeliscis luant. Adhibe igitur te illis aequum iudicem, non iniquum, hoc est severum, non indulgentem. Nam quae maior iniquitas quam amicum fallere de te sibi omnia promittentem? Non eo usque ingenio delicato sum ut amici hominis[2] lituras fastidiam.[3] Quin forte nec tu nec quispiam crederet quam haec mea mihi non satisfaciant, quam, in his etiam quae magis placent, metuam tamen ne sim, ut inquit ille, Suffenus.[4] Quare operam tuam, quaeso, in re honesta et liberali, amicissimo homini ne deneges.[5]

Vale.[6]

that your own people, until now objects of ignorance for so many centuries, were famous, illustrious men.

Farewell.

: III :

Giovanni Pico della Mirandola[1] to Angelo Poliziano

Since I have arranged my poetic trifles, by which I made sport of   1
my love affairs for as long as youth allowed, into five books, I am
sending you the first of these and intend to send you the rest, provided that in this one I find in you a friend instead of a flatterer.
For they come to you on the strict condition that they be chastised
and spanked and that they pay the price for their errors by enduring fingernail and skewers.[2] Apply yourself to them as a fair judge,
not an unfair one—in other words, strict, not indulgent. For what
could be more unfair than to deceive a friend who counts on you
for everything? I am not so sensitive that I would be bothered by
the erasures of a man who is my friend.[3] On the contrary, probably neither you nor anyone else would believe how little satisfied I
am with these poems of mine and how, even regarding the parts
that I somewhat like, I still worry that I am being (as you-know-
who says) a Suffenus.[4] And so, in this fine and noble undertaking,
please do not withhold your aid from a man who is very much
your friend.[5]

Farewell.[6]

17

: IV :

Angelus Politianus Ioanni Pico Mirandulae s. d.

1 Ne, tu homo es lepidus qui me cum tuis Amoribus committere
tentes quique adeo severe et tetrice a me, homine haud sane rugosae frontis,[1] tam bellos accipi pueros postules. Unus (aiunt)
Amor Pana deum palaestra provocatum[2] supplantavit. Tu me con-
certare cum toto Veneris grege quam putas posse? Sed tamen hoc
tu exigis, tu, inquam Pice, cui denegari quicquam sit plane nefas.
Quare aliquot exoravi ex iis ut se a nobis vexari paulum pateren-
tur. Neque ego iudicis (ita me semper ames) sed Momi personam
indui, quem ferunt sandalium Veneris tandem culpasse cum Vene-
rem non posset. Confodi igitur versiculos aliquos, non quod eos
improbarem, sed quod tanquam equestris ordinis cedere reliquis
veluti senatoribus videbantur atque patriciis. Plebeium nihil
offendi.[3] Sed et in his non tam iudicium tibi quam voluntatem[4]
defuisse certo scio, quando et Nasoni tuo decentior (ut aiunt) facies videbatur in qua naevus esset.[5]

2 Remitto ad te eos atque addo Stoicum comitem, quem utinam
Talione tantum referiant ipsi ac non plane habeant ludibrio.
Utcunque erit, habet senecio[6] hic superciliosus ubi patientiam
suam exerceat. Non erit iam quod clamet ὦ Ζεῦ βρέχον τὰς πε-
ριστάσεις. Non Bitus et Bacchius[7] melius compositi.

3 Reliqui quos petis negant ferre lucem. Tu me ama, id quod mutuo facies.
Vale.[8]

: IV :

Angelo Poliziano to Giovanni Pico della Mirandola

My, you are a wit to match me with your *Loves* and to require that   1
such attractive boys be received by me—though I hardly am the
type to wear a furrowed brow—with such nasty strictness. They
say that Love all by himself challenged Pan, a god, to the ring and
threw him on his back.[1] How do you suppose that I can wrestle
with Venus's whole team? Nevertheless, you—yes, you, Pico, who
can be refused in nothing, no matter what it is, without gross sac-
rilege—insist on this. And so I prevailed upon a few of them to
endure a little abuse from me. But I chose to play the part not of a
judge (may you always love me this much!) but, rather, that of
Momus, who, as the story goes, criticized Venus's sandal, since he
could find no fault with Venus herself. Thus I pricked a few little
verses, not because I rejected them, but because they seemed to
give way to the others, like members of the equestrian order before
senators and patricians. I ran into nothing plebeian.[2] And yet I am
sure that herein lies a failure, not so much of judgment as of will,
since, as they say, a face looks prettier with a mole, even to the eyes
of your Naso.[3]

I am sending them back to you and am adding a Stoic compan-   2
ion.[4] Let's hope they limit their return blows to "an eye for an eye"
and do not make an utter fool of him. Whatever happens, the cur-
mudgeon will have a chance to test his patience. No longer will
there be reason for him to exclaim, "O Zeus, pour rain upon these
misfortunes." Bitus and Bacchius weren't better matched.[5]

The others you ask for say they cannot bear the light of day.   3
Return my love with your own.
Farewell.[6]

: V :

Ioannes Picus Angelo Politiano s. d.

1 Nec urbanius unquam nec hilarius acceptos se Amores mei praedicant quam his proximis diebus apud te, et quod amice quidem
confossi sunt, cum sibi gratulantur maxime, tum tibi plurimum
debent. Quis enim nolit ab isto ense mori? Dolent tamen indul-
gentius id factum esse quam oportebat, atque in eo sunt ut dubi-
tent amore ipso in Amores te caecutientem factum meos, ac ita demum dubitant ut iudicio tuo alioqui gravissimo in sua causa non[1]
satis confidant. Confidunt tamen et iam sese vinculis asserunt;
domi esse nesciunt; libertatem et publicum secure postulant.

2 Sed quid de Epicteti tui festivitate dicam? O rem iocosam et
risu dignam Catoniano. Vix erat in limine cum pandens sinus,
'En,' inquit, 'obelos, en sagittas, si nescitis Graece, en me, si ex vestris quisquam audax fuerit paratum referire.' Quis cachinnis tem-
perasset, cum Stoicus homo tam lepide iocaretur? Abstinuimus
profecto telis, et quod interminatus erat repositurum sese iniuriam, et quod ita cutis occalluerat, ut tam leves ictus non admitte-
ret. Qua igitur veneratione debuimus, senem excepimus, qui ut
demum apud nos consedit, philosophari coepit de moribus, et id
quidem Latine, non tam ob id, quod apud Latinos erat, nam et
erant in eo consessu qui Graeca noverat, quam quod Latine ipse

: V :

Giovanni Pico to Angelo Poliziano

My *Loves* declare that they never have enjoyed a reception more 1
stylish or entertaining than that which greeted them over the
course of the past few days at your house. Even as they themselves
take full credit for the friendly way in which you did it, they
are enormously in your debt for pricking them at all. Yes, who
wouldn't want to die on the receiving end of that sword of yours?
Still, they regret that this was done more gently than it should
have been. They even go so far as to consider the possibility that,
blinded by love itself, you see my loves only dimly, to the point
that their confidence in your otherwise unsparing judgment wa-
vers regarding their own case. All the same, they do have confidence, and already they are loosing themselves from their bonds;
they do not know how to stay at home; they fearlessly demand
freedom and a public.

But what can I say about the sense of humor your Epictetus 2
has? It really was funny, even worth a laugh from Cato. He was
barely on my doorstep when he bared his chest and said, "Behold
the *obeloi*, behold (in case you don't know Greek) the arrows, behold me — ready to strike back if anyone from your side is feeling
reckless." Who could keep from laughing while the man, though a
Stoic, offered such witty entertainment? We swore off weapons altogether, both because he had threatened to repay violence with
violence and because his skin was too thick to be susceptible to
such soft blows. Therefore we received the old man with the respect we owed him. And when at last he took his seat among us,
he began to discourse on moral philosophy, and he did so in Latin,
not so much because he was among Latin speakers, for some of
those sitting among us were acquainted with things Greek, as be-

beneficio tuo luculentius saperet. Sed nec operam perdidit, quandoquidem non prius loqui desiit, quam nos ex Peripateticis Stoicos fecerit, et apathian illam omnes approbaverimus, ut iam videre sit paulo ante delicatos homines, iam factos omnium tolerantissimos, qui lacessiri quidem possimus ab aliis, laedi a nobis tantum, qui fato reluctemur nunquam, et quae nostra non sunt, sic fieri demum velimus ut dii volunt, et eos nec culpemus unquam, nec accusemus, nihil doleamus, nihil expostulemus, servire, vinci nesciamus, re, non oratione, philosophemur, et qui novicii sumus, nos ipsos ut adversarios observemus, aliorum de nobis opinionem atque id genus[2] alia, quae externa sunt, negligamus potius quam reiciamus, ad diem curremus, ut hospitium viatores, habeamus ea denique non habeamur, silentium amemus, nequicquam evomatur non concoctum; et nobis alii raro, et nos aliis nunquam risum pariamus, et ut uno Epictetum totum verbo complectar, et substinere adversa, et abstinere voluptatibus abunde didicerimus.

3   Vide quam singulatim[3] ad Epictetum tuum effinxerimus vitam nostram. Vide quam et cito, ne hac quoque parte Stoici non essemus qui nos admonitos volunt, tandiu deficere hominem, quandiu non proficit, id quod, quanquam in caeteris admiratus sum, in me tamen uno, vel maxime, qui cum semper in Lycio vel Academia, nunquam in Porticu sim versatus,[4] ita victus sum oratione senis ut in eius sententiam non pedibus modo, sed manibus quoque et toto corpore discesserim.[5]
    Vale.

cause, thanks to you, his wisdom shines more brightly in Latin. Nor were his efforts in vain, given that he did not stop speaking until he had turned us from Peripatetics into Stoics and all of us had endorsed the principle of freedom from emotion. The result is that one can now see men who a little while ago were addicted to pleasure but who now are second to none in their ability to endure anything: we can be attacked by others but injured only by ourselves; we never resist fate; we want things which do not pertain to us to turn out in the end according to the will of the gods, whom we never reproach or blame; we experience no grief or pain; we make no demands; we are incapable of servitude or defeat; our philosophy is real, not rhetorical, and being novices, we regard ourselves as adversaries; rather than challenge others' opinions of us (and other things that are likewise beyond our control), we ignore them; like travelers to a place of repose, we hasten to our appointed day (when that day finally comes, ours is not the loss but the gain); we adore silence; nothing comes out of our mouth that we have not chewed on thoroughly; others seldom give us reason to laugh, and we never give reason to others; and, to give you all of Epictetus in a nutshell, we have learned beyond measure how to endure adversity and abstain from pleasure.[1]

Note how we have fashioned our life point by point after the model of your Epictetus. Note too how quickly we have done so, not wanting not to be Stoics in this respect as well, since they want us to heed this warning: a man's failure is measured in time spent without profit. Though I often have been surprised by such change in others, I am especially so in my own particular case, for, although I have always frequented either the Lyceum or the Academy, never the Portico,[2] the old man's discourse has so convinced me that I have gone over to his way of thinking, making the move not just with my feet, but with my hands too — indeed, with my whole body.

Farewell.[3]

: VI :

Angelus Politianus Ioanni Pico Mirandulae s. d.

1 Tanti mihi sunt literae tuae, mi Pice, ut nullo pacto credam posse me illis rescribendo satisfacere. Tanta rursus tua est humanitas, ut te boni consulturum quicquid a nobis proficiscatur existimem. Si verba suppeterent animo, laudare pro merito ingenium, literas, eloquentiam tuam conarer. Sed vereor ne laudes cogar tantas, ut Flaccus inquit, culpa deterere ingenii. Quare imitabor Timantem, quodque exprimere penicillo non possum, velo contegam. Quod si mihi hortandus est, qui ipse omnibus exemplo sit, ita ego meum Picum ut ille Mycenaeus Teucrum hortabor, βάλλ' οὕτως.

2 Tibi autem debere me multis nominibus intelligo, quae singula enumerare non est consilium, sed accessit meritis erga me tuis Manuelis nostri viri docti elegans epistola, Hymettio illo, unde scilicet eam legit, melle atque omni nectare dulcior. Eum nos plane Glaucum reddidimus, χάλκεα χρυσείων commutantes. Quis enim nescit quam illi ἐπιχώριοι τοῖς Ἕλλησιν ἀττικισμοὶ degenerent citra mare? Sed tamen hoc ipso minus eius obelos metuimus: quod in Latio nati sumus, sicut Latina cum scribimus perperam, hoc nos tuemur, quod Graecissare putamur, atque ut vespertiliones, dum neque mures plane neque aves sumus, utrisque tamen nos probare tentamus.[1]

Vale.

: VI :

Angelo Poliziano to Giovanni Pico della Mirandola

Your letter means so much to me, my dear Pico, that I do not 1
think there is any way I can do justice in reply. But then again,
your kindness is such that I count on your being happy with whatever issues from me. I tell you this: if the right words would come,
I would try to offer your talent, your literary learning, your eloquence the praise they deserve. But I fear that I would be forced
"for want of talent to diminish merits" of such magnitude, as Horace says.[1] And so I shall imitate Timanthes, and what I cannot express with the brush, I shall conceal with the veil.[2] But if he who
is by himself a model for everyone needs encouragement from me,
I will encourage my Pico as that Mycenaean encouraged Teucer:
"Keep shooting like that!"[3]

I realize that the ledger of my debts to you is long, and I do not 2
intend to list each and every item, but add to your services on my
behalf our learned Manuel's[4] elegant letter, sweeter than either the
honey of Hymettus[5] (his source, of course) or any nectar. Trading
"bronze for gold," we have turned him into a complete Glaucus.[6]
For who doesn't know how those Atticisms native to the Greeks
degenerate on this side of the sea?[7] And yet the very fact that we
were born in Latium makes us fear his daggers less, in the same
way in which, when we write bad Latin, we protect ourselves behind the assumption that we are Hellenizing, and like bats, even
though we are not fully mice or birds, we try to make ourselves
convincing to both.[8]

Farewell.

: VII :

Angelus Politianus Ioanni Pico Mirandulae suo s. d.

1 Audio te versiculos amatorios quos olim scripseras combusisse, veritum fortasse ne vel tuo iam nomini vel aliorum moribus officerent (non enim, puto, quoniam minus exierint apte) sicuti Plato suos dicitur. Nam quantum repeto memoria, nihil illis tersius, dulcius, ornatius, quos quia vocabas Amores tuos, placuit mihi nuper, velut in Amores ipsos abs te crematos, ita ludere Graecis versibus:

2 Πολλάκι τοξευθεὶς φλεχθείς θ᾽ ὑπὸ Πῖκος Ἐρώτων
οὐκ ἔτλη προτέρω, πάντα δ᾽ ἀφείλεθ᾽ ὅπλα,
τόξα, βέλη, φαρέτρας, καὶ νηήσας τά γε¹ πάντα
ἧψεν ὁμοῦ σωρὸν λαμπάσι ληϊδίοις.
Σὺν δ᾽ αὐτοὺς μάρψας, ἀμενηνὰ χερύδρια δῆσεν
ταῖς νευραῖς, μέσσῃ δ᾽ ἔμβαλε πυρκαϊῇ²
καὶ πυρὶ φλέξε τὸ πῦρ. τί δ᾽ ὦ ἄφρονες αὐτόν, Ἔρωτες,
τὸν Πῖκον Μουσῶν εἰσεποτᾶσθε πρόμον;

: VIII :

Ioannes Picus Mirandula Angelo Politiano s. d.

1 Quod proximis literis tuis me tantopere laudaris, debeo tibi tantum quantum ab eo absum ut merito lauder. Id enim debetur cuique quod gratis dat, non quod persolvit. Quare et ipse id totum

: VII :

Angelo Poliziano to his dear Giovanni Pico della Mirandola

I hear that you have burned the erotic epigrams you wrote   1
some time ago, worried, perhaps, that they might prove detrimen-
tal either to your reputation or to others' morality, just as Plato is
said to have done with his. Not, I assume, because they turned out
badly. For if memory serves, nothing was more polished, more
pleasant, more splendid than these. Since you called them your
Loves, I decided the other day to amuse myself in Greek verse as
follows, as if describing those very Loves being consigned to the
flames by you:

Pico, often pierced and set aflame by Loves   2
    More would not bear, but took their every arm,
Bows and arrows, quivers too, and all amassed.
    The heap he torched with stolen flames.
They themselves he seized, and tied their tender hands
    With strings, and hurled them on the pyre.
Fire he burned with fire: why then, o foolish Loves
    to Pico, Prince of Muses, did you fly?[1]

: VIII :

Giovanni Pico della Mirandola to Angelo Poliziano

Given the degree to which you compliment me in your most re-   1
cent letter, I am in your debt to the precise extent that I am unde-
serving of your praise. A debt to someone corresponds to what he
gives freely, not to what he pays as due. Thus I myself owe you the

tibi debeo quod de me scribis, cum in me tale sit nihil; cum id mihi ipse nullo pacto deberes, id totum tuae fuit humanitatis et singularis in me benivolentiae. De caetero si me examinaris, nihil invenies nisi tenue, humile, angustum. Novicii sumus atque tirunculi, qui ex inscitiae tenebris pedem modo movimus, promovimus fere nihil. Benigne nobiscum agitur si inter studiosorum ordines referamur. Habet docti nomen quiddam aliud quod sit tibi et tui similibus peculiare; mihi tam grandia non conveniunt, cum eorum quae in literarum studiis sint praecipua, nihil non solum exploratum habeam, sed nec adhuc etiam nisi per transennam viderim. Conabor quidem, id quod nunc ago, talis esse aliquando qualem nunc me praedicas et esse aut iudicas aut certe velles.

2   Interea imitabor te, Angele, qui te Graecis excusas quod sis Latinus, Latinis quod Graecisses. Simili et ego utar perfugio, ut poetis rhetoribusque me approbem propterea quod philosophari dicar, philosophis quod rhetorissem et musas colam. Quanquam[1] mihi longe aliter accidit atque tibi, quippe ego dum geminis sellis (ut aiunt) sedere volo, utraque excludor, fitque demum, ut dicam paucis, ut nec poeta nec rhetor sim, neque philosophus. Tu ita utrunque imples ut utrunque magis haut satis constet, qui et Graecam et nostram[2] Minervam ita pulchre amplectaris, quasi cinnus[3] utriusque linguae, ut quae insiticia sit, quae genuina,[4] non facile discerni possit. Nam ut de Latinis taceam (de his enim cui e primo loco cesseris?) quis credat, ut de Hadriano ille, Romanum

full sum of what you write about me, since in me there is nothing of the sort. Since you did not owe me this in any way, it belongs fully to your kindness and extraordinary good will towards me. Otherwise, if you look at me closely, you will find nothing that is not weak, common, limited. We are beginners, young recruits who have only just set foot outside the gloom of ignorance; we barely have taken a single step. Things are going well for us if we are counted among the students on their benches. To call someone "learned" suggests something else, something peculiar to you and others like you. Such lofty titles do not fit me, since not only do I have no first-hand knowledge of those matters which are of chief importance in literary studies, but I have not even caught sight of them except through the garden gate. But I shall try (I am already working on it) to be one day the kind of person you now prematurely say I am, the sort of person you judge — or at least want — me to be.

Meanwhile, I shall imitate you, Angelo, excusing yourself for your Greek by saying you are Latin, and for your Latin because you are trying to be Greek. I too shall employ a similar dodge in order to make myself acceptable to poets and orators, because I claim to be philosophizing, and to philosophers, because I orate and worship the Muses. Nonetheless, things turn out far differently for me than they do for you, since, while I want to sit, as they say, in two seats,[1] I am excluded from both, and to be brief, the end result is that I am neither orator nor philosopher. You so fulfill both roles that it is not quite clear which you do better. For you so beautifully embrace both Greek talent and our own — like a cocktail of the two languages — that it cannot easily be determined which is foreign and which is native. Indeed, to say nothing of your Latin compositions (for regarding these, to whom have you relinquished first place?), who would believe "that a Roman could speak such good Greek," as a certain someone says about Ha-

hominem tam Graece loqui? Iurabat Emanuel noster, dum tuas legeret, non esse tam Atticas Athenas ipsas.

3   Is es mi Angele (facessat adulatio) cui ex nostris unus aut alter (ne dicam, nemo) conferendus sit. Quod si plures essent tales, non haberent haec saecula cur inviderent antiquitati. Incumbe, quaeso, et literas quantum potes a situ recipe, ne nitor ille Romanae linguae iniuria[5] temporum penitus obsolescat. Excude semper aliquid novum, quod rem Latinam adiuvet et illustret, et quae domi habes, fac tandem exeant in communem studiosorum utilitatem.[6]
Vale.[7]

: IX :

Hermolaus Barbarus Angelo Politiano suo s. d.

1   Post discessum tuum Venetiis, ad te scripsi nunquam, de te saepe. Nec scripsi modo saepe,[1] sed etiam locutus sum de te, quotiens incidebat. Incidebat autem cum volebam, volebam semper. Omnino mihi multus in ore Politianus est, eritque dum vixero. Nam quantum ipse de te conceperim, cum primum te cognovi, quantum porro de doctrina tua literae sibi sperent et spondeant, facilius cogitare possum animo quam dicere.

2   Postulo autem a te quasi meo iure duo: primum, uti vivere diu studeas, non tibi—sed et tibi sane, dum literis primum et bonis

drian?[2] Our friend Manuel, as he was reading your letter, swore
that Athens itself is not more Attic.

My dear Angelo, you are the sort of person (let flattery be far   3
from my mind) to whom just one or two of our contemporaries —
lest I say no one — ought to be compared. But if there were more
men like you, our age would have no reason to be jealous of antiquity. Work hard, I beg you, and, to whatever extent you can, rescue literature from its decay, so that the brilliance of the Roman
tongue may not grow entirely dim through the damaging effects of
time. Always be hammering out something new that can lend aid
and luster to the Latin cause. And see to it that whatever you have
at home finally comes out, to the advantage of all scholars alike.[3]
Farewell.[4]

: IX :

Ermolao Barbaro to his dear Angelo Poliziano

Since you left Venice[1] I have sent you no letters, but many have I   1
written about you. Not only were you the frequent subject of my
writing, but I also spoke about you as often as the occasion arose.
Actually, the occasion arose whenever I wanted it to, and that was
always. The name of Poliziano is constantly on my lips, and so it
will be for as long as I live. I can contemplate more easily than I
can express in words how fine an opinion I formed of you when
we first met, how much in turn the world of letters is hoping
for — indeed, is counting on — as a result of your learning.

But I claim the right to make two requests of you. The first is   2
that you endeavor to live for a long time, not for your own sake —
well, for your own sake too, of course, as long as you do so primarily for the sake of literature and the liberal arts, which, for heaven's

artibus, quibus hercule succurrendum est, ruinosis et nutantibus brevique casuris, nisi per solertissimos homines ope summa prospiciatur, alterum, uti aut tu me socium in haec adhibeas aut a me adhibitus aequo animo patiare. Sin gravaris, in famulatu ero tibi cum iusseris. Ultro nomen do, profiteor invocatus et maxime voluntarius. Ardeo cupiditate iuvandi recta studia. Nullus est tam magnus labor, nullum munus in literis tam sordidum quod defugiam, quanquam omnis fere functio quae pertinet ad literas non potest esse non honesta, non splendida, non magnifica.

Vale.[2]

: X :

Angelus Politianus Hermolao Barbaro suo s. d.[1]

1 Tu vero, Hermolae, ita mihi omnia, vel praesenti prius, vel deinde absenti, praestitisti, ut, si officia duntaxat, non autem animum atque voluntatem remetiamur, ingratus proculdubio sim moriturus. Et quidem ea causa est cur tibi nec agam gratias nec egerim hactenus, quod intellego non orationem modo nostram sed plane facultatem omnem imparem esse tuis erga me meritis. Nam quod mihi in tua epistola tantum tribuis quantum ego nec agnosco nec fateor, vel ob id certe mihi gratum est, quod amicius quam verius sentiens, magis fortasse nos diliges. Verba porro quibus, velut me militem, bonus imperator hortaris, ut rectis studiis, utroque quasi

sake, need help, for they are crumbling and tottering and any moment now will collapse unless measures are taken by experts using all means at their disposal. The second request is that you either use me as an ally in these efforts or else patiently allow yourself to be so used by me. If you do not find me burdensome, I shall be in your service whenever you give the word. I am signing up without being asked, enlisting without being drafted—a complete volunteer. I burn with desire to come to the aid of virtuous studies. In the field of literature, no effort is so great, no job so menial that I would turn my back, though virtually no assignment pertaining to literature can fail to be honorable, illustrious, magnificent.

Farewell.[2]

: X :

Angelo Poliziano to his dear Ermolao Barbaro

You, Ermolao, have provided me with everything, first when I was   1
present, then when I was absent, and to such a degree that, even if
I calculate just what you have done for me and not what you have
planned or wished to do, I unquestionably will die guilty of ingratitude. This, in fact, is the reason why I do not thank you now nor
have done so hitherto—namely, because I realize that my every capacity (not just my power of speech) is inadequate in the face of
the things you have done that deserve my thanks. I find it particularly gratifying that, in your letter, you credit me with more than I
recognize or acknowledge, since this means that you are basing
your opinion of me more on friendship than on the truth and so,
perhaps, will like me somewhat more. The words with which you
then urge me, as a good general urges a soldier, to come to the rescue of virtuous studies—in trouble, as it were, on both flanks—

cornu laborantibus succurram, eo me minus moverunt, quod sane quam paucos tui similes video quos duces sequar. Ut enim non dubitat Agamemnon quin sit brevi Troiam capturus si sibi[2] decem dentur συμφράδμονες Nestoris similes, ita[3] si Hermolai mihi denter decem sub quibus meream, facile sperem literas, cum Graecas tum Latinas, e barbaria media receptum iri. Te tamen et laudo et admiror, qui adeo accisis rebus atque afflictis, spem tibi aliquam feceris adhuc reliquam. Quapropter mihi etiam vel ob id 'audentem extrema cupido est certa sequi.'[4]

Vale.[5]

: XI :

Angelus Politianus Hermolao Barbaro suo s. d.

1 Quod ad te iamdiu nihil, Hermolae, dederim literarum non tam meis velim quam tuis occupationibus adscribas. Occupationes autem non minus equidem studia ipsa literarum et sapientiae quibus usquequaque invigilias quam istos accipio discursus obeundae legationis et rei gerendae publicae. Quid igitur vel ineptius vel inhumanius quam aut Musarum sacris operanti obstrepere, aut agenti rem seriam, trichas[1] veluti intempestivas obicere? Neque vero causa fuit cur timuerim ne (quod est apud Aristotelem tuum) nostram quoque amicitiam silentium dirimeret. Non enim sic in amore mutuo languemus ut simus inter nos machinis retinendi.

have less of an effect on me, given that I see so very few men like you whom I might follow into battle. Just as Agamemnon does not doubt that Troy would soon be captured if he were given ten advisors like Nestor,[1] I too, if I were given ten Ermolaos under whose command I might serve, might readily hope that both Greek and Latin letters will be recovered from the heart of barbarism.[2] You have my praise and my astonishment, since, even in such a mangled, ruined state of affairs, you still have left yourself a ray of hope. And so I too, if only for this reason, have "steady desire to follow the darer of desperate measures."[3]

Farewell.[4]

: XI :

Angelo Poliziano to his dear Ermolao Barbaro

Please attribute the fact that I have not sent you a single letter in   1
such a long time, Ermolao, not so much to my own responsibilities as to yours. And as I see it, your responsibilities include precisely those literary and intellectual pursuits over which you are always burning the midnight oil, no less than the back and forth of participating in delegations and conducting state business. What, therefore, could be more improper or inconsiderate than to make noise and distract someone who is performing the sacred rites of the Muses, or to have the bad timing to throw baubles in the path of someone doing something serious? Naturally there was no reason to worry that silence would cause an interruption in our friendship as well. (This can be found in your Aristotle.)[1] We are not so weak in our love for one another that we need to be held together in an artificial way.

2   Sed nec silentium quispiam interpretetur ubi neuter cessat honorifice de altero et loqui et scribere. Cave enim putes, Hermolae,
non diem dixerim sed horam pene ullam praeterire in qua non ego
de ingenio, de literis, de prudentia, de consilio, de humanitate, de
candore, de studiis denique tuis prope declamitem. Testis Medices
Laurentius meus, testis hic item Mirandula Picus, heroes arbitror
duo, non viri, quos aut auditores habeo laudum tuarum attentissi-
mos, aut benevolentissimos praedicatores. Iam apud eruditam iuventutem et familiarium cohortem tantum de te loquendo pro-
fecimus ut unus utique habeare non solum doctissimus sed et
humanissimus et prudentissimus. Porro autem ut epistolas, ut orationes omiserim, in quis de te semper a nobis illustris mentio
facta, vel haec ipsa quae mox edentur, Miscellanea nostra, cum
quidem, ut Horatius inquit, dignus vindice nodus incidisset, te
scilicet una cum Laurentio Picoque iudicem sibi contra rudem inscitiam nuncupaverunt.

3   Neque vero tu quoque ociosus aut occasionibus imparatus in
me semper, etiam ultra fortasse quam patior, ornando extol-
lendoque sic ut temet pulcherrime ab hoc epistolarum silentio crebris de me sermonibus redemeris. Non igitur amicitiam nostram
blandimentis istis et assentationibus indecoris et ineptis atque optimo cuique maxime suspectis, addo etiam vulgaribus, fovemus.
Non tamen ullo loco vel studio desumus alter alteri, vel officio.
Speciosa ista et popularia benevolentiae ostentamenta quasique fucum et praestigias neque tu, arbitror, desideras, et ego abominor.
Vino, aiunt, vendibili suspensa hedera nil opus. Et nos ergo faciem

But really, no one should understand as "silence" a situation in   2
which neither ceases to speak or write about the other with esteem. Do not dare think, Ermolao, that a day—nay, scarcely a single hour—passes in which I do not make your talent, literary
learning, knowledge, wisdom, refinement, integrity, and finally
your studies practically the subject of an extemporaneous speech.
My dear Lorenzo de' Medici is my witness, as is Pico della Mirandola, both of them in my judgment not men but demigods, whom
I employ either as attentive listeners to or as devoted singers of
your praises. Already among young men of erudition and the
ranks of courtiers we have accomplished so much by speaking
about you that you, and you alone, are regarded not only as the
most learned of men but also as the most refined and wisest. I
should, besides, say nothing about my letters, nothing about my
lectures, in which I always make a glowing mention of you. Even
my forthcoming publication, the *Miscellanea*, at a point at which,
as Horace says, "there comes a knot of its redeemer worthy,"[2] appeal to you by name, along with Lorenzo and Pico, to be their
judge in the case against rude ignorance.

You too, however, in the way in which you are always putting   3
me on a pedestal, maybe even beyond what I can bear, have not
been idle or unequipped with opportunities to redeem yourself
most beautifully for this epistolary silence by frequent conversations about me. We do not, therefore, nourish our friendship with
those words of flattery others use and those silly, unseemly expressions of adulation that sound entirely suspicious to any gentleman
and even, I might add, to ordinary people. Nevertheless, neither of
us at any point disappoints the other in terms either of support or
of dutiful service. I do not think you want—and I despise—those
shallow and common performances of affection which are like
masquerades and magic tricks. As the saying goes, wine worth
buying doesn't need to advertise.[3] And so let's spurn every pre-

strepitumque omnem (sic doctos decet) aspernemur, atque amicitiae (quod dicitur) personam detrahamus.

4   Caeterum ut eo tandem deveniam qua gratia tibi hanc epistolam scribere institueram: cum Franciscus Gaddius Florentinus, qui paulo ante legatus istic agebat, vir utrique nostrum coniunctissimus, forte, ut fit, in sermone apud Laurentium Medicem nuper iniecisset desiderare te volumen, si quod hic emendatum Dioscoridis haberemus, statim nobis Laurentius, ut est homo tui studiosissimus, pro more, auctoritateque mandavit, ut eam rem quamprimum, quam diligentissime curaremus. En tibi igitur librum, mi Barbare, satis emendatum, ni fallor, certo veterem. Tu cum fueris usus, ad me remittes, non tam (quae tua est diligentia) incolumem, quam doctissima ista notatum manu, quo pretium volumini aliquod ex te atque auctoritas accedat.

Vale.[2]

: XII :

Hermolaus Barbarus Angelo Politiano suo s. d.

1   Si surdis etiam brutisque rebus amicitiae et inimicitiae suae non aliunde quam a coelo constant, quo et affectus caecos et quae graeci ἀναιτιολόγητα vocant referimus accepta, quidni sentiat hanc vim et homo? Quanquam[1] interest quod stolida illa et muta

tense and empty noise (as befits the learned) and, as they say, take off the mask of friendship.

But let me finally come around to why I set about writing you   4
this letter. On one of those frequent occasions when Francesco Gaddi[4] of Florence, who not long ago spent time in your city as an envoy, a man very attached to both of us, happened to be in conference with Lorenzo de' Medici, he remarked in passing that you needed a copy of Dioscorides,[5] if we had an accurate one here. Lorenzo, being your very devoted supporter, immediately instructed me, in accord with his custom and his authority, to take care of the matter as soon and as thoroughly as possible. And so here you have your book, my dear Barbaro — a fairly accurate copy, unless I am mistaken, and, at any rate, an old one. I ask you, when you have finished with it, to send it back not so much in good condition (I trust you to be careful) as annotated by that very learned hand of yours, thus lending the volume additional value and authority from your personal supply.

Farewell.[6]

: XII :

Ermolao Barbaro to his dear Angelo Poliziano

If even brute, insensate things derive their attractions and repul-   1
sions from no place other than the heavens — source, in the accepted view, both of invisible influences and of what the Greeks call "the unmotivated" — why should human beings not also experience this force?[1] The difference, however, lies in the fact that, in relation to one another, dumb and unthinking entities separate or cohere, each type according to its own properties, by the agency of the heavens alone, whereas judgment and shared customs attach

semper inter se pro natura quaeque sua dissident aut concordant unius coeli merito, sed hominem homini plerunque mores et iudicia conciliant, nec minore glutino quam istaec siderum[2] defluvia ferruminant. Huiusque[3] generis est amor qui nos invicem innexuit et Herculeo nodo iunxit.[4] Nihil mirum si nec spatio temporis excutitur,[5] nec locorum intercapedine convellitur, nec officiorum silentio polluitur, nec alia quavis negligentia rubigine decoloratur. Certa opinione virtutis et doctrinae tuae natus, eadem opinione conservatur, alitur, augetur. Te volente nolenteque perennat, tandiu hercule futurus, non (dico) me quandiu ames, sed quandiu amare cogas, et iste ingenii et eruditionis tuae fulgor obversetur oculis. Tunc amare potero desinere, cum tu rem Latinam deserere. Sed de hoc satis.

2   Dioscoridem accepi. Gratias et tibi et Gaddio nostro tam multas ago ut quas Laurentio meo agam, homini clarissimo, humanissimo, doctissimo non habeam, habeam quas non ago. Atque utinam quandocunque possim referre.[6] Multis nos magnus ille vir in dies et studiis accumulat et officiis adobruit. Ego contra diu noctuque retracto ac recogito, non quemadmodum rationem cum eo parem faciam (quis enim possit hoc, nisi alter Hercules, aut certe alter Laurentius?), sed quemadmodum plane intelligat me apud eum eo loco esse cupere quo qui magnitudinem aeris alieni et professione nominis et magnae fidei compensatione redimunt.

Vale.[7]

people to one another, binding them together by no lesser glue than that involved in stellar emanations. To this category belongs the love that has tied the two of us to one another, joining us in a Herculean knot.[2] This is not to be sloughed off by the passage of time, or torn apart by a geographical gap, or compromised by the quieting of services rendered, or discolored by the rust provoked by any other lack of maintenance. Born of conviction regarding your excellence and learning, it is preserved, nourished, increased by the same conviction, and whether you like it or not, it will endure, lasting, I swear, not as long as you love me, I would say, but as long as you force me to love, and as long as the brilliance of your genius and erudition appears before me like a vision. I shall be able to stop loving you when you abandon Latinity. But enough on this subject.

I received the Dioscorides. I send you and our dear Gaddi so 2 many thanks that I have none left to send my Lorenzo, the most illustrious, generous, and learned of men. What I do not send, I sense as gratitude: If only I might one day repay my debt thereof![3] Day by day that great man showers me with a mounting supply of support and overwhelms me with service on my behalf. For my part, I spend day and night mulling over, not how I can square my account with him (for who could do this except for another Hercules, or at any rate another Lorenzo?), but, instead, how I can make him fully aware that I long to be there with him, in the company of men who discharge their mass of debt by declaring what they owe and then balancing the credit extended to them with an equally great measure of fidelity.[4]

Farewell.[5]

: XIII :

Angelus Politianus Hermolao Barbaro[1] suo s. d.

1 Explicare non possem literis, Hermolae, quanta mihi laetitia pran-
denti nuper secum Laurentius Medices te patriarcham factum esse
Aquileiensem nuntiaverit. Ego vero tanto sum ex ea re gaudio tan-
taque voluptate perfusus ut in ipso quoque discubitu (quid enim
manifesta negem?) gestierim, exilierim, laetum felicemque nun-
tium, vix ipse me capiens, proclamaverim.

2 Et nunc gratulor tibi, gratulor doctis omnibus, gratulor saeculo,
Hermolae: tibi quod hoc etiam tuarum virtutum praemium dixerim an testimonium publice acceperis (nam quanvis antea quoque
multis magnificisque[2] fueris ornamentis affectus, tamen hoc unum
procul excellit atque eminet, non modo quia maius aut quia genere
diversum, sed quod per eum, quasi gradum, brevi putaris altius as-
censurum), doctis vero quod is vir ad maximas proveheris dignita-
tes cui semper hoc hominum genus atque haec secta vitae plurimum placuit (etenim summo loco natus, amplis opibus innutritus,
egregiis honoribus perfunctus, et fastigium disciplinarum prope
omnium tenes, et professores ac studiosos artium bonarum, quanvis humili fortuna plerunque sumus, ita complecteris et amas ut
aeque cunctis tuae quasi maiestatis fasces ac vexilla submittas),
saeculo autem, quod insigne aliquod habet quo iam stare audacter
adversus et vetustatem possit et posteritatem, scilicet quia veluti
recuperasse nunc oculos caeca prius fortuna videri potest, dum cu-

: XIII :

Angelo Poliziano to his dear Ermolao Barbaro[1]

I cannot express in a letter, Ermolao, how great my joy was when   1
Lorenzo de' Medici, the other day when I was having lunch with
him, divulged the news that you had been made patriarch of
Aquileia. I was filled with so much pleasure and delight by the fact
that this had happened that right there in the dining room (for
why should I deny what everyone knows?) I waved my hands,
jumped for joy, and, barely able to control myself, shouted out the
happy and auspicious news.

And now I congratulate you, I congratulate all learned men, I   2
congratulate our age, Ermolao. You I congratulate because you receive publicly what I know not whether to call the reward for or
the proof of your virtues. For although you have been awarded
many distinguished honors in the past, this one far surpasses the
rest and stands apart, not only because it is greater, or because it is
different in kind, but because by way of it, as by a stepping stone,
you are soon expected to climb higher. I congratulate the learned
because you, the sort of man who has always liked this class of
people and this way of life, have been promoted to the most illustrious ranks. Born of the highest station, reared on ample resources, and having discharged offices of great distinction, you occupy the summit of almost every discipline, and you so embrace
and cherish those who are devoted to liberal studies (though we
generally are of humble position) that you lower the flags and rods
of what one might call your sovereignty before all comers, without distinction. I congratulate our age because it has some badge
to wear with which it can now stand boldly face-to-face with
both antiquity and posterity, particularly since Fortune, previously
blind, seems now, as it were, to have regained its eyes, while it has-

mulare honoribus eum gestit in quo virtutum pene omnium quasi quidam concentus exauditur

3   Tu igitur, etsi virtute ipsa clarior es atque, ut puto, laetior quam virtutis praemio, debes tamen hanc et temporibus et literis diligentiam: ne fortunae desis neu vota nostra destituas, sed incubas instesque favori quantum potes, non quidem ambitu infami, qui philosophum dedecet, sed his potius artibus quae te carum bonis, admirabilem prope universis reddiderunt. Equidem, quod ad me attinet, quando aliter suffragari non licet, illud usquequaque praestabo, ne quam occasionem vel tui celebrandi nominis vel conciliandae tibi colligendaeque benevolentiae praetermittam.

Vale.[3]

: XIV :

Hermolaus Barbarus Angelo Politiano suo s. d.[1]

1   Quod ex secundis rebus meis laetitiam incredibilem conceperis, neque novam rem fecisti, nec mihi non praevisam, imaginationeque praesumptam. Novi quanta propensione atque adeo inductione animi provinciam duram et inexplicabilem susceperis ornandi et tollendi nominis mei, quam constans, pertinax, et adductus in eo fueris, quam rem tuam videaris agere, cum meam agis. Itaque nihil sum miratus, quod rationibus tuis consultum

tens to shower with honors one in whom a kind of harmony of all
the virtues is heard.

Therefore, even if your fame and, I think, your satisfaction are 3
due more to virtue itself than to virtue's prize, you nevertheless are
bound, by your obligations to literature and to our times, to take
pains not to forsake your fortune or abandon our prayers but instead to use, to the greatest possible extent, this favor shown you
as a support and a step. You should do this not, of course, out of
disgraceful ambition, which ill suits the philosopher, but rather for
the sake of those arts which have made you dear to good men
and a marvel practically to the whole world. And as for me, when
circumstances permit no other form of support, I always and
everywhere will offer this: to overlook no opportunity either to
celebrate your fame or to procure and accumulate for you the
favorable disposition of others.

Farewell.[2]

: XIV :

Ermolao Barbaro[1] *to his dear Angelo Poliziano*

Just because you say you derived incredible joy from the fact that 1
things have gone well for me does not mean that you did anything
that was new or that I had not anticipated and enjoyed thinking
about in advance. I know with how much eagerness as well as
mental energy you have taken on the laborious and complicated
task of embellishing and elevating my reputation, how reliable,
persistent, and serious you have been in this, how you seem to be
managing your own affairs when you really are managing mine.
Therefore I was not at all surprised that you believed the measure
was taken with your interests at heart, when actually it provided

putaveris cum meis est provisum. Habeo tibi et semper habebo gratias, non solum ut amico et benivolo, sed ut Politiano, id est ut[2] homini doctissimo. Plus enim est a Politiano quam ab amico laudari. Testimonium et iudicium amici fallitur; Politiani etiam amantis non fallitur.

2   Laurentio non minus principi tuo quam meo in dies plura et maiora debeo. Testis est ipse. In magno versor periculo ne in tanto meritorum eius erga me cumulo et ingratus et barbarus esse videar.

Vale.[3]

: XV :

Pomponius Laetus Angelo Politiano s. d.

1   Serius quam opinabaris ab amicissimo fieri distuli ad te mittere quod summo opere legere optabas. Causa fuit nescioquis qui se intra paucos dies daturum Quintilem et Sextilem mihi pollicitus est, remque is longius opinione mea traxit. Ipse tandem, ut creditori, qui vel praecipuus es, satisfacerem, quae apud me erant diligentissime exscripsi. A Venusia Apulorum adlata sunt marmorea in tabula. Obscuro loco ibi latebant fragmenta aliarum tabularum. Ubi annus integer erat coniungi nequiverunt, quod multa deerant. Illinc translata Arianum. Summa cura quae superest tabula servatur.

2   Mitto et quaedam monimenta rerum eodem in loco reperta et placitura tibi, ut existimo, amatori vetustatis. Romae fere idem,

for my own. To you I am and always shall be grateful, not only as one is to a friend and well-wisher, but as one is to Poliziano, that is, as to the most learned of men. Being praised by Poliziano means more than being praised by a friend. The testimony and judgment of a friend is unreliable, but not that of Poliziano, even in the case of someone he loves.

Every day my debts to Lorenzo, no less your prince than mine, 2 grow in number and magnitude. He himself is my witness. In the face of the mountain of things he has done for me, I find myself running the serious risk of seeming ungrateful—and "barbarous."

Farewell.[2]

: XV :

Pomponio Leto to Angelo Poliziano

I put off sending you what you most earnestly desired to read for 1 longer than you were expecting a friend to do. The reason was this person who promised to give me Quintilis and Sextilis[1] within a few days but who dragged the thing out for longer than I expected. At long last, in order to satisfy you who are my chief creditor, I myself carefully copied out the ones here with me. They were brought, written on a marble tablet, from Venosa, in Apulia. In the same place lay fragments of other tablets, hidden from view by their obscure location. They could not be joined anywhere to make a complete year, since many pieces were missing. Everything was transported from there to Ariano. The surviving tablet is being preserved with the utmost care.

I am also sending some inscriptions found in the same place 2 that are sure to please you, I think, as a lover of antiquity. Roughly the same thing in Rome. But much older. Missing the last part,

sed multo ante. Verum fine caret. Si habere cupis, rescribe, quanquam quid hoc dixerim, cum facile intellegam te plurimum id quaerere? Sed videbatur optabilius si poposceris. Scias omnia quae apud me sunt tua esse.

3   Duo a te sum petiturus. Alterum studio, alterum auctoritate conficies. Illud est apud Valerium Flaccum in quinto libro, cum loquitur de Chalybibus populis, apud quos ferrum repertum est: quid sibi velit 'indigena'? Quod sequitur corruptum est. Et statim duo carmina quae sequuntur fabulam habent mihi incognitam. Forte Apollonius aliquid de ea re scribit. Tuum limatissimum iudicium expecto, quod, mea sententia, quicunque profitemur literas, veneremur necesse est. Sed de ingenio nescioquid scripturus sum.[1]

4   Illud alterum erat, ut unicis literarum fautoribus, Laurentio ac filio, me commendes. Ab Laurentio tua opera obsecro impetres literas non vulgares, sive ad Ioannem Tornabonum, sive ad oratorem Florentinorum, in commendationem Fabritii contubernalis mei, qui, ut praedicat, notissimus est Laurentio. Aliasque Florentiae negocia Reguli Faventini egit. In praesentia cum sit expediturus quaedam honestissima in Curia Romana, auctoritatem Laurenti, quae plurima est, vehementer accedere cupit. Effice tu, homo non minus literatissimus quam integerrimus, ut voto fruamur.

Bene valeas.

Romae, xvi Calendas Apriles MCCCCLXXXVIII

however. Write back if you want to have it. But what am I saying, since it's easy for me to see you asking for it, plenty. But I decided it was preferable to make you insist. Know that everything in my house is yours.

I'm going to make two requests of you. One you will fulfill 3 by study, the other, by your influence. The first involves a passage of Valerius Flaccus, book five, where he is talking about the Chalybes, by whom steel was invented.[2] What could that *indigena* mean? What follows is corrupt. And the two verses that immediately follow contain a legend unknown to me. Maybe Apollonius says something about this? I await your most polished judgment, which, in my opinion, absolutely everyone who teaches literature has to worship. But I'm planning to write something or other on the subject of your genius.[3]

The other request was that you recommend me to those peer- 4 less patrons of letters, Lorenzo and his son. I urgently ask you to obtain from Lorenzo by your own means a letter of recommendation, written (not in the vernacular) either to Giovanni Tornabuoni[4] or to the Florentine ambassador, for my protégé Fabrizi,[5] who, according to what he tells everyone, is very well known to Lorenzo. In places other than Florence he managed the affairs of Regolo from Faenza. At present, since he is about to work through some very respectable matters in the Roman Curia, he earnestly desires Lorenzo's additional authority, which is considerable. Most literary and honorable of men, see to it that we get our wish.

Stay well.

Rome, March 17, 1488

: XVI :

Angelus Politianus Pomponio Laeto s. d.

1 Quas a te nuper accepi literas ita gratas habui, mi Pomponi, ut me ab iis putem immortalitate donatum. Sed et semenstre calendarium mire fuit gratum, et quam ais tabulam bello Marsico factam, quae si eadem est quam Romae obiter legerim, vereor ut satis ex fide sit exscripta, siquidem Aimilius, non Aemilius erat in saxo, quam eandem diphthongum etiam super[1] ipsa Panthei testudine adnotaveram.

2 Quod vero etiam (si diis placet) de obscuris poetarum me consulis, homo omnis literaturae consultissimus, atque[2] id mihi ex amore tribuis quod tibi ex vero debetur. Intellego quam tibi debeam, quam mihi faveas, quantum oneris sustineam. Dicam tamen quod sentio, tibique si non rem ipsam, studium certe meum voluntatemque probabo.

3 Versiculi ipsi quos vere mendosos putas hi sunt videlicet:

Indigena aeterni rupem Iovis, hinc tibi Mavors
dant virides post terga lacus, ubi deside mitra
foeta legat, partuque virum fovet ipsa soluto.

hos equidem ita legendos arbitror:

Inde Genetaei rupem Iovis, hinc Tibarenum
dant virides post terga lacus, ubi deside mitra
foeta ligat, partuque virum fovet ipsa soluto.

: XVI :

Angelo Poliziano to Pomponio Leto

I am so pleased by the letter I just received from you, my dear 1
Pomponio, that I think I have been granted immortality by it. But
the six-month calendar was wonderfully welcome too, as was what
you say is a tablet produced during the Marsian War. If this latter
is the same one which I skimmed when I was in Rome, then I am
worried that it has not been transcribed accurately, given that
"Aimilius," not "Aemilius," was on the stone.[1] I had noted the
same diphthong also atop the very dome of the Pantheon.

But in that you, the leading expert on all literature, consult me 2
(so please the gods!) even about obscure passages in the poets, you
bestow on me out of love what is truly owed to you. I am aware of
how much I owe you, of how much favor you are showing me, of
how great a burden I am assuming. Nevertheless, I shall say what
I think and prove to you, if not my actual answer, then at least my
effort and my willingness to try.

The verses which you rightly think corrupt are as follows: 3

Indigena aeterni rupem Iovis, hinc tibi Mavors
dant virides post terga lacus, ubi deside mitra
foeta legat, partuque virum fovet ipsa soluto.

They should in my own opinion be read as follows:

Inde Genetaei rupem Iovis, hinc Tibarenum
dant virides post terga lacus, ubi deside mitra
foeta ligat, partuque virum fovet ipsa soluto.[2]

[Next comes the rock of Genetean Jupiter; then they put to
their backs the green lakes of the Tibareni, where the

ut sit sensus: post Chalybas, promontorium Genetaei Iovis dant post terga, hoc est praeternavigant. Tum virides lacus Tibarenorum, virides scilicet quoniam pecore abundant adque³ ob id pascuis. Quibus scilicet Tibarenis mos est uti a parturientibus, iamque etiam partu liberatis, uxoribus viri in lecto mitrati collocentur, et ipsi vicem puerperarum foveantur, curenturque. Quod ex Apollonio mira brevitate tralatum, cuius in libro secundo sunt hi versus:

Τοὺς δὲ μετ᾽ αὐτίκ᾽ ἔπειτα Γενηταίου Διὸς ἄκρην
γνάμψαντες σώοντο παρὲξ Τιβαρηνίδα γαῖαν.
ἔνθ᾽ ἐπεὶ ἄρ κε τέκωνται ὑπ᾽ ἀνδράσι τέκνα γυναῖκες,
αὐτοὶ μὲν στενάχουσιν ἐνὶ λεχέεσσι πεσόντες,
κράατα δησάμενοι, ταὶ δ᾽ αὖ⁴ κομέουσιν ἐδωδῇ
ἀνέρας, ἠδὲ λοετρὰ λεχώια τοῖσι πένονται.

4   Addunt interpretes Apollonii scriptum id etiam a Nymphodoro in τισι Νόμοις.⁵ Tum Genetaeum promontorium a Genete fluvio vocatum, in quo templum sit hospitalis Iovis, quem ξένιον⁶ appellant. Idem eodem libro sic scribit Apollonius:

ἄγχι δὲ ναιετάουσι πολύρρηνες Τιβαρηνοί,
Ζηνὸς Εὐξείνοιο Γενηταίην ὑπὲρ ἄκρην.

Quo loco πολύρρηνες ab agnorum copia dicti, unde virides lacus erudite dixit Valerius, ob pascua, ut arbitror. De Tibarenis etiam Orpheus in Argonauticis post Chalybas meminit statim, et eosdem Strabo libro xii Tibarnos appellat.

pregnant woman wraps her husband in the idle turban, and, after childbirth, *she* looks after *him*.]

The resulting sense is this: After the Chalybes they "put to their backs" the cape of Genetean Jupiter; that is to say, they sail past it, followed by the "green lakes of the Tibareni"—green because they abound in livestock and thus in pastures. These Tibareni have a custom by which men, with their heads wrapped, are positioned in bed by their wives in labor (and even after they have given birth), and they themselves, instead of the women in labor, are looked after and taken care of. This is adapted, with remarkable economy, from Apollonius, whose verses (in book two) are as follows:

Right after these they round the cape of Genetean
Zeus and then dart past the land of the Tibareni.
In that place, when women bear their husbands children,
not they but the men, with their heads wrapped, fall into bed
and groan, while the women in turn see to it that their men
are fed and prepare for them the child-bed baths.[3]

The commentators on Apollonius add that the same thing was written by Nymphodorus[4] in his *Local Customs*. The cape is called "Genetean" after the river Genes, because on it there was a temple of Jupiter the Host, whom they call Xenios. Apollonius again, in the same book, writes,   4

Nearby dwell the lamb-rich Tibareni,
past the Genetean cape of Zeus the Good Host.[5]

Here they are called by a Greek word meaning "lamb-rich" because of the large number of lambs. Prompted by this, Valerius, in an erudite turn, calls the lakes "green," on account of the pastures, in my opinion. Orpheus too, in his *Argonautica*, mentions the Tibareni immediately after the Chalybes, and Strabo in book twelve calls the same people the "Tibarni."[6]

5   Quod autem de Eribote quaesieras, fuit is filius Teleontis, de
quo sic idem scribit Apollonius:

Εἵπετο δ' Εὐρυτίων τε καὶ ἀλκήεις Ἐριβώτης,
υἷες ὁ μὲν Τελέοντος, ὁ δ' Ἴρου Ἀκτορίδαο·
ἤτοι ὁ μὲν Τελέοντος ἐυκλειὴς Ἐριβώτης,
Ἴρου δ' Εὐρυτίων. σὺν καὶ τρίτος ἦεν Ὀιλεύς·

6   Literas contubernali tuo commendaticias ad oratorem Floren-
tinum paulo negocio impetrabimus a Laurentio Medice, qui si
mihi quasi uni e minutioribus literatis nihil non indulget, cur quicquam tibi literarum principi deneget?

7   Vale, et si quid te dignum ex antiquitate habes, participa,
quaeso, nobis, tui cupidissimis. Et Vasinio dic salutem meis verbis.

Florentiae, iiii Calendas Maias[7] MCCCCLXXXVIII

: XVII :

Pomponius Laetus Angelo Politiano[1] *s. d.*

1   Iam tempus appetit, eruditissime et candidissime Italorum, ut Lucretii libros remittas, ut vir integer fidem solvas. Dabis ferendos ad
urbem Petreio, homini fidei summae, qui celebritatem tui nominis
cum caeteris nostri ordinis amat, colit, veneratur. Nam quisquis
est qui de se bene senserit gratulari plurimum debet saeculo nostro, cum tales habeat viros quales maiores nostri in summa gloria
habuisse duxissent. Data opera Florentiam se confert ut te saepius
visat et ut totus ex lima tua pendeat. Utinam et mihi liceret. Cum

As for what you ask about Eribotes, he was the son of Teleon. 5
Again it is Apollonius who writes about him, as follows:

Eurytion followed, and valiant Eribotes,
one the son of Teleon, the other, of Actor's son Irus,
that is, famed Eribotes was the son of Teleon,
and Eurytion, of Irus. A third, Oileus, was with them too.[7]

The letter of recommendation to the Florentine ambassador for 6
your protégé we shall have no trouble obtaining from Lorenzo de'
Medici, who, if he indulges me, as one of literary studies' minor
figures, in everything, why should he refuse you, Prince of Letters,
anything at all?

Farewell, and if you have anything worthwhile from antiquity, 7
please share it with me, someone who completely adores you. And
say hello to Vasinio for me.

Florence, April 28, 1488

: XVII :

Pomponio Leto to Angelo Poliziano[1]

The time is ripe, most learned and fair of the Italians, for you to 1
send back the books of Lucretius and pay off your credit without
damage to your reputation. Give them, for delivery to the city, to
Petreio,[2] a highly trustworthy fellow who, along with other members of our circle, loves, fosters, worships the fame your name enjoys. Indeed, anyone who is not insecure[3] should warmly congratulate our age, since it possesses the sort of men the possession of
whom our ancestors counted toward the summit of glory. He has
gone to some trouble to get himself to Florence so that he can see
a great deal of you and never lift his eyes from your file.[4] If only I
were allowed to do the same! When I think about the lofty

de altitudine tui ingenii cogito, non possum non admirari cur nostri gracculatim et sturnatim (ut ita loquar) ad te non advolent.

2 Legi opus tuum, in quo apertissime doctrina quadam singulari veteres ab inferis revocasse videris. Sed parcius in praesentia. Praedicatione mea non indiges: satis enim tuo labore clarus es. Verum quoties de aliquo sublimi interpretatio est, unus Politianus occuris. Ego quid de perspicacissimo ingenio tuo sentiam una epistola et longa quidem explicui, quanquam in ea re quid longum esse potest? Credo distulisti carmina Lucretii remittere propter variarum disciplinarum occupationem. Opsecro atque optestor: effice ut ad suum Quirinum redeant.

3 Habeo quaedam vetustissima monimenta, quae cum videris opstipesces admiraberisque, quae nuper effossa erutaque, et inventa in illa tua observatione reperiantur. Qua de re divinitatem quandam in te esse intellego, ut vere animus tuus sit de coelo sumptus ignis. Dii te servent.

4 Commenda me Medicibus patri et liberis, literarum patronis. Deinde plurima salute Demetrium impertias.

Vale.

Romae, ante v Calendas Iunias

: XVIII :

Angelus Politianus Pomponio suo s. d.

1 Lucretium Petreio dedi quem tibi iam redderet. 'Vah, tam sero,' inquis. Fateor. Sed non plus neglegentia mea quam tuae humani-

heights of your genius, I cannot help wondering why my circle doesn't flock to you jackdaw-like and starling-wise, so to speak.

I have read your book, in which you plainly seem, by a kind of 2 unparalleled learning, to summon the ancients back from the underworld. But I'll limit what I say right now. You do not need public praise from me: You are famous enough as a result of your own hard work. Indeed, every time there is a question about the meaning of something sublime, you alone present yourself by name. I have explained what I think about your extremely acute intellect in a letter—indeed, a long one, though on this subject, what can be long? I'm sure you put off sending back the verses of Lucretius because of the time you spend on multiple learned disciplines. I beg and beseech you to see to it that they return to their Quirinus![5]

I have some very ancient inscriptions at which, when you see 3 them, you will stare in stunned silence, because things just dug and pried out of the ground turn out to be discoveries already known to those powers of observation you have. From this I recognize that there is a kind of divine quality in you—though truly your mind is fire taken from heaven. May the gods keep you.

Put in a good word for me with the Medici, father and chil- 4 dren, patrons of letters. Finally, give Demetrius[6] a big hello.

Rome, May 28

: XVIII :

Angelo Poliziano to his dear Pomponio

I gave Petreio the Lucretius to return to you, which by now he will 1 have done. My, you say, how late! I admit it. But as a result no more of my negligence than of confidence in your kindness and

tatis fiducia, dum alia ex aliis in quibus opera ponatur occurrunt, dilatus hic in quadriennium liber est, qui vel triduo potuerat apsolvi. Caeterum ego Pomponi mei memor, qui quidem nescit offendi, a Politiano praesertim, praetuli audacter officio commodum.

2   Petreio nondum frui licuit ut optabam, probo et antiquis moribus homine. Iam tum peregre aberam cum ille Florentiam, statimque peregrinationem meam rusticatio excepit. Spero, tamen, dierum paucorum iacturam, ut in urbem revertimus, inrupta (quod aiunt) copula sarciet.

3   Quas in me laudes confers, quanquam agnoscere salva fronte non ausim, tamen ob id gratissimas habui, quoniam cum nec irrisio in istos mores nec adulatio cadat, necesse est laudatio haec aut ex amore in[1] me nimio, aut ex vero proficiscatur, quorum cum sit utrunque mihi gloriosum, alterum diu in votis, alterum etiam supra vota est.

4   Monimenta illa quae narras antiquitatis iam iam tractare, complecti, adorare gestio. Per fortunas imperti, si quid habes, quod excellat.

5   Medices nostri unice tibi favent. Demetrius autem salutem sibi a te dictam totidem verbis remuneratur.[2]

Vale.

In Faesulano, vi Idus Augustas MCCCCLXXXXI

: XIX :

Baptista Guarinus Ioanni Pico Mirandulae s. d.

1   Nondum concedo secundum te litem dari oportere. Nam facile possum tuas istas captiones in te ἀντιστρέφειν. Si tibi prae-

generosity, while one thing after another came up that required attention, this book was put off for four years, when it could have been thoroughly dealt with even in three days. Instead, mindful of my Pomponio, who does not know how to be offended, especially by Poliziano, I confidently placed convenience before duty.

It has not yet been possible to enjoy the company of Petreio as I 2 had wished. He's a good man, with character you do not find today. I was already on my way out of town when he arrived in Florence, and a stay in the country immediately followed my journey. But as soon as I return to the city, what they call "a bond not put asunder"[1] will mend, I hope, the loss of a few days.

For the praise you bestow on me, though I should not acknowledge it if I want to avoid embarrassment, I nevertheless am grateful, and for this reason: since neither scorn nor flattery is consistent with your character, your words of praise must necessarily arise either from excessive love for me, or else from the truth. Though either would bring me glory, I have long hoped for the first, but the second is beyond even my fondest hopes.

As for those inscriptions from antiquity you describe, I absolutely cannot wait to handle, to embrace, to adore them. If you have anything that stands out, then for heaven's sake share it.

Our Medici give you their unrivaled support. Demetrius repays, by the same number of words, the hello said to him by you. Farewell.

The Villa at Fiesole, August 8, 1491

: XIX :

Battista Guarini to Giovanni Pico della Mirandola

I do not yet concede that this dispute should be decided in your 1 favor. For I can easily turn those sophistic arguments of yours

ceptor sum, cur mihi non obsequeris? Si non sum, cur me praeceptorem appellas? Neque ideo nomen hoc recuso, quod te discipulum spernam, quem mihi praeceptorem assero, sed quod tuam
doctrinam et veneror et praedico, in qua te neque unguium meorum nota, neque transversi calami signo, neque miniata caerula,
neque obelisco denique aut asterisco, tantum promovisse mihi
conscius sum. Sed in novum quoddam vindiciarum genus, ut video, incidimus, dum tu mihi eam possessionem asserere contendis
qua ego cedere conor. Quae unquam rhetorum causa huius generis
actorem aut reum habuit? Ego, mi Pice, nunquam in hac pugna
tibi herbam porrigam, nisi prius bona cum gratia composuerimus
ut, quando aliter non succumbuis, uterque nostrum alteri praecep-
tor pariter et discipulus iudicetur.

2   Sed omissis iocis seria agamus. Et Heptaplus tua et tu ipse merito placere potes, cum omnia doctorum hominum puncta ita sis
assecutus ut, ne in tabellae quidem latebra, livor ullus appareat.
Idem in reliquis scriptis facilius tibi datum iri sperandum est cum
usus etiam accesserit, qui solet in scribendo magister haberi optimus. Quod ad me attinet, gaudeo vehementer laudato viro et ab
omnibus ac ubique laudando Laurentio me in ore esse. Addito
praesertim Politiani calculo, cuius ego copiosam et arcanam multi-
plicis disciplinae lectionem ita complector, ut admirer, ita admiror,
ut commendare non desinam. Quo fit ut extra doctrinae aleam me
ab illo poni, triumphi instar existimem.

3   Quod librorum meorum indicem petis, id mihi et laboriosum
est et inutile. Satis erit si pro tempore postulatis meis inservies.
Nunc Martianum Capellam et Senecae Quaestiones Naturales

against you. If I am your teacher, why do you not humor me? If I am not, why do you call me your teacher? Nor do I refuse the label because I reject you (whom I claim as my own teacher) as a student but because I greatly admire and publicize your learning, in which I am fully aware that you have made huge progress without any fingernail-marks of mine, or signs of erasure, or red pencil, or, finally, any dagger or asterisk. But as I see it, we are entering upon a new kind of property-claim when you seek to declare that I have possession of something which I am trying to abandon. What law-school case of this sort has ever had a real plaintiff or defendant? In this fight, my dear Pico, I myself will never throw in the towel, unless we first combine our assets amicably, so that (seeing that you will not give in otherwise) each of us can be judged to be equally teacher and student of the other.

But enough joking: let's get down to business. You have every   2
right to be pleased both with your *Heptaplus*[1] and with yourself, since you have so completely won all the votes of the learned that not even in the secrecy of the ballot-box does any resentment leave its mark. One should hope that the same will be granted to you even more readily in your future written works, when you will have the additional advantage of experience, which in writing tends to be regarded as the best instructor. As for me, I am exceedingly glad to be on the lips of that celebrated man, who should be celebrated everywhere and by everyone, Lorenzo, especially when you throw in Poliziano, whose extensive and arcane reading in various branches of learning I hold so dear that I long to possess it, and such is my longing that I do not stop praising it to others. And so it is that I regard my being raised by him above any vicissitude of value[2] as nothing short of a triumph.

As for the list of my books you ask for, you are making a diffi-   3
cult and pointless request, as far as I am concerned. It will be good enough for you to attend to my requests as they arise. Right now I would like Martianus Capella and the *Natural Questions* of Seneca,

opto, si modo emaculati sint codices. Nam qui apud nos sunt opera Sibyllae indigent. Eos[1] si impressos emere possim, gratius mihi erit. Sin minus, non longo postliminio tui ad te redibunt.

4 Vale specimen bonarum disciplinarum, meque amare perge.
Ferrariae, Nonis Decem. MCCCCLXXXVIIII

: XX :

Angelus Politianus Baptistae Guarino suo s. d.

1 Ostendit epistolam mihi nuper ad se tuam Ioannes Picus Mirandula, princeps omni laude cumulatissimus. In ea cum tu mihi multum tribueres ex recenti Miscellaneorum foetura, tum vero seorsum in sceda syllabas notasti aliquas in quibus[1] meam nonnihil diligentiam requirebas. Sed hoc posterius tamen, ita cunctanter, ita suspitiose fecisti,[2] quasi denique metuisses ne me laedi gravius putarem sicubi abs te non doctissimo solum viro sed optimo quoque redarguer.

2 Ego igitur, quanquam dissimulare non possum laudationem mihi tuam fuisse pro eo ac debuit omnino gratissimam, tamen ut eam quoque plausibilius exciperem, causa fuit in primis quod abunde fidem blanditiis illis tuis comes addita libertas, ne dixerim castigatio, faciebat. Etenim non ego avidius refellam quam refelli

as long as they are not corrupt copies. For the ones here await the efforts of a Sibyl. If I can buy them printed, that would be more to my liking. If not, then yours will come home to you by an undeferred right of return.

Farewell, paragon of liberal studies. Keep loving me. 4

Ferrara, December 5, 1489

: XX :

Angelo Poliziano to his dear Battista Guarini

Giovanni Pico della Mirandola, that prince overflowing with all 1 manner of praise, has shown me your recent letter to him. In it, although you make much of me over the recent birth of my *Miscellanea*, you nevertheless, on a separate sheet, list a few syllables in which you detect a degree of inattentiveness on my part.[1] But you present this as an afterthought, so hesitantly, so cautiously, as if in the end you were afraid that I might think myself grievously offended if on any point I were contradicted by you, not only the most learned of men, but also the best. Although I cannot hide the fact that your praise gave me enormous pleasure on its own terms, as it should have, nevertheless, the principal reason that it sounded to me like genuine applause was that the addition of candor, not to say correction, as a companion to your flattering words lent them credence.

I should, therefore, be no more enthusiastic about contradicting 2 you than I should be about allowing myself to be contradicted. And I should be happier about being myself free from the deceptions of what people think, given that these are the principal illnesses of the mind, than I should be about freeing others from them. Rather, your judgment should act altogether as a touch-

63

me patiar, et opinionum fallaciis, quasi morbis animi praecipuis, multo etiam libentius ipse caream quam caeteros liberem. Tuum vero mihi omnino quasi pro lapide Lydio iudicium debet esse. Nam ut illo purum dinoscitur aurum ab adulterino, sic apud me de tua facile sententia verum videtur posse falsumque discerni. Nec est id tam quod bene de propriis mihi studiis spondeam, quam quod ita disputare soleo de ambiguis ut plus invento vero gaudeam quam victoria. Quanquam autem abs te tantae auctoritatis homine provocatio non est, tamen pro tua singulari humanitate, quaeso, benigne audias quid ad ista respondeam.

3   Negas probare te quod 'imolare' prima brevi, quod item 'matutinus' prioribus correptis syllabis enuntiaverim. Ego vero tametsi rudis in primis, non adeo tamen obtusi sim pectoris, in versibus maxime faciundis, ut spatia ista morasque non sentiam. Verum cum mihi de Graeco pene ad verbum forent antiquissima interpretanda carmina (fateor) affectavi equidem ut in verbis obsoletam vetustatem, sic in mensura ipsa et numero gratam quandam, ut speravi, novitatem. Nec autem putabam fore ut, cum Vergilius, acerrimi vir iudicii, versus aliquoties Homeri vatis exemplo caudam trahentes effinxerit, non etiam mihi tale quippiam, praesertim Graeca vertenti, concederetur. Quocirca versiculos feci de³ industria, prominuli quasi ventris, qui medii pedem quaterna tempora superantem caperent ex argumento προκοιλίους appellatos, qualis apud Homerum, puta, sit ille, Πατρόκλου ποθέων ἀνδροτῆτά τε καὶ⁴ μένος ἠΰ

4   Sed quoniam quod ego studio novitatis quaesiveram syllabarum scilicet ignorantioni plerique tribuebant, mandavi statim quibus

stone for me. For just as this is used to distinguish gold from alloy, so too here does it easily seem possible to separate truth from falsehood regarding your verdict. Nor is there any reason why I so trust my own judgment regarding my own scholarly efforts other than the fact that I habitually discuss points of uncertainty in a way that leaves me happier with the discovery of the truth than with winning my case. Although there is no appeal beyond you, a man of such great authority, nevertheless, in keeping with your unparalleled kindness and generosity, I ask you to listen indulgently to what I say in response to your points.

You say you do not approve of the fact that I pronounce *imolare* 3 with a short first syllable, and likewise *matutinus* with the first two syllables shortened. Although I am, above all, unsophisticated, I would not be so thick in the head, especially when it comes to versification, as not to hear those quantities and intervals. But I admit that, since I needed to translate very ancient poetry essentially word for word from the Greek, I did indeed strive for what I hoped was a kind of agreeable novelty in actual length and rhythm, just as I strove for archaism in my vocabulary. And since Vergil, a man of razor-sharp judgment, sometimes fashioned verses that, on the model of his bard Homer, wore a pinned-on tail,[2] I did not expect that something of the sort would not be allowed to me as well, especially when translating from the Greek. Thus I deliberately produced some little verses with, as it were, a bit of a tummy, since in the middle they contain a foot that exceeds four beats, on the basis of which they are called, in Greek, "potbellied." Think, for example, of the line in Homer, "Craving the manhood and vigorous brav'ry of his Patroclus."[3]

But since what I had pursued in the interest of novelty many 4 people attributed in just this way to ignorance of syllable-lengths, I immediately wrote those friends I especially could, instructing them, in the event that any copies had reached them, to bring

maxime potui amicis, ad quos ulla modo exemplaria pervenissent, ut versiculos eos, velut in quadram, redigerent ad hoc exemplum:

luce feri, nam lux superis gratissima divis

et item:

O puerae emicuit rubor (haud mora)[5] matutinus.

Cuius enim stultitiae, vel cuius potius improbitatis fuisset agere diutius etiam bonam fabulam quam continuo populus exsibilaret? Itaque magnopere a te peto, cures mihi primo quoque tempore, non ausim dicere tua, sed scholastici alicuius manu, locum sic utrunque, in omnibus quotquot istic erunt exemplaribus, emendandum. Nam ut tibi potestas venalium quoque fiat, ipsi continuo per literas cavebimus.

5   Iam vero, quod 'liquentibus' prima correpta dici vix permittis, equidem in eo Vergilium sequebar, cuius illa certe sunt notissima:

principio coelum ac terras camposque liquentes

et

ignemque horribilemque feram fluviumque liquentem.

Nec me fallunt 'aut cum[6] liquentia mella' sic apud eundem posita ut quantum scilicet in tempore, tantum sit in intellectu discriminis.

6   Sed et 'orichalcum' brevi secunda dictum reprehendis, quae tamen syllaba diphthongo notatur. Ad hoc:[7] illo ipso quem tum locum interpretabar, οὔτ᾽ ἐς ὀρείχαλκον dixerat Callimachus, unus mihi tum quidem prae caeteris sequendus, quanquam alias quoque gravissimus auctor. Nam quod Statius aliter usurpat, iure suo, videlicet una diphthongum litera defraudat, quod et in 'Pliadum' vocabulo non reformidat. Postremo quaeris, idem ut, cur et 'Boeotia' scribam; sed enim quaerere ego quoque vicissim poteram cur tu 'Boetia' potius, nullo scilicet in has vocales Graecarum transitu,

these little verses back to square, so to speak, in accord with the following:

luce feri, nam lux superis gratissima divis

And likewise,

O puerae emicuit rubor illico matutinus.

Going on with the performance of even a good play which the audience relentlessly booed would have represented what kind of stupidity, or rather, what kind of impudence? Therefore I myself must earnestly request that you see to the emendation as indicated of the two passages for me at the first available opportunity (I dare not say by your own hand, but by that of someone from the school) in all the copies that are there, however many they may be. I shall myself see to it right away by letter that you be given authority over the ones for sale as well.

But to continue. As for the fact that you find it difficult to al- 5 low *liquentibus* to be said with the first syllable shortened, in this I was actually following Vergil, of whom surely the following are very well-known:

principio coelum ac terras camposque liquentes[4]

and

ignemque horribilemque feram fluviumque liquentem.[5]

Nor do I fail to realize that *aut cum liquentia mella* in the same author is placed in such a way as to produce a corresponding difference in sense and quantity.[6]

You also object that *orichalcum* was pronounced with a short 6 second syllable (even though this syllable abbreviates a diphthong).[7] I reply that in that very passage which I was then translating, Callimachus had said οὐδ' ἐς ὀρείχαλκον, and I had to follow him in preference to anyone else in this particular instance

quem modo vel praecepta tradiderint vel rationes persuaserint vel auctoritas comprobaverit, nisi forte vulgus imperitum respicimus, nullo prorsus habendum numero apud eruditos, quorum te princi-pem semper existimavimus. Adde quod hanc nostram vocis istius scripturam, sicut e Graeco primum demigravit, intemeratam ser-vant exemplaria, quaecunque adhuc incorruptae vetustatis indole censentur.

7   Haec igitur habui nunc quidem quae pro mea causa dicerem. Verum quando tu unus omnium aetatis nostrae professorum cele-berrimus aliter sentis, nihil iam credo mihi, sed ad Pyrrhonios plane[8] deficio, nec esse prorsus aut affirmo posthac aut nego quic-quam sicuti nobis vel a sensibus ipsis vel ab animo denique reprae-sentatur. Cupio tamen et de caeteris quid sentias audire, tanto maiorem tibi habiturus cottidie gratiam, quanto ab erroribus me vel saepius vel liberius vel postremo etiam severius vindicaveris.

Vale.

(although also elsewhere he was my most important authority). As for the fact that Statius uses the word differently,[8] he does so on his own authority, for he plainly cheats the diphthong out of one letter, which he does not hesitate to do as well with the word *Pliades*. You then ask, in the same way, why I also write *Boeotia*. But I in turn could just as well have asked why you instead write *Boetia*, that is to say, without the adaptation of Greek vowels to our own which in one way or another either rules dictate or logic suggests or authoritative sources sanction—unless by chance we turn our attention to the untrained masses, surely of no account among the learned, whose prince I have always considered you to be. Add to this the fact that any and all manuscripts reckoned to be native to an antiquity not yet corrupted present, inviolate, my same way of writing this word, just as it first made the transition from Greek.

Well, then. These are the things I had to say in my own defense. But when you, the single most applauded professor of our age, have a different opinion, I no longer trust my own judgment at all but entirely defect to the Skeptics, and subsequently I neither affirm nor deny that anything exists at all in the form in which it is presented to us either by the senses themselves or, eventually, by the mind. Nevertheless, I long to hear what you think about the rest, and my debt of gratitude to you will be in proportion to the frequency, or the freedom, or finally even the severity with which you deliver me from my errors. 7

Farewell.

: XXI :

Baptista Guarinus Angelo Politiano suo s. p. d.

1 Gaudeo mirifice, interprete Pico nostro, Palladio magis quam Martio, datam esse nobis occasiunculam ut de communibus studiis aliquid per literas colloquamur. Sic enim fore spero ut amor in doctrinam tuam meus amicitiam inter nos conflet. Quod autem ita cunctanter et meticulose ad Picum ipsum nonnulla de aureolo Miscellaneorum tuorum libro scripsi, id neutiquam mirare debes. Ita sunt horum temporum mores, ut si quis liberius quid proferat, bellicum cecinisse videatur. In me, Angele mi suavissime, ut nullus est loliginis succus, ita est candida et sine labe simplicitas. Doctos omnes amo coloque, et novos nescio quo modo magis etiam quam veteres admiror, quippe cum hoc tempore et librorum iactura et morum aliquorum ignoratio et multarum rerum desuetudo anxiam laboriosamque pariat emergendi difficultatem. Quare ignosces mihi si ex aliis animum spectavi tuum. Quia tamen te maxime diligebam, ut hominem eruditissimum, cupiebamque sine exceptione ab omnibus te[1] posse laudari, ideo quae sentiebam a lividulis fortasse notatum iri, ea tibi clandestina aliqua via nota fieri desideravi. Delectatus sum vehementer tua ista probitate, qua neque tulisti aegre te commoneri, et rogasti ut de caeteris idem facerem, quia eis te gratiam habere profitearis qui ab erroribus te vindicaverint. Non ego tantum mihi arrogo, ut quod tu ignoraveris, ego id

: XXI :

Battista Guarini to his dear Angelo Poliziano

I am fantastically pleased that, through the mediation of our 1
friend Pico, a follower more of Pallas than of Mars, we have been
granted some limited opportunity via letters to say something to
one another about the studies we have in common. Indeed, my
hope is that my love for your learning will fan the flames of friendship between us. You, however, should by no means be surprised
that I so hesitantly and timidly wrote a thing or two, just to Pico,
about that golden book, your *Miscellanea*. Present expectations are
such that, if anyone expresses an opinion with relative freedom,
everyone thinks he has commenced formal hostilities. Angelo my
sweet, just as there is in me no "cuttle-fish juice,"[1] so is my natural
simplicity spotlessly white. I love and cherish all learned men, and
somehow I admire the new ones even more than those of old, especially given that, in our day, the loss of books, ignorance of various customs, and the discontinuation of numerous practices en-
gender anxious and laborious difficulty for anyone trying to break
forward. Forgive me, therefore, if I judged your character on the
basis of others. But since I admired you most especially, given that
you are the most erudite of men, and I was hoping that you would
be able to be esteemed by all without exception,[2] I wanted things
which I sensed might attract the attention of petty, envious individuals to become known to you by some hidden route. I have derived tremendous pleasure from your integrity, by which you have
not taken criticism badly, asking me to provide the same regarding
the remainder, since you claim a debt of gratitude to anyone who
delivers you from errors. I do not think so much of myself that I
suppose I know something of which you are ignorant. But it regularly happens to every writer that, rereading their own writings

me scire credam. Sed scribentibus omnibus id usu venire solet, ut in scriptis suis, dum nova sunt, relegendis, vel obaudiant vel conniveant (ut taceam opiniones nonnullas quarum inventionibus applaudunt), quod ni ita esset, non in praeceptis haberemus, 'Nonumque prematur in annum.' Si quid autem a me bene dictum videatur, Terentianum illud, non tamen assentatorie, respondebo: 'Ridiculum. Non enim cogitaras. Caeterum idem istuc, tute melius quanto invenisses.'

2   Ut aliquando ad rem veniam: dabo operam, ut qui residui sunt apud mercatorem libri tui non nisi ex tua sententia exeant. Ego sumptu meo habueram librum ipsum apud me hospitem. Posteaquam tamen etiam gratis alterum fratrem in contubernio esse voluisti. Usus sum tua liberalitate ut ego munificus esse possim et ut tibi plus debeam. Leoniceno et Pictorio munus tuum tradam, cum abs te responsum accepero.

3   Magnificis Laurentio et Pico me commendes rogo.
Vale.

Ferrariae, iiii Calendas Ianuarias MCCCCLXXXVIIII

: XXII :

Angelus Politianus Baptistae Guarino suo s. d.

1   Bene habet. Amicos undique Miscellanea nobis aut comparant aut excitant. Undique epistolae ad nos vel de nobis excellentium virorum plenae studii, plenae laudum, vel proximae duae abs te. Quam ingenuae, bone Deus, quam simplices, quam liberales, quantis postremo et quibus aspersae amoris notis! Mitto enim

when they are new, they either hear themselves amiss or have their eyes half-shut, to say nothing of the various ideas the discovery of which they applaud. If this were not so, we would not number among our maxims, "Keep it back till the ninth year."[3] But if anything I said seems right, I shall reply with those lines of Terence (though without flattery): "That's ridiculous! You just hadn't thought about it. Otherwise you would have come up with the very same thing yourself, and much better."[4]

But let me get down to business. I shall make every effort to see 2 to it that whatever copies of your book are left on the merchant's shelf will not leave except as you indicate. I already had a copy living in my own house at my own expense. But later you wanted, free of charge, a second brother to share his room. I took advantage of your liberality so that I too could be generous — and even deeper in your debt. I shall pass your gift on to Leoniceno and Pittorio[5] once I have received your reply.

Please put in a good word for me with those Magnificents,[6] 3 Lorenzo and Pico.

Farewell.

Ferrara, December 29, 1489

: XXII :

Angelo Poliziano to his dear Battista Guarini

Excellent. From all quarters my *Miscellanea* either produce new 1 friends or scare up old ones. And from all quarters come letters, full of enthusiasm, full of praise, written either to me or about me by distinguished men. Especially the latest two from you. Dear God, how direct, how natural, how gracious — sprinkled, finally, with signs of love notable for their size and kind. To say nothing

quam elegantes et doctae. Proprium videlicet hoc eius domus in qua duntaxat etiam ipsa bonarum artium sunt incunabula. Quos igitur mihi tanta ista seu iudicia seu studia vestra admovere aculeos, immo vero quos ad scribendum subdere stimulos debent? Item[1] facile contemno, quas et contempsi tamen semper, ineptias malevolorum, et nugas vere dixerim abortivas (prius enim pene emortuae quam editae), tuis mihi suffragantibus epistolis, etiam Phoenice vivacioribus. Ego vero alacer iam doctorum clamoribus adiutus ad huius calcem curriculi propero. Quin[2] (si modo tu non aspernaris) curabo extet ad posteros in reliquis meis scriptis perpetuum non dixerim doctrinae tuae, quo quidem minus eges, sed certe benevoli inter nos animi testimonium.

2   Vale, Pictoriumque nostrum candidissimum hominem salvere iube meis et Pici verbis.

Florentiae, quinto Idus Ianuarias MCCCCLXXXVIIII

: XXIII :

Baptista Guarinus Angelo Poliziano suo s. d.

1   Nolim existimes maxima esse tuarum laudum praeconia quae ad te in epistolis praescribuntur.[1] Multo enim maiora sunt quae studiosi humanitatis in animis suis ex libro tuo taciti concipiunt, aut cum in coetu sunt, de te colloquuntur. Uno ore omnes omnia bona dicunt, doctrinam tuam praedicant, extollunt, admirantur. Nemo est qui pretio deterreatur quominus Miscellanea domi habeat unde discat. Haec sunt vera eruditionis testimonia, in quibus nulla est placendi adulandive suspicio. Quo magis miror dubitari a te an cupiam scriptis tuis famam meam immortalem fieri. Quasi

of how elegant and learned they were. Signature, in a word, of the home of nothing less than the cradle of arts and letters. When such great things, be they judgment or scholarship, come from the Guarini, they spur me on, or better, they goad me to write. In the same way I scorn, as I always have, the inane comments of spiteful people—what I might truthfully call aborted babble, given that it is basically dead on arrival—since your letters, more enduring than the Phoenix, give me a vote of confidence. Indeed, aided by the shouts of the learned, I now rush eagerly toward this race's finish-line. Better still, unless you say no I shall see to it that in my future writings there remains for posterity a lasting record not, I would say, of your learning (proof of which you hardly need) but certainly of our friendly feelings for one another.

Farewell. Say hello from me and Pico to our friend Pittorio.   2

Florence, January 9, 1490

: XXIII :

Battista Guarini to his dear Angelo Poliziano

Please do not imagine that the most important singings of your   1
praises are the ones outlined in letters to you. Far greater are those which, as a consequence of your book, students of human learning silently imagine. Or else they converse about you when they gather. With one voice everyone says every possible positive thing. The proclaim, exalt, adore your learning. No one is deterred by the price from having the *Miscellanea* at home from which to take lessons. These are the genuine proofs of erudition, in which there is no suspicion of efforts to please or flatter. This leaves me all the more surprised that you have any doubt about whether I want my fame to be made immortal by your writings. As if my heart were

cornea mihi sit fibra, non id ego quoque expetam, in quod fertur humanae naturae proclivitas.

2   Illud tamen monuisse aut saltem rogasse velim: ut et morsibus viventium et laudationibus (non enim adulationes appellaverim) quam minime in scribendo utaris. Nam praeterquam quod ea res dignitati scribentis officit, multi sunt qui magis affectionibus animi id scribendi genus quam vero iudicio acceptum referant. Non temere hoc dici putes. Audio enim persaepe quae de reliquis circunferantur. Et tamen liberum tibi in hisce rebus examen relinquo, quem etiam plus videre arbitror.

3   Salutem tibi Pictorii nostri verbis dico. Tu vero Magnificis Laurentio et Pico me commendabis.

Vale.

Ferrariae, xvi Calendas Februarias[2] MCCCCLXXXX

made of stone, and I too did not covet that to which human nature is prone!

All the same, I would like to have advised or, at least, asked 2 you, when you write, to be as sparing as possible in either sinking your teeth into or offering praise (to say nothing of adulation) to people who are still alive. Such a practice interferes with the dignity of the writer, but even beyond that, there are many who attribute this kind of writing more to emotion than to genuine judgment. Do not suppose I say this offhandedly. All the time I hear what circulates about everyone else. Nevertheless, I leave the final analysis in these matters entirely up to you, who, I think, see even more.

Hello from our friend Pittorio. Put in a good word for me with 3 those Magnificents, Lorenzo and Pico.

Farewell.

Ferrara, January 17, 1490

LIBER SECUNDUS

Angelus Politianus Philippo Beroaldo suo s. d.

1 Legit epistolam mihi nuper ad se tuam Picus hic Mirandula noster, plane flos illibatus ingeniorum, cuius in extrema clausula nostri quoque sic honorificam mentionem faciebas ut, in quodam veluti literatorum consessu, proximos videlicet ab illo mihi gradus
assignaveris. Hanc igitur ego tuam (si modo ita vocetur) sententiam quamvis audire citra ruborem, gnarus inscitiae meae, non poteram, tamen quod ab insigni quadam benivolentia proficiscebatur,
ita gratanter accepi ut vix tantundem fuerim voluptatis habiturus
si mihi esse illa quae de me pronuntiabas vera persuasissem. Nam
quamvis testimonio conscientia repugnet, laetor tamen alicui talem me videri posse qualem tua me fingit, hoc est hominis eruditissimi, praedicatio. Quare statim dictavi hanc tibi epistolam,
Beroalde, qua ducerem quantopere mihi tuum tale laudationis officium blandiatur, simulque darem fidem nulli me prorsus occasionem defuturum, rerumque posthac et temporum plane omnis arti-
culos excussurum, donec tibi pro studio erga me tali et animo
tandem quoquo modo referam gratiam.

Vale.

Florentiae, xvii Calendas Februarias MCCCCLXXXVIIII

BOOK II

: I :

Angelo Poliziano to his dear Filippo Beroaldo[1]

Our friend Pico della Mirandola, decidedly an unplucked flower 1
of talents, recently read me your letter to him. In its final phrase
you make such a flattering mention of me too that, in what one
might imagine as an assembly of literary persons, you assign me a
seat in the next row, right after him. Although I, being aware of
my ignorance, could not hear your judgment (assuming one can
call it that) and keep from blushing, nevertheless, given that it was
the result of some kind of remarkable kindness, I am so glad to
have received it that my pleasure would be rather less if I were to
persuade myself that those things you assert about me are true.
For, although what I know to be true stands in the way of your
testimony, I rejoice all the same that I can appear to someone to be
the sort of person your assertion (that is to say, the assertion of a
man of maximum erudition) represents me as being. Therefore,
Beroaldo, I immediately dictated this letter to you, so that in it I
might give an account of how much the kind of favor you do me
by your words of praise flatters me, and at the same time, offer my
pledge that I shall overlook no occasion whatsoever and that, from
now on, I shall exhaust the potential of each and every passing
moment until I finally shall repay my debt of gratitude for your
kind-hearted interest in me.

Farewell.

Florence, January 16, 1489

: II :

Philippus Beroaldus Angelo Politiano suo s. d.

1 Perlegi oppido quam libens literas illas quas ad me nuperrime dedisti, et quia tuae sunt et quia literatae. Miscellanea tua doctissimum te esse testantur, epistolae humanissimum. Turpe est vinci eruditione, humanitate vero turpissimum. Inde fit ut mihi non minutula labecula inspergatur, sed maxima labes, et ea quidem ineluibilis infigatur, cum abs te vincar in utroque. Assurgebat iam primum literatio nostra tuae politissimae literaturae, neque id dissimulanter. Iam vero et illa quoque, quae in me alioquin non improbari solet, humanitas tuae cedit humanitati adeo ut tibi comparatus possim merito inhumanus iudicari. In aliena tibi epistola, salutem transeunter adscripseram; tu, quae tua dexteritas est, e vestigio me per epistolam resalutasti quae sua plane politura Politianum ostentat artificem totaque est officii benivolentiaeque refertissima.

2 Cui ut breviter respondeam: non opus est, mi Politiane, ut mihi gratias agas ob meum de singulari tua virtute vel testimonium vel iudicium. Etenim si nolo videri mendax et vanus, id faciam quod facio necesse est. Praeterea persuasissimum habe me in primore fronte animum gestare, nec a labiis dissentire praecordia: concordat in me scriptio cum mente, lingua cum pectore, et de promptuario nostro sincera promuntur citra omnem fucatam simulationem. Eruditio tua illa interior atque politior a nemine non paulo

: II :

Filippo Beroaldo to his dear Angelo Poliziano

I read every word of the letter you just sent me with the greatest 1
possible pleasure, both because it was from you and because it was
scholarly. Your *Miscellanea* prove that you are extremely learned;
your letters, that you are extremely generous and kind. It is disgraceful to be surpassed in erudition, but it is exceedingly so to be
surpassed in kindness. The result is that I am marked, not by a
tiny little spot, but by a massive stain—and this sets, indelible,
since I am surpassed by you on both counts. First of all, our gram-
mar-school learning gives up its seat to your very polished philology—and it does so without hidden motives. Next, however, even
that quality for which, in other circumstances, I tend not to be
criticized—my kindness—is so far inferior to your kindness that,
compared to you, I quite rightly can be judged unkind. In a letter
to someone else, I had added, in passing, a hello to you. Here is
your willingness to do a good turn: you immediately returned my
hello in a letter which, by its polish, plainly showed Poliziano to
be its maker,[1] all of it replete with dutiful service and good will.

Let me offer a brief reply. My dear Poliziano, there is no reason 2
for you to thank me for my testimony or judgment regarding your
unparalleled talent. For I am obliged to do what I do if I do not
want to seem an empty liar. Rest entirely assured, moreover, that I
wear my thoughts on my brow,[2] and that my deepest feelings do
not disagree with my lips. In me, text concurs with mind, tongue
with heart, and from my mouth comes a ready supply of sincerity
that avoids any rosy-cheeked deception. Anyone more than minimally civilized looks up to that erudition of yours as more profound, more polished. I look up to it—and love it too. This happens now, and the same thing will continue to happen in the

humaniore suspicitur; a me et suspicitur et amatur. Hoc in praesentia fit, hoc idem fiet in posterum. Sum et ero tuarum laudum, si non idoneus, saltem benivolus buccinator. Olim istic iecimus amicitiae inter nos mutuae fundamenta, quae cum id temporis a nobis glutino literario fuerint ferruminata, superest ut eodem deinceps ferrumine immisso ad fastigium extollantur, quod ad amussim fiet et libellam, si epistolae inter nos ultro citroque discurrerint, si fuerit inter nos, si non cottidiana, saltem hebdomatica literarum reciprocatio, quae in fulturis amicitiae stabiliendis laterculorum aut calcis[1] haud dubie vicem repraesentant. Patefactae sunt amicitiarum fores, quarum me futurum subinde hospitem polliceor.

3   Vale, decus literarum, et quod Pico polyhistori meo nomine debes, eidem meo nomine resolvito.

Vale.[2]

: III :

Nicolaus Leonicenus Angelo Politiano suo s. d.

1   Munus Miscellaneorum tuorum, quae tuo nomine Baptista Guarinus nuper mihi tradidit, ingenti me voluptate affecit. Nam etsi a politioris humanitatis studiis iampridem feriatus sim, gaudeo tamen a doctissimis atque amicissimis hominibus mihi aliquando occasionem praestari ad ea studia redeundi quae me in adolescentia maxime delectarunt. Quanquam (ut verum fatear) postquam opus id perlegi, visus sum non in alienis agris cum dispendio, sed in proprio solo magna cum utilitate versari. Inveni in eo non modo quae ad literaturam ac poetarum et oratorum cognitionem pluri-

future. I am and will be a trumpeter of your praises — if not the right trumpeter, then at least a good-hearted one. There where you are, we once upon a time laid the foundations of our mutual friendship, and since back then we cemented these together with the mortar of writing, it remains that they, by the application of layers of the same cement, be raised to the roof. This will be done according to plumb and level if letters run back and forth between us, if between us there is, if not a daily exchange of letters, then at least a weekly one. These, in fixing fast the supports of a friendship, unquestionably serve the purpose of alternating layers of bricks and mortar. The doors of friendship are open wide, and I promise to be their frequent visitor.

Farewell, crowning achievement of literature. And from my account reimburse Pico the polymath what you owe him *on* my account.[3]

Farewell.[4]

3

: III :

Niccolò Leoniceno[1] to his dear Angelo Poliziano

The gift of your *Miscellanea*, which Battista Guarini recently delivered to me on your behalf, brought me immense pleasure. For although I long ago retired from the studies of more polished humanity, I nevertheless rejoice that, now and then, an opportunity is provided by very good friends for me to return to those studies which enormously delighted me in my youth. But to tell the truth, after I read the entire book, I seemed not to be wasting time in someone else's fields but, rather, to be making good use of it on my own turf. In it I found not only things which contribute a great deal to literature and to the understanding of the poets and

1

mum conferunt, sed et medicorum et philosophorum sententias
docte atque eleganter abs te explicatas et in veriorem lucem educ-
tas quam in aliorum libris perlegantur. Quae res non mediocrem
mihi spem affert fore ut aliquando philosophia universa, quae iam
pridem apud barbaros barbara facta est, Angeli Politiani opera Latine loqui incipiat.

2 Habuisiti, ut scribis, a teneris annis praeceptores praestantissi-
mos, sub quibus et Platonicam et Aristotelicam disciplinam imbi-
bere potuisti. Nunc vero, ut ex tuis scriptis accepi, frueris consuetudine Pici nostri, principis nunquam satis laudati, cuius doctrinae
imitatione summum sapientiae culmen, quemadmodum iam in
oratoria ac poetica facultate eminentissimum obtines locum, brevi
attingere poteris. Nisi utrunque amarem, utrique plurimum debe-
rem, inviderem felicitati vestrae, quibus in praeclarissima Italiae civitate, sub Laurentio Medice ac Petro filio, eximiis aetate nostra
virtutis atque ingeniorum patronis, per summum ocium ingenue
philosophari contingit.

3 Utinam ego is essem quem vos tertium socium tantis rebus
adiungere non indignum iudicaretis. Si facultas daretur vobiscum
vivere, vobiscum emori vellem. Nam quid suavius, quid conducibi-
lius esse in vita potest quam cum amicissimis, iisdemque et inte-
gerrimis et undecunque doctissimis, quales vos estis, vivere? Sed
erit, ut spero, ut reliquum iam ingravescentis aetatis meae vobiscum traducam, non modo propter consuetudinis suavitatem,
sed etiam ut commentemur quonam modo pereunti doctrinae ac
vitae hominum potius, quos multorum inscitia Ἄϊδι προϊάπτει,
consulamus.

4 Vale. Magnifico Petro tuo, in cuius olim pueri dum Florentiae
essem me gratiam insinuasti, nunc iam iuveni atque una cum ae-

orators, but also opinions of physicians and philosophers, inter-
preted by you with learning and elegance, and exposed to a more
accurate light than that of their cursory reading in books by others. This offers me no small hope that, one day, by the efforts of
Angelo Poliziano, all of philosophy, which, living among barbarians, long ago became barbarous too, will begin to speak Latin.[2]

From a tender age, you had, as you write, the most pre-eminent 2
instructors, under whom you had the chance to imbibe Platonic
and Aristotelian teaching. But now, as I learn from your writings,
you enjoy the regular company of Pico our prince, who is never
praised enough, by the imitation of whose learning you will be
able to reach the highest summit of wisdom, just as you now occupy the loftiest position in oratorical and poetic skill. If I did not
love both of you and owe a great deal to each, I would envy your
good fortune. For it has fallen to the two of you to philosophize
freely in complete leisure in the most splendid city of Italy, under
Lorenzo de' Medici and his son Piero, patrons of talent and genius
who are exceptional in our day.

If only I were the sort of person whom you might judge not un- 3
worthy to add to your company as a third partner in such great
undertakings! If the possibility were given to live with you, I
would want to die with you. For what in life could be sweeter or
more profitable than to live with very good friends who are, at the
same time, the kind of very honorable and (in every respect) very
learned men that you yourselves are. But a way will be found, I
hope, for me to spend the rest of my life, already growing heavy
with years, with you, not only because of the sweetness of your
company, but also so that we can deliberate how on earth to come
to the aid both of learning, now perishing, and, more importantly,
of the lives of those people whom the ignorance of many matters
"is hurling into Hades."[3]

Farewell. If you do not mind, put in a good word for me with 4
Piero the Magnificent, into whose good graces you once insinuated

tate virtutibus ac dignitate, ut audio, aucto, si tibi videtur, me plurimum commendabis.

Ex Ferraria, quinto Calendas Februarias

: IV :

Angelus Politianus Nicolao Leoniceno suo s. d.

1 Non tu munus accepisti, quin immo dedisti potius, ut qui dignum me habueris cuius etiam nugas lectitares—nisi magis iniuria sit haec: Florales agentem spectari a Catone. Feriatum diu te dicis a literis politioribus. At ego, si talem scribere epistolam qui feriatur potest qualem tu misisti nuper, omnium elegantissimam, censeo esse mihi quoque quacunque occasione feriandum. Sed ita est profecto: bonae istae artes, literae, philosophiaeque vestrae non prius tenentur singulae quam simul omneis. Omneis vero aetate nostra tu, si non solus, certe cum paucis, hoc est cum uno aut altero, ad summum tenes. Sed de reliquis alias.

2 Galeni vero commentarios vidi nuper quos tu plane Latinos fecisti. Auguror (nec me, puto, fallit augurium) plurimum posteritati collaturos. Nam saeculo etiam huic nostro nondum audeo sperare, quoniam prava consuetudine sic pene quidam homines obbrutuerunt ut glandem adhuc defendant repertis frugibus, similesque mihi Gryllo videntur illi qui cum Ulysse disputat apud Plutarchum nec ullis adduci rationibus potest ut a sue rursus in hominem redire velit, quem prius ex homine Circe mutaverat[1] in suem.

me when he was a boy and I was in Florence, though he is now already a young man, having grown, as I hear, not only in years, but also in authority and marks of excellence.

From Ferrara, January 28

: IV :

Angelo Poliziano to his dear Niccolò Leoniceno

You did not receive a gift; rather, you gave one by judging that I   1
deserved for you to read, closely, even my trifles—unless it does more harm than good to be watched by Cato while you celebrate the festival of Flora![1] You say that you long ago retired from more polished literary pursuits. But if someone in retirement can write the sort of letter (as elegant as they come) you just sent me, then I think that I too should retire at every available opportunity. But it really does happen this way: no sooner are those noble arts and literatures and philosophies of yours possessed singly than they are possessed all together at once. In our day you, if not alone, then in the company of a few, that is, of one or two, possess all of these to perfection. But let us save the rest for another occasion.

I recently saw the commentaries of Galen that you turned   2
seamlessly into Latin. I hope (and I do not think my hope deceives me) that they will be of considerable use to future generations. For I do not yet dare hope that they will be so to this age of ours, since, given the perverse habits of our day, men have become so nearly like beasts that, despite the discovery of grain, they still defend the nut. Indeed, to me they seem similar to that man Gryllus, who discusses things with Ulysses in Plutarch and who is not able to be moved by any arguments to want to be turned back from a pig into a person.[2] (For Circe had earlier changed him from a person into a pig.)

3   Gratulatio tua, quod philosophiae me totum dediderim, mirum
quantum mihi bonae spei addidit.[2] Perseverabimus, igitur, praesertim cum bene cesserit adhuc quod hactenus publice specimen
dedimus, non modo docendo, set etiam disputando. Facit animos,
credo, Picus hic noster, qui cum diu comparem sibi non inveniat in
arena, certanti mihi laborantique tamen unice favet. Isque cum
mihi tale quiddam forte qualem Glauco illi Carystio pater accla-
mavit, τὴν ἀπ᾽ ἀρότρου, terram (medius fidius) ipsam subiicere
videtur Antaei pedibus.

4   Atque utinam tu quoque nobiscum viveres eodem contubernio.
Crederem fore ut et Musae huc omnes, si modo ullae usquam sunt
Musae, cum suis et nemoribus et fontibus (ne dixerim, cum sua
modo supellectile), commigrarent, et indoctorum barbarorumque
phalanges, quae totum fere orbem signis positis exultantes tenent,
facile te et Pico ducibus fugarentur.[3]

5   Laurentius Petrusque Medices, hoc est cum filio suavissimo pater humanissimus, certatim te diligunt, occasionemque sibi dari
volunt qua benivolentiae ipsorum aliquando erga te uberiorem[4]
fructum plenioremque percipias.

Vale.

It is incredible how much extra confidence your congratulations 3
for dedicating myself entirely to philosophy have given me. I shall
stay the course, therefore, especially since what up to now I have
offered publicly as a sample, not only in lectures but also in debates, has met, so far, with good results. Our friend Pico, I think,
not only by teaching, but also by discussing, gives me courage.
Long unable to find an equal partner in the arena, he nevertheless
favors me above the rest, while I struggle and exert myself. And
when he gives me something along the lines of the "just like with
the plow!" that the father of Glaucus shouted to his son,[3] I swear
it seems as if the very ground were being thrown beneath the feet
of Antaeus.[4]

If only you too were living here with us, under the same roof! 4
Then I would believe that all the Muses (assuming that there are
any Muses left anywhere) would pack up and move here, along
with their groves and fountains (I cannot say "with just their furniture"!), and that the battalions of uneducated and barbarian
men who, their standards planted, jubilantly occupy nearly the entire world, would easily be chased away, with you and Pico as our
leaders.[5]

Lorenzo and Piero de' Medici, that is to say, that most generous 5
father along with his most gentle son, compete in their affection
for you, and they want an opportunity to be given them by which
you may one day harvest fuller and more abundant fruit of their
good will toward you.

Farewell.

: V :

Nicolaus Leonicenus Angelo Politiano suo s. d.

1   Quemadmodum non multum dolenter fero ab hominibus illaudatis vituperari, ita plurimum gaudeo a viris nunquam satis laudatis commendari.[1] Nam etsi illi aut odio aut invidiae livore occaecati[2] omnibus detrahunt, hi vero plura quandoque amori ac benivolentiae tribuunt quam veritati, non parum tamen interesse censeo hocne an illo affectu quicquam agatur. Quis enim Thersitae maledicenti ac nemini parcenti credat, Nestori vero, a cuius ore melle dulcior distillat oratio, non assentiatur? Ego sane, etsi nihil me esse sciam, tuae tamen orationis persuasione ac lepore ductus, aliquod iam nomen ac decus censeo possidere. Neque in animum inducere possum quin tuum de me iudicium nonnulli sint approbaturi, si non illi qui, ut in tua elegantissima epistola scribis, iam[3] obbrutuerunt et a glande nesciunt desuescere, saltem ii quos recta studia delectant,[4] 'exigui sane numero, sed bello vivida virtus.' Horum armis atque auxiliis fretus, barbarorum phalanges, atque eorum qui a nobis[5] ad illos defecerunt, impetus insolentiasque contemnam.

2   Tu modo, mi Politiane, eum te mihi exhibe qui semper fuisti erga me, hoc est mei honoris ac dignitatis acerrimum defensorem. Laurentium vero ac Petrum Medices, hoc est cum patre filium humanissimum, in me dilectione certantes, quandoquidem tu ille fuisti 'qui mihi quodcunque hoc regni, qui sceptra Iovemque' tua

: V :

Niccolò Leoniceno to his dear Angelo Poliziano

Just as I do not much mind when I am censured by people unwor- 1
thy of praise, so I take very great pleasure in being commended by
men who are never praised enough. Indeed, although the former,
blinded either by hatred or by the malice of envy, disparage everyone, whereas the latter at times base more on love and good
will than on truth, I nevertheless think it matters whether something is done in one mood or the other. For who would believe
Thersites, hurling abuse and sparing no one? Who, however,
would not agree with Nestor, from whose mouth drips speech
sweeter than honey?[1] I tell you, even though I know that I am
nothing, I am led by the persuasiveness and charm of your speech
to think that I already possess some fame and glory. Nor can I
unconvince myself that a number of people will accept your judgment about me — if not those who, as you put it in your most elegant letter, are already become like beasts and know not how to
break the habit of the nut, then at least those whom proper studies delight, "a tiny group," to be sure, "but one of spirited valor in
war."[2] Supported by their arms and aid, I scorn the battalions of
the barbarians and the violence and insolence of those who have
defected from our side to theirs.

As for you, my dear Poliziano: just keep showing me that you 2
are the sort of person you always have been towards me, that is to
say, an extremely fierce defender of my honor and esteem. And as
for Lorenzo and Piero de' Medici (that is to say, that son who is,
along with his father, the most civilized of men), who compete in
their affection for me, well, given that you were the one who, by
your favor and authority with them, "won for me whatever I have

apud illos auctoritate ac gratia conciliasti, studeas in eodem erga
me amore conservare.

Vale.

: VI :

Angelus Politianus Nicolao Leoniceno suo s. d.

1 Dictata illa tua, Nicolae, quibus Avicennae refellis inscitiam do-
cesque medicos iuniores quanta in caligine rerum versentur, nescio
plusne mihi voluptatis an doloris attulerint. Nam et gavisus mirifice sum res eas quibus hominum vita salusque continetur ab eo
potissimum viro editas esse in lucem quem ego semper ingenii dis-
ciplinarumque merito plurimi fecerim, et indolui rursus generis
humani vicem, quod in se grassari tandiu impune tristem hanc
inscitiam[1] patiatur, atque ab iis interdum vitae spem pretio emat,
unde mors certissima proficiscatur. Quis enim non videat plus esse
a medico quam a morbo periculi, siquidem et morbus alius pro
alio curetur, et alia pro aliis remedia afferantur?

2 Quod si te prisca illa, Nicolae, tulisset aetas, in qua pro meritis
praemia reddebantur, ne deorum quidem honoribus caruisses, nisi
forte maius esse credimus unum aut alterum (quod Aesculapius
fecit) a morte quam omneis pariter homines (quod ipse facis) a
mortis etiam periculo eripere. Quare perge, obsecro, qua instituisti
via, scilicet ut una opera et immortalem tibi gloriam parias, et omnibus vere hactenus mortalibus aegris vitam salutem concilies.

of a kingdom, and my might, and the favor of Jupiter,"[3] do what you can to keep them in their present state of love toward me.

Farewell.

: VI :

Angelo Poliziano to his dear Niccolò Leoniceno

I do not know, Niccolò, whether those lessons of yours,[1] by which you refute the ignorant beliefs of Avicenna[2] and teach a newer generation of physicians the extent of the fog of ignorance in which they make their way, brought me more pleasure or pain. For on the one hand, I was marvelously happy that those matters by which human life and health are conserved were brought to light by that particular man whom I have always rated most highly on the basis of his intelligence and learning. On the other hand, it pained me to consider the current condition of the human race, which for such a long time has allowed this depressing ignorance to victimize it and has gone on buying, at a price, the expectation to live from those very persons who are the source of certain death. Who, indeed, cannot see that more danger comes from a doctor than from disease, since treatment is for one disease instead of another, and these remedies are used instead of those?

But if that bygone age, in which achievements received corresponding rewards, had produced you, Niccolò, then you would not have lacked the honors even of the gods, unless perhaps we think it more important to rescue one or two people from death (as Aesculapius did) than to rescue all men equally from even the risk of death (as you yourself do). And so I beg you to continue on the road on which you began, so that by this one enterprise you beget immortal glory for yourself and restore life and health to all those sick people who, until now, were sure to die.

3   Quod autem Plinium quoque redarguis nostrum, quasi cisthon
pro hedera acceperit, in hoc ego (ut libere agam et amice) longe a
te dissentio. Nec autem verebor eius viri patrocinium suscipere audacter qui fuerit de vita et literis tam praeclare meritus, praesertim
adversus te, hoc est adversus eminentem philosophum, cui nihil
veritate ipsa debeat esse antiquius. De vestris enim illa sunt scholis: 'Amicus Socrates, amicior veritas,' et item, 'Amici ambo, plus
tamen habendum honoris veritati est.'

4   Plinius igitur, ut quidem tu ais, perinde atque Avicenna cisthon
ab hedera non distinguit, errore, si quidem ita sit, maximo,
quando cisthos ab hedera plurimum et figura et colore et viribus
differat. Addisque mirandum de Plinio magis quam de Avicenna,
quoniam Graece linguae peritus, secernere a cisso, hoc est ab hedera, cisthon debuerat. Argumentum affers quamobrem alterum
ab altero non separet, quod in libro Naturalis Historiae sexto decimo hederam dividat in marem ac foeminam, floremque utriusque similem dicat esse rosae silvestri, tum idem libro quarto et vigesimo cisthon quoque illam, sub qua nascitur hypocisthus, in
marem dividat et foeminam, marique rosaceum, foeminae album
tribuat florem, postremo quod etiam cisthi huius fecisse inter hederas mentionem se dicat. Quocirca sic videris posse colligere:
cum Plinius libro quarto et vigesimo mentionem se de cistho inter
hederas fecisse doceat, cuius tamen vocabulum nusquam superius
inter hederas citetur, facilis coniectura est, cisthon ab eo hederae
nomine comprehensam, praesertim qui sic hederam quemadmodum et cisthon in marem foeminamque partiatur, et in hederis florem describat cisthi.

5   Iam quoniam quid tibi videatur exposui, quid ego contra opiner
edisseram. Nego usquam a Plinio inter hederas cisthi mentionem

But as for the fact that you also contradict our friend Pliny for,   3
apparently, mistaking *cisthos* for ivy—well, on this score, if I may
speak freely and as a friend, I very much disagree with you. Nor
shall I shrink from boldly taking up the defense of a man who
contributed so famously to life and letters, especially against you,
that is, against an outstanding philosopher, to whom nothing
should be more time-honored[3] than the truth. Indeed, the following are from your school: "Socrates is a friend, but the truth is a
better one," and along the same lines, "Both are friends, but more
honor should belong to the truth."[4]

In any case, Pliny, according to you, just like Avicenna, does not   4
distinguish *cisthos* from ivy. Provided this is true, his is quite a
blunder, since ivy is extremely different from *cisthos* with respect to
its shape, color, and therapeutic properties. You add that there is
more reason to be surprised about Pliny than about Avicenna,
since Pliny, fully competent in Greek, should have been able to
distinguish *cisthos* from *cissos*, i.e., from ivy. You advance the following explanation of how he does not separate the one from the
other: in book 16 of the *Natural History*, he divides ivy into male
and female and says that the flower of both is similar to the woodland rose; then, in the same way, in book 24 he also divides the
cisthos under which sprouts the *hypocisthis* into male and female and
assigns the rose-colored flower to the male and the white to the female; finally, he says that he had also mentioned this *cisthos* among
the ivies.[5] On the basis of all this you seem to be able to deduce
the following: since Pliny in book 24 indicates that he had mentioned *cisthos* among the ivies, but this term is cited among the
ivies nowhere earlier in the text, the obvious conclusion is that
cisthos is included by him in the meaning of "ivy," especially given
that he divides ivy into male and female, just as he does *cisthos*.

Now that I have explained what seemed to you to be the case, I   5
shall set forth my contrasting view. I deny that *cisthos* is mentioned
among the ivies by Pliny anywhere other than in book 24, where

factam, praeterquam libro quarto et vigesimo, ubi illam praeclare distinxit ab hedera. Nam quod tibi sumis, quasi Plinii testimonium, alibi eum de cistho inter hederas locutum, hoc ego neutiquam concedo. mihi enim ubi hoc ait, in quarto et vigesimo scilicet libro, disserere de cistho adusque illam tantum clausulam videtur quae sic est apud ipsum: 'sub his maxime[2] nascitur hypocisthis.' post id autem statim interpungitur, ac de integro sic verba incipiunt: 'quam inter hederas diximus, cissos, erythranos ab isdem appellatur, similis hederae.' nec autem vereor (quae tua est in literis elegantia[3]) quin figuram agnoscas cuiusmodi apud Ovidium est: 'Quam legis a rapta Briseide littera venit,' et iterum, 'Quam,[4] nisi tu dederis, caritura est ipsa, salutem, mittit Amazonio Cressa puella viro.' quod si illud 'quam' referre ad id malis quod antegreditur, cogeris ad hypocisthida potius (haec enim statim prior) quam ad cisthon referre. Deque hypocisthide tacet omnino superius, hoc est libro sexto decimo, inter hederas, cum de erythrano tamen loquatur.

6   Quid quod nec cisthon alibi usquam nominat inter hederas, nec maris foeminaeque discrimen tam cisthi proprium quam omnium plane arborum virgultorumque videtur, quod nec idem Plinius dissimulat? Quid quod flos quoque diversus perhibetur, in hedera quidem maris et foeminae concolor, in cistho autem plane discolor? Nam quod hederaceum silvestri rosae comparat, non tam colorem insinuari quam lanuginem puto qualis intra rosas est. Unde etiam hederae florem χνοώδη Theophrastus appellaverit.

7   Satis igitur, ut arbitror, apparet nihil esse quod nos fateri cogat Plinium libro sexto decimo cisthon inter hederas retulisse, qui tamen idem libro quarto et vigesimo sic hederae cisthon quemadmo-

he quite clearly distinguishes it from ivy. Indeed, what you assume for your argument to be the word of Pliny—that he somewhere else spoke about *cisthos* among the ivies—I do not grant you in the least. As I see it, at the point at which he says this, there in book 24, he is discussing *cisthos* only up to the phrase which runs as follows: "under these sprouts the *hypocisthis*." Immediately after this comes a period, and then the text starts from scratch as follows: "What I spoke about among the ivies, *cissos*, is called *erythranos* by the same people and is similar to ivy." Given the elegance of your letter, I am not worried that you will fail to recognize a turn of phrase paralleled in Ovid: "What you are reading, a letter, has come from stolen Briseis,"[6] and again, "What she herself will lack unless you offer it too—*salus*—a girl from Crete sends to her Amazonian man."[7] But if you prefer to apply *quam* to that which precedes it, you will be forced to apply it to *hypocisthis* (for this comes immediately before), rather than to *cisthos*. And he is completely silent about *hypocisthis* earlier in the text, i.e., in book 16, among the ivies, where, however, he speaks about *erythranos*.

What of the fact that nowhere else does he name *cisthos* among   6 the ivies, and the distinction between male and female appears to be not so much an unique property of *cisthos* as one common to absolutely all trees and bushes, something the very same Pliny does not hide? What of the fact that a different flower is also produced? (In ivy it is of the same color whether it belongs to a male or female plant, whereas in *cisthos* they are of completely different colors.) As for the fact that he compares the ivy-flower to the woodland rose,[8] what is implied is not so much the color as the downy surface that is characteristic among roses. This is why Theophrastus too called the ivy-flower *chnoôdê*.[9]

It is therefore clear enough, I think, that nothing compels us   7 to say that Pliny in book 16 reckons *cisthos* among the ivies. The same author, in book 24, nevertheless connects *cisthos*, just like *chamaecissos*, to ivy, not because he believed *cisthos* and ivy to be the

dum et chamaecisson adnexuit, non quia cisthon hederamque esse idem crediderit, sed quod eam Graeci[5] vicino (sic enim inquit) vocabulo appellent. Quare ne quenquam similitudo vocabuli falleret, ibi potissimum distinctiones adhibuit ubi confusionis occasio nascebatur. Nec eo contentus etiam cisthi proprietates prorsus ab hedera diversas adiecit. Nusquam enim hederam sic ante descripserat ut aut maiorem thymo aut ocimi[6] foliis aut postremo albo esse flore docuerit. Quamobrem quis iam dubitet 'Secundum' Plinium pronuntiari oportere, quem ne suspitio quidem ulla istius erroris attingat.

8   Illud obiter mirari me fateor: quid ita tibi in mentem venerit ledon herbam (seu tu ladam mavis, unde et ladanum vocetur) Latinam vocem arbitrari? Prorsus quasi non et Dioscorides et alii veteres Graeci passim ut patria vernaculaque utantur tam, hercules, quam et ladano.

9   Haec habui, mi Nicolae, quae tibi pro Plinio (verane an falsa nescio, sed mihi tamen verisimilia) obiicerem, quae si tibi doctissimo homini probabuntur, laetabor equidem Latinum auctorem non in eadem esse alea qua barbari. Sin minus, expecto iam quid ad haec nostra qualiacunque respondeas. Etenim cum gravissima sit apud eruditissimum quenque Plinii auctoritas, aut non tentanda fuit, aut aliquanto fortius quam certe adhuc fecisse videris convellenda.

Vale.[7]

same thing, but because the Greeks refer to the latter by (for this is what he says) "a closely related word." For this reason, in order to prevent the similarity of the words confusing anyone, he engages their distinctions at the very point at which there arises an occasion for confusion. Still not content, he also adds that the properties of *cisthos* are entirely different from ivy. For nowhere previously had he described ivy in a way that would indicate it to be either "larger than thyme" or characterized either by "basil-leaves" or, finally, a "white flower." Since not even any suspicion of that error you describe touches Pliny, who could now doubt that he should be pronounced "Fortunate"?[10]

I admit that, in passing, I am surprised by the following: Why   8 did it occur to you to decide that the herb *ledon* (or if you prefer, *lada*, source also of the word *ladanum*) is a Latin word? As if, in short, Dioscorides[11] and other ancient Greeks do not use it all the time as a native, indigenous word, as much, by Hercules, as they also use *ladanum*.

These are what I have, my dear Niccolò, by way of objections   9 to you on Pliny's behalf. I do not know whether they are true or false, but to me they seem plausible. If they receive the approval of a very learned man like yourself, then I shall certainly rejoice that this Latin author is not on the same scale[12] as are the barbarians.[13] But if not, then I am waiting to see what you will say in reply to these objections of mine, such as they are. For given that Pliny's authority carries considerable weight for anyone who is especially erudite, either it should not have been challenged, or it should be overturned rather more vigorously than you certainly seem so far to have done.

Farewell.[14]

: VII :

Nicolaus Leonicenus Angelo Politiano suo s. d.

1 Gaudeo plurimum, Angele vir doctissime, studium meum in refellenda inscitia barbarorum qui de medicina scripserunt abs te, nunquam satis laudato viro, probari. Non enim ego id de te sentio quod forte plerique qui in ea haeresi sunt, hominem eloquentem non posse de aliis disciplinis iudicare, quasi earum peritia carere sit necessarium ei qui bonarum literarum ac politioris humanitatis studiis fuerit imbutus. Novi ego tuum perspicacissimum ingenium, novi fervens iam inde a pueritia studium, non minus ad philosophiae doctrinam quam ad oratoriam atque poeticam capessendam,[1] in quibus omnibus tantum profecisti ut tua te patria inclita Florentia omnium liberalium artium utatur praeceptore.

2 Nec sane mirandum te unum esse perpaucorum qui aetate nostra eloquentiam cum sapientia iunxerunt, cum in eiusdem sapientiae studio habeas ducem ac comitem divino virum ingenio, Ioannem Picum Mirandulam nostrum, cum quo dies ac noctes in omni doctrinarum meditatione versaris, ac praeterea tibi omnia ad ingenue philosophandum adiumenta suppeditet favor ac gratia Laurentii Medicis, maximi hac tempestate studiorum patroni, qui missis per universum terrarum orbem nuntiis in omni disciplinarum genere libros summa ope conquirit, nulli sumptui parcit quo tibi ac reliquis praeclaris ingeniis bonarum artium studia aemulantibus instrumenta abundantissima paret. Audivi te referente vocem illam praeclaram ex Laurentii ore prodiisse, optare tanta sibi

: VII :

Niccolò Leoniceno to his dear Angelo Poliziano

I am overjoyed, Angelo, most learned of men, that my dedication 1
in refuting the ignorance of barbarian writers on medicine has met
with the approval of a man who is never praised enough, namely,
you. Nor have I had the opinion about you which, perhaps, many
in this school of thought have: that an eloquent person is unable
to make judgments about other disciplines. As if a lack of compe-
tence in these were obligatory for one who has been imbued in
studies of fine literature and more polished humanity! I have come
to know your very penetrating intellect, as well as your fervent enthusiasm, going back to your boyhood, for acquiring knowledge of
philosophy no less than that of oratory and poetry. In all of these
you have made such great progress that your illustrious homeland,
Florence, employs you as teacher of all the liberal arts.

Nor is it especially surprising that you are one of the few who 2
in our day combine eloquence with wisdom, since in the pursuit of
the same wisdom, you have as your guide and companion a man
of divine intelligence, our dear Giovanni Pico della Mirandola,
with whom you pass day and night in every exercise of the fields
of learning, and since, besides, the support and favor of Lorenzo
de' Medici, today's greatest patron of studies, procure for you every resource for philosophizing freely. With emissaries dispatched
throughout the entire world, he uses every resource to acquire
books in all branches of learning, and he spares no expense to acquire an overflowing supply of tools for you and the other brilliant
intellects that strive after the studies of the liberal arts. I have
heard (you yourself told me) that there once came from Lorenzo's
mouth a remarkable line to the effect that he hoped that such
great incentives for emending books would be offered to him by

abs te ac Pico nostro ad libros emendos praestari incitamenta ut
tandem, deficientibus sumptibus, totam supellectilem oppignerare
cogatur. Cum igitur omnia et animi et fortunae bona in te cumula-
tissima sint, nihil est quod, Angelo Politiano pro me contra barbaros pronuntiante, quempiam deinceps timere debeam qui illorum
patrocinium sit suscepturus.

3   Quod autem, ut iure a me barbaros reprehendi iudicasti, ita
non approbas quod Plinium, de vita ac literis optime meritum, intra eandem cum barbaris aleam posuerim, cuius tanta sit apud pe-
ritissimum quenquam auctoritas ut aut eam tentare non debuerim,
aut si omnino convellendam duxeram, fortius id a me fieri quam
adhuc fecisse videar oportuerit, si me forte hisce verbis, ut qui mecum amice omnia potes, temeritatis atque impudentiae tacite accusas, qui tantae existimationis virum per calumniam quodam modo
deprehendere² quaesiverim, habeo iam excusationem mihi ex tua
epistola paratam. Fateris enim vera esse quae in scholis nostris lec-
titantur, 'Amicus Plato, magis³ amica veritas, sed cum ambo sint
amici, pium esse veritatem in honore praeferre.'

4   Cum igitur ita sentirem, Plinium non minus quam caeteros in
hederae descriptione alterius plantae quae apud Graecos κισθὸς
appellatur⁴ nominis vicinitate deceptum, quoniam⁵ hedera a Graecis κισσὸς dicatur, indicia non sine errore miscuisse, nolui, quantum in me erat, pati⁶ veritatem ipsam in obscuro iacere. Quod
autem fortius atque evidentius hunc a me errorem indicari opor-
tuisse censes, scito non fuisse tunc⁷ animi mei propositum Plinii
auctoritatem pessundare. Nam cum illa dictabam, praecipua erat

you and by our dear Pico that, when his money finally began to
run out, he would be forced to pawn all his furniture. Since, therefore, all the goods of mind and fortune are superabundant in you,
there is no reason for me, when Angelo Poliziano declares for me
against the barbarians, to fear anyone who subsequently may take
up their defense.

Just as, however, you have determined that the barbarians are   3
rightly faulted by me, so you do not approve of my placing Pliny,
who contributed so excellently to life and letters, on the same scale
as the barbarians, and whose authority in the eyes of each and every expert is so great that either I should not have challenged it or,
if I thought it needed to be completely overturned, then this
should have been done by me more vigorously than so far I seem
to have done. Regarding all this, if by chance with these words you
(being someone who can try anything with me without offense)
are tacitly accusing me of recklessness or impudence, because I
sought somehow to catch a man of such great reputation by slan-
dering him, I already have a defense ready for myself out of your
own letter. For you admit the truth of what is taught in our
school: "Plato is a friend, truth is a better one, but although both
are friends, the respectful thing is to place truth first in honor."

I was, in fact, of the opinion that Pliny, no less than others, in   4
his description of ivy, deceived by the similarity of the name of another plant, which in Greek is called *kisthos*, since ivy is called *kissos*
by the Greeks, had confused his information, not without error. I
did not want, therefore, as far as I was able, to allow the actual
truth to lie hidden in the dark. As for the fact that you think that
this error should have been revealed by me more vigorously and
clearly, know that it was not then my intention to ruin Pliny's authority. For when I was saying these things, my quarrel was primarily with the barbarians. And so, in the course of a discussion
of ivy, the nature of which, I was trying to show, was not sufficiently known to Avicenna, in mentioning some others I also

mihi contentio cum barbaris. Atque ideo cum de hedera sermo ha-
beretur, cuius naturam non satis Avicennae cognitam fuisse probare contendebam, obiter ac veluti quodam in transcursu Plinium
quoque in aliorum mentione nominavi, quem tamen non dixi una
cum Avicenna ac reliquis errasse, sed videri in eodem cum aliis errore versari. Vide quam modestius de Plinio, quam de aliis tunc
sim locutus quos non videri[8] eodem errore deviare sed plane aber-
rare asseveravi. Quod si is mihi animus tunc fuisset, aut nunc
etiam esset, Plinii errata in lucem patefacere, potuissem et tunc et
nunc quoque possem integrum de eisdem implere volumen. Pauca
tamen e multis hoc in loco censui aperienda, ut intelligas me non
temerario iudicio sed certissimis rationibus adductum ut existimarem Plinium in hederae descriptione, quemadmodum in multis
aliis ad medicinam pertinentibus, aberrasse.

5   Illud vero mihi primum tecum conveniat, tam apud Graecos
quam apud Latinos atque etiam barbaros, Dioscoridem esse summum auctorem, atque praecipuum cui in herbarum ac fruticum
descriptionibus fides sit adhibenda. Nam et Plinius ipse[9] non minus hunc quam Theophrastum in hac parte secutus videtur, ut qui
utranque linguam, et Graecam et Latinam, noverit, sententias in-
tegras Dioscoridis, quasi verbum ex verbo, a Plinio translatas
agnoscat. Galenus praeterea, homo tum in omnium liberalium artium tum in medicinae praesertim disciplina praecipuus, in suo de
simplicibus medicamentis libro se a describendis herbarum imagi-
nibus supersedisse fatetur, quoniam abunde in hoc studio fuerat a
Dioscoride satisfactum. Nec Serapio Arabs, herbas describere ag-
gressus, aliis eas notis indicavit quam Dioscorides, quamvis et
ipse, non recte in omnibus imitando Dioscoridem, libros suos in-
numeris implevit erroribus, quos nisi sperarem aliquando[10] in lucem fore detegendos studio ac diligentia inclyti praesulis Hermolai
Barbari, Patriarchae Aquileiensis, viri omnium disciplinarum peri-

named Pliny, in passing and on the side. I did not, however, say that he had made a mistake along with Avicenna and the rest, but that he seemed to be situated, along with the others, in the same error. See how respectfully I spoke about Pliny, and how I then spoke about the others, who, I said, seemed as a result of the same error not to step off the path but, rather, to have lost the road altogether. But if I had been or even now were of a mind to expose Pliny's mistakes to the light, I could have then and could now fill an entire volume of the same. All the same, I have decided that, here and now, a few of these (out of many) ought to be disclosed, so that you may realize that I was led not by rash judgment but by the surest of reasons to suppose that Pliny, in his description of ivy, as in many other matters pertaining to medicine, had gone astray.

First, however, let us agree that, equally among Greek, Latin, and barbarian writers, Dioscorides is an authority of the highest level, and that he should be relied upon especially in his descriptions of herbs and bushes. Indeed, even Pliny himself in this category seems to have followed him no less than he followed Theophrastus, to the extent that someone who knows both Latin and Greek recognizes whole sentences of Dioscorides imported, essentially word for word, by Pliny. Furthermore, Galen, a leading figure in the study of all the liberal arts, but especially in that of medicine, acknowledges that he has refrained from describing the appearances of herbs because more than enough had been done on this subject by Dioscorides. Nor did the Arab Serapion,[1] having set out to describe herbs, distinguish them by any characteristics other than those Dioscorides had used, although, because he himself did not properly imitate Dioscorides in all matters, he filled his own books with countless errors. And if I were not hopeful that one day these will be brought to light by the careful efforts of our illustrious protector, Ermolao Barbaro, Patriarch of Aquileia, expert in all disciplines,[2] I would be pointing them out myself, a good deal more willingly than I am about to list, presently, those

5

tissimi, libentius sane aliquanto[11] notarem quam hosce Plinii in praesentia sim recitaturus, tum quia magis me iuvat contra homines barbaros quam Latinos agere, tum quia maius humano generi ex Serapionis inscitia quam ex Plinio[12] periculum imminet, siquidem aetate nostra omnes fere medici in simplicium medicaminum cognitione Serapionem sequuntur, Plinium autem nec legendum quidem existimant, quod eum in numero grammaticorum vel oratorum, non autem philosophorum aut medicorum habendum iudicent.

6   Ego vero, etsi non infitias eo Plinium omnium doctrinarum studia excoluisse, multa tamen de quibus in suis de naturali historia libris conscripsit non satis illi comperta atque explorata fuisse crediderim. Ex quo illud secutum est, ut cum non ea scriberet quae ipse novisset sed quae potius a diversis auctoribus varie scripta collegisset, saepius diversa pro eisdem atque eadem pro diversis retulisse videatur. Quam quidem rem me tibi homini doctissimo facile probaturum spero si, paululum seposito affectu, non tanquam Plinii patronus sed potius iudex haec quae in Plinio notaturi sumus errata diligentius perpendere atque examinare volueris.

Vale.[13]

: VIII :

Angelus Politianus Ioviano Pontano s. d.

1   Etsi magnum te dolorem Ferdinandi regis interitu cepisse non dubito, propterea quod in illo et auctoritas et sapientia tanta fuit

of Pliny, the reasons being, first, because I enjoy speaking out against barbarians more than Latin-speakers, and second, because a greater danger looms over the human race as a consequence of Serapion's ignorance than as a consequence of Pliny. This is because in our day nearly all doctors follow Serapion in the recognition of simple medicines, but they do not consider it necessary even just to read Pliny, since they think he should be counted among the grammarians or the orators, but not among the philosophers or the physicians.

I myself, however, even though I do not deny that Pliny refined 6 the studies of all branches of learning, nevertheless tend to believe that many of the things he wrote about in his books on natural history were insufficiently researched and confirmed by him. The consequence of this was that, since he wrote things of which he did not have first-hand knowledge but which, variously recorded by different authors, he had instead collected, he fairly often seems to refer to things as different when they should be the same, and to things as the same when they should be different. Indeed, I hope that I shall easily prove this to you, given that you are an extremely learned man, if, having set aside your affection for a little while, acting not as Pliny's patron but rather as his judge, you will be willing to weigh and examine carefully the errors we are about to point out in him.[3]

Farewell.

: VIII :

Angelo Poliziano to Gioviano Pontano[1]

Although I do not doubt that you have experienced great grief at 1 the passing of King Ferdinando,[2] for the reason that the degree of authority and wisdom in him we remember in scarcely any other

quantam vix in rege unquam alio meminimus, tamen cum mecum ipse considero quis ei regi rex succedat, pene esse nefas arbitror vel te vel quenquam ex iis qui rebus vestris favent, quorum de numero nos quoque sumus, maiore aliquo in luctu moestitiaque versari. Nam cum vobis regni haeres (quod felix faustumque sit) Alfonsus alter, maximus natu, filius obtigerit, cuius excellens ingenium, singularis virtus, incredibilis sapientia bello et pace claruit, ingrati profecto fuerimus, si non quantum relictum sed quantum sit ademptum respexerimus, praesertim cum subsidiis tot tantique regnum fulciatur.

2   Dux enim suffectus Calabris Ferdinandus, alter Alfonsi filius, quem et ipsum nobis fama refert omnibus corporis animique dotibus excellere, sicut multis magnisque rebus, non dubium iam regiae cuiusdam indolis specimen dederit. Accedit eo Federicus, magna prudentia, magna dexteritate, magno usu rerum, sed maiore in regem fratrem benivolentia, fide, pietate. Mitto necessitudines alias, opes, exercitus, duces, socios, studia, popularium praesidia, munimenta, propugnacula, quae nullis pene humanis viribus labefactari posse videantur. Opem vero divinam quis, rogo, vel sperare vel polliceri sibi magis potest quam qui Turcos impios ferro ignique sequens non tam ab oppido Hydrunte quam, ut mihi videtur, ab Roma ipsa, quam primum petebant, atque adeo a sanctissimis illis altaribus expulerit?

3   Quapropter, tametsi magna omnino fata est iactura Ferdinandi obitu, tamen quoniam vigiliam quasi suam filio tradidit, regemque pro se quem potissimum voluit reliquit, in omni genere laudis ex-

age's king, nevertheless, when I think to myself what king succeeds this king, I almost think it blasphemous for you or anyone who supports your interests, in which number we too are counted, to spend time on any extended grieving or sorrow. Indeed, since there has fallen to you as heir to the kingdom (propitious and prosperous may it be![3]) a second Alfonso, his oldest son,[4] whose outstanding intellect and unparalleled virtue and unbelievable wisdom have been conspicuous in peace and in war, we would be utterly ungrateful if we regarded not how much we have been left but, rather, how much has been taken away from us, especially since the kingdom is bulwarked by supports that are so numerous and so great.

For example, the Duke Suffect of Calabria, the other Ferdi- 2
nando, son of Alfonso,[5] who too, according to report, excels in all physical and intellectual gifts, just as in great and numerous deeds, already will have provided indisputable evidence of a certain royal quality. There is, in addition, Federico,[6] notable for his great wisdom, great readiness, and great experience — but also for his even greater good will, loyalty, and respect toward his brother the king. I omit the other members of the family, the resources, the armies, the generals, the allies, the support, the protection of his countrymen, the defenses, the fortifications, of a sort which seem capable of being shaken by practically no human force. Who, I ask, can more expect or promise for himself divine aid than the man who, pursuing the infidel Turks with sword and fire, expelled them not so much from the town of Otranto[7] than (as I see it) from Rome itself, which was their first goal, and thus from those holiest of altars?

For these reasons, even though a great loss has been sustained 3
in the death of Ferdinando, nevertheless, since he turned over his watch-post, as we might say, to his son and left in his place the king whom he most especially wanted, an outstanding one in every category of merit, those of you in the service of the king should in

cellentem, non debetis ullo pacto, mi Pontane, quicunque inter officia regis estis, moerori vos dedere, sed animo praesenti (quod equidem te facere arbitor) praesto esse, diligentiamque omnem vestram videlicet ad eum (quantum quidem fieri potest) cura, labore, molestiaque levandum conferre. Te vero etiam seorsum gratias agere Deo maximo convenit, quod eum quem in hanc spem a tenero educasti, quem disciplinis ornasti, quem praeceptis instituisti, regem iam vides, atque ita regem, non modo ut regno pulcherrimo isto quidem atque opulentissimo, sed ut etiam orbis terrarum imperio dignissimus habeatur.

4   Haec ego ut ad te scriberem praecipuus quidam meus erga te principesque tuos amor impulit. Sed et multum quoque adhortatus est alumnus hic meus idemque patronus nostraeque rei publicae columen, Petrus Medices, excellenti iuvenis et animo et ingenio, quo nihil fieri potest, mi Pontane, tui amantius. Nam regi ipsi tuo quam sese idem totum penitusque tradiderit nihil attinet scribere, praesertim ad te, cui nota sunt omnia. Sed tamen ita de illo semper et honorifice loquitur et amanter, ut caeteris pene reliquis nihil faciat.

5   Atque haec hactenus. Quod autem superioribus diebus excusasti diligenter occupationes tuas, propterea quod epistolae cuidam nostrae non responderas, nimis officiosus homo es, ut video, nimis humanus. Me enim quamvis omnino equidem literas tuas gratissimas haberem, nihil delectare potest quod cum tua ulla molestia tribuatur. Tantum illud ignoscas velim quod, dum studio in te meo et amore obsequor, non sum veritus semel iterumque tuis occupationibus obstrepere. Licet autem per me tibi, dummodo amare non desinas, non solum non respondere ad literas meas, sed ne legere eas quidem, si ita sit commodum.

Vale.

no way, my dear Pontano, surrender yourselves to grief, but you should instead serve the current king with devotion (which of course I assume you yourself are doing) and apply all your combined care to the following clear purpose: that of relieving him (to the extent possible) of concern, labor, and annoyance. It is fitting, however, that you yourself give separate thanks. For the one you raised from a tender age with this expectation, whom you equipped with learning, whom you formed by instruction, you now see as king, and king in such a way that he seems eminently worthy not only of that most beautiful and rich kingdom of yours, but even of the command of the entire world.

What drives me to write these things to you is most of all my love towards you and your leading citizens. But my simultaneous protégé and patron, pillar of our Republic, Piero de' Medici, a young man of outstanding spirit and intellect, than whom nothing more devoted to you could exist, my dear Pontano, also gave me much additional encouragement. For it is pointless to put in writing—especially to you, to whom all is well-known—how complete and heartfelt is his dedication to the person of your king. But let me at least say that he speaks about him so frequently and flatteringly he leaves nothing for anyone else. 4

Enough about all that. As for the fact that, a few days back, you carefully asked forgiveness for the demands on your time, because you had not responded to a certain letter from me, well, you are, from my point of view, too responsible, too kind. Although I certainly am overwhelmingly grateful for a letter from you, no gift which had caused you any trouble could give me pleasure. Please just forgive me for the fact that, in my devotion and love for you, I once or twice did not scruple to make noise in the face of demands on your time. As far as I am concerned, you are allowed (as long as you do not stop loving me) not only not to respond to my letters, but if convenient, not even to read them. 5

Farewell.

: IX :

Hieronymus Donatus Ioanni Pico Mirandulae s. d.

1 Quae meae partes esse debuerant, eas omnes tibi sumpsisti, Pice doctissime, te ipsum apud me neglegentiae insimulans et in eo crimine, cuius ego apud te maxime reus sum, excusationem quaerens. Parum tibi videtur alios ingenio et eruditione praecellere, nisi modestia quoque et humanitate vincas non solum alios, sed te ipsum. At vero, obsecro, harum virtutum munera ita amplectaris ut nobis quoque aliquam obeundi officii nostri occasionem relinquas, ne dum harum omnes tibi partes vindicas, nos inhumani atque inciviles habeamur, qua ego in re (quae mea est impudentia) iam non excuso neglegentiam meam, sed accuso humanitatem tuam.

2 Quod scribis te non temporariam mecum sed perpetuam amicitiam statuisse, non solum ea causa tibi me plurimum debere intelligo, verum etiam recte mihi amicitiam definisse videris, quae temporaria cum sit, iam amicitia esse non potest. Illud scito: me eam in meorum ornamentorum delectu seposuisse. Quid enim mihi accidere potest praeclarius quam a tanto viro non laudari solum sed etiam amari?

3 Hermolaus noster incredibilem doctrinarum tranquillitatem et studiorum φιλοπονίαν curat, maxima utilitate eruditorum. Video esse summum ac rarum quiddam quod sperare possunt literae, eo incolumi. Eius ego consuetudinem, quam mihi tantopere invides, eadem penu servo qua et amicitiam tuam. Nihil praeterea adeo θαυμαστὸν censeo quod assequi ingenio et eruditione non possis, praesertim quia audio te τῆς ἑλληνικῆς παιδείας χάριν

: IX :

Girolamo Donà[1] to Giovanni Pico della Mirandola

Most learned Pico, you have taken for yourself the entire role that   1
should be mine, for you accuse yourself of negligence in my regard
and seek forgiveness on the very charge of which I myself am
enormously guilty regarding you. To you it seems too little to surpass others in genius and learning unless you outdo not just others
but even yourself in modesty and kindness. But I beg you to embrace the duties connected with these virtues in such a way that
you leave us too some possibility of fulfilling our obligations, lest,
while you claim for yourself all aspects of said virtues, we be regarded as rude and unkind. On which score, such is my impudence that I no longer excuse my own negligence but, rather, accuse your kindness.

As for the fact that you write that you have established with me   2
not a temporary friendship, but a permanent one, not only do I realize that I owe you a very great deal on this account, but you also
seem to me to have properly defined friendship, which, when it is
temporary, can no longer be friendship. Know this: I have reserved
friendship for the choicest category of my badges of honor. For
what more glorious thing can happen to me than by so great a
man not only to be praised, but to be loved?

Our friend Ermolao fosters an unbelievable detachment for   3
learning and industriousness for study, to the great profit of the erudite. I see that there is something lofty and rare for which literature can hope, as long as he is around. I store his intimacy in the
same inner chamber in which I keep your friendship. Furthermore, I consider nothing to be so astonishing that you cannot
achieve it by your genius and learning, especially since I hear that
you have left home to go there for the sake of a Greek education. I

istuc demigrasse. Quod ego consilium ita laudo ut magis laudare non possim. Nam οὐδὲν γλυκύτερον ἢ πάντ᾽ εἰδέναι.

4   Ego Politianum tibi invideo, hominem fertilissimi et facundissimi ingenii, cuius Rusticum nuper legi. Visus est mihi splendor aetatis nostrae et πᾶν ἐπ᾽ ἀλαθείᾳ πεπλασμένον ἐκ Διὸς ἔρνος, cui ea de me polliceri te meis verbis postulo quae ab homine amicissimo expectare potest. Utor autem te internuntio in auspicanda mihi cum eo benivolentia, cum fretus humanitate tua, tum quod τῶν Μουσῶν καπυρῷ στόμα per te, qui eruditissimus es, me conciliari convenit.

5   Vale, et puta nihil mihi tuis literis esse iucundius. Plura laxiore ocio ad te scribam.

Venetiis, xvii Kalendas Ianuarias MCCCCLXXXIIII

: X :

Angelus Politianus Hieronymo Donato[1] *suo s. d.*

1   In epistola quadam tua ad Picum nostrum cum me pleraque delectassent, tum ut ad te scriberem subinvitavit iudicium quod affers[2] de Rustico nostra,[3] utinam quidem tam verum quam honorificum, quod ego tamen non iudicium adeo de me sed studium potius in me ac beneficium interpretor.[4] Neque enim ita mihi sum inexploratus ut tibi, amicissimo homini, atque[5] ob id minus integro iudici, plus de me credendum statuam quam ipse[6] mihi, nisi forte ita me ludit illa poetarum (quod Horatius inquit) amabilis insania ut

so commend this decision that I cannot commend it any higher. For "nothing is sweeter than knowing everything."[2]

I envy you Poliziano, a man of most fertile and fluent genius, 4 whose *Rusticus*[3] I recently read. He struck me as being a shining light of our age and "a tender shoot all shaped by Zeus in line with truth."[4] I ask you, on my behalf, to pledge to him from me those things he can expect from a very friendly person. I shall use you as intermediary in inaugurating friendly relations with him for me, not only relying on your kindness, but also because, since you are most erudite, it is only fitting that I be commended to "the clear-sounding voice of the Muses"[5] through you.

Farewell, and calculate that nothing is more delightful to me 5 than a letter from you. I shall write you more things when I have a more extensive break.

Venice, December 16, 1484

: X :

Angelo Poliziano to his dear Girolamo Donà

Although numerous things in a recent letter of yours to our friend 1 Pico caused me pleasure, it was the opinion you offer of my *Rusticus* that gave me the nudge to write to you.[1] If only it were as true as it is flattering! I understand it, however, not so much as an opinion about me as, instead, support for me, and a favor. I am not such a stranger to myself as to decide that, on the subject of myself, more than I trust myself I should trust you, who, being a very friendly person, are for this reason a less impartial judge. Unless by chance, to use Horace's words, that "gentle madness" of the poets so "makes sport of me" that I never come to grips with myself and never return the knapsack from my back to my chest.[2] But

nunquam congrediar mecum, nunquam de tergo in pectus manticam revocem. Quod si poeticen sequitur, velut umbra corpus, 'caecus ille amor sui,' qui φιλαυτία dicitur quaeque plerosque infatuat, 'et tollens vacuum plus nimio gloria verticem,' fateor iam nunc, piget me candidatum poetices haberi, tam ingrata vice, tam tristi ac poenitenda mercede. Alioqui ne Lycius quidem ille me stultior χρύσεα χαλκείων demutaverit ἑκατόμβοια ἔννεαβοιῶν.

2   Caeterum nihil minus debemus tibi, vel sentienti de nobis vel sentiri ab aliis postulanti quae nec agnoscat conscientia nostra nec ferat pudor. Sive enim, ut caeteros fallas, ne tua quidem ornamenta, hoc est laudum tuarum supellectilem, mihi invides, sive ipse falleris potius, meaque te vel vitia delectant, utrunque amoris est, et quidem non vulgaris, siquidem Achilles quoque Patroclo sua arma induit, et Alcaeum vatem naevus etiam in articulo pueri delectabat. Quare, si me amas, id quod scio, iam scilicet dubitare non potes quin ego te redamem, siquidem aiunt amorem nullo magis emi quam se ipso. Neque tamen sicut amantem mutuo amo, ita laudantem vicissim te laudo; quippe in reponendis beneficiis lex est illa Hesiodi custodienda, ut eadem mensura reddas, aut etiam cumulatiore, si possis. Sed cum tu (quas habes orationis divitias), cum tu, inquam, isto ingenio vir, istaque doctrina, in me unum e medio homunculum laudes tantas, ipso (quod aiunt) horreo, congesseris, qui possum ego, de reditu maligni incultique soli, saltem alterum tantum tibi, nedum⁷ plus aliquid, remetiri, nisi tamen, velut Echo illa, tuas tibi voces regeram atque refundam? Sed

if, like a shadow after a body, that "blind self-love" (which is called *philautia* and which makes a fool of many a person) "and vainglory lifting its empty head beyond excess"[3] follow poetic art as its consequence, then—let me say for the record—I'm vexed to be considered poetry's nominee, so thankless is the office, so depressing and regrettable the reward. If I were not, then not even that Lycian who traded "gold for bronze, a hundred oxen's worth for that of nine"[4] would be stupider than me.

However, my debt to you is no smaller because you hold opinions about me (or ask that they be held by others) which neither my conscience can acknowledge nor my sense of propriety bear. Whether, in order to fool others, you do not grudge to see me decked out in your own equipment (i.e., that of your accomplishments), or, alternatively, you yourself are fooled and admire even my defects, both are attributable to love—indeed, no common love, since Achilles too dressed Patroclus in his own armor, and Alcaeus admired even a mole on his boyfriend's knee.[5] And so, if you love me, as I know you do, then you surely can no longer doubt that I love you back. For love, they say, costs nothing more than—itself. Nevertheless, though I in turn love you loving me, I do not in the same way reciprocally praise you praising me. My reason? In repaying favors, one must maintain observance of that law of Hesiod, according to which you should give back in equal measure, or even, if you can, in more abundant measure.[6] But since you, given the wealth of expression you have, since you, I say, a man in possession of that genius and that learning of yours, have heaped upon me, a single insignificant person from the crowd, so much praise—a whole barn-full, as they say[7]—how can I measure back even just an equal amount, to say nothing of something extra, from the yield of my barren and uncultivated soil, unless, in spite of it all, I reflect your words and send them flowing back to you, like Echo?[8] But I worry that, if I forfeit whatever you have given me and send you back those words of praise which I possess

2

vereor ne si quaecunque dederis resignavero, tibique laudes tuas quas precario possideam remissero, nudum ipse me statuam et, ut illa Aesopi cornicula plumis ablatis, moveam risum.

3   Atqui tamen nec illud saltem me potes ingrati reum peragere, cum vicariam pro me solutionem sponte suscipiat ac meas parteis sublevet sacer hic—Picus dicam, an Phoenix?—cuius tu semper in ore illo es, Musarum Gratiarumque pleno, quo scilicet inspirante nos quoque impellimur ad te, supra etiam quam valemus, sed tamen adhuc infra quam cupimus,[8] efferendum. Nam par quidem tanto perferendo oneri ipse est solus. Nos autem de eo sic pendemus ut de magnete[9] Platonis anuli ferrei, ipseque in nos vim quandam arcanam depluit, quasi ἐνθουσιασμόν, qui plus etiam posse nos cogit quam sponte possumus. Ipse quasi pausarius modos et incitamenta dat nobis laudandi tui, laudandi una tecum Hermolai Barbari, hominis, ut mihi quidem videtur, unius ex reliquiis aurei saeculi, quamvis ipse longe doctior, et non illi sanctiores. Sed ingressos plerunque nos super vobis aliquid ῥαψῳδεῖν, tam multa in caelum aura levat ut Icarium quandoque casum formidemus. Vides autem nunc quoque me, quasi νυμφόληπτον, etiam in epistola nescioquid exhibere διθυραμβικώτερον. Quid tu igitur frontem obducis? An scilicet te fugit indulgendum hoc mihi, quicquid est furoris, vel quod omnis paulo humanioris iuxta adamo ac sum (quod dicitur) amussis alba, vel quod tibi quoque non abhorrens videor a Musis, Picoque item ipsi, et fortasse Hermolao, triumviris scilicet literariis, qui si me vel tantillum probatis, iam nunc medium ostendo digitum, non popello tantum, et litera-

by your permission, I shall put my naked self on display and, like that crow of Aesop stripped of its feathers, shall make people laugh.[9]

At least, however, there's one thing you cannot do — prosecute me for ingratitude — since this divine Pico (or should I say Phoenix?[10]), on whose lips you always are and who is full of Muses and Graces, undertook payment on my behalf, of his own free will, and lightened my share of the load. Needless to say, it is by his inspiration that I too am driven to extol you even beyond my capacity, though still less than I would like. For he is the only person equal to the task of carrying this heavy responsibility. I am as dependent on him as Plato's iron rings are on the magnet.[11] And he in turn rains down into me a certain secret power, a kind of divine possession that forces me to have capabilities in addition to those I have on my own.[12] Like a boatswain, he marks time and spurs me on, showing me how to praise you[13] and, along with you, Ermolao Barbaro, one of those people (it seems to me) left over from the Golden Age,[14] although he is more learned by far, and they were no more virtuous. But often, having set out to rhapsodize something about the three of you, so much of a breeze lifts me toward heaven that I fear sooner or later an Icarian fall.[15] Even now, you see that I, more or less under a spell even in a letter, am producing something rather dithyrambic.[16] Why then are you frowning? Could it possibly escape you that I must be indulged in whatever kind of frenzy[17] this is, either because I am equally in love with everyone who is a little more than minimally civilized and am, as they say, an "unmarked ruler,"[18] or because I do not seem hideously incompatible with the Muses from your point of view either, just as I do not seem so to Pico or (I hope) Ermolao — in other words, to the Triumvirs of Letters. If you three are showing me even a modicum of approval, then I am already giving the finger not only to the rabble and the schoolmasters, but even to

3

toribus, sed philosophis adeo ipsis, ne excepto quidem Platone, sed Florentino.
Vale.

: XI :

Hieronymus Donatus Angelo Politiano suo s. d.

1   Ego vero, Politiane doctissime, tui erga me amoris fructus gratissimos et iucundissimos cepisse me sentio, neque aliunde uberiores honorificentioresque proventus expecto. Nam et in amicitia respondisse te video αὐτῷ τῷ μέτρῳ λῴον, et te (id quod nunquam dubitavi) non Politianum modo, verum et πολιτικώτατον esse percipio, sociata tam rara exactaque eloquentia infinitae prope humanitati atque modestiae. Quod si rationes negociorum meorum excussero atque invicem retulero, nihil me ab eo die quo ad Picum novissime scripsi praestantius lucrifecisse comperiam tua hac epistola — dii boni, quantum Attica, erecta, exculta, quantum denique amabili, ut in ea summus amor, summa eruditio contendere videantur, neque facile utrum excellat dignosci possit. Utriusque rei evidentissimas causas coniectari facillimum est. Eruditio enim divino ingenio, studio infatigabili, tota ex te ipso summa est. Benivolentia vero non ingentissima esse non potest qua me, Pico auctore, complexus es. Ego tamen iam antea amare te coeperam, sed defuit illa εἰς ταὐτὸν συνάγουσα ὁμιλία, qua tamen in posterum beneficio literarum non indigebimus.

the philosophers. Not even Plato is spared — unless he be the Florentine one.[19]

Farewell.

: XI :

Girolamo Donà to his dear Angelo Poliziano

I am truly aware, most learned Poliziano, that I have gathered 1
fruits of your love for me that are most welcome and delicious,
and I do not expect more copious harvests, or ones which do me
more honor, from any other source. For I see that, even with respect to friendship, you respond "with the same amount, and even
more."[1] And I recognize that which I have never doubted, namely,
that you are not only Poliziano, but also pure Politeness, since
such rare and perfect eloquence has been united with almost
boundless kindness and forbearance. Indeed, if I scrutinize the
ledger of my transactions and record each value in turn, I shall discover that, since that day on which I most recently wrote to Pico, I
have received as profit nothing more impressive than this letter of
yours. Dear gods, how Attic,[2] elevated, refined, and, finally, how
affectionate! To the point that, in it, supreme love seems to contend with supreme erudition, nor is it easy to tell which is winning. It is a very simple matter to deduce the reasons for each of
these, since they are extremely obvious. Given your divine intellect
and tireless study, your erudition is supreme entirely as a consequence of you yourself. On the other hand, the friendly feeling
with which you have embraced me cannot fail to be huge — since
Pico is responsible for it. Mind you, I had already begun to love
you, but that "communion fusing into one"[3] was missing, which,
however, we shall not lack from now on, thanks to letters.

2   At tamen meminisse te suspicor (fere enim quinquennium agitur cum apud nos versabaris) te Hermolao ac mihi, tunc parentis et patrui morte squalido ac pullato, carmen illud aureum de sacrilega ac sanguinaria Iuliani caede recitasse, ex quo nunquam apud me eruditorum hominum mentio facta est quin mihi ex omnibus primus occurreres. Mox in tua illa Rustico elegantissima, magnus a me semper habitus, maior inventus es. Quamobrem id tibi persuasum velim: ea te mecum amoris et officium fundamenta iecisse ut nullo casu ruere, nulla vi convelli possint, cuius fructus candidissimos et mihi omnium longe gratissimos, hoc est literas tuas, expecto. Neque solum literas, sed interdum quoque amoenissimas Musas, quae cum ad me venerint, tunc maxime Theocriti carmen illud suavissimum cantabo:

τᾶς μοι πᾶς εἴη πλεῖος δόμος, οὔτε γὰρ ὕπνος
οὔτ᾽ ἔαρ ἐξαπίνας γλυκερώτερον, οὔτε μελίσσαις
ἄνθεα, ὅσσον ἐμοί Μῶσαι Πωλιτιανοῦ φίλαι.

3   Vale, et me ama, a quo amaris plurimum.
Venetiis, vi Idus Iunias MXVD[1]

: XII :

Hieronymus Donatus Angelo Politiano suo s. d.

1   Salve, Politiane mi. Tam diu humanissimis literis tuis respondere distuli ut putem me nunc potius ad te scribere quam rescribere.

Yet I suppose you remember—to be sure, nearly five years have 2
passed since you stayed with me—that you read to Ermolao and
me, when I was dressed in black and filthy over the deaths of my
parent and uncle, that golden poem about the sacrilegious and
bloody murder of Giuliano.[4] From that point on, no reference to
"erudite men" was made in my presence but that you first of all
sprang to mind. Soon thereafter, having always been considered
great by me, you were found to be greater in your very elegant
Rusticus. Please, therefore, rest assured that you have laid such
foundations of love and obligation with me that they cannot
crumble from any calamity, cannot be uprooted by any violent
power. I await their fairest fruit, for me by far the most welcome
of all—namely, letters from you. And not just letters, but, now
and then, those most delightful poems too. Especially then, after
these have reached me, I shall sing that most gentle song of
Theocritus:

Of this may all my house be full. Not sleep
nor spring's surprise more sweet, nor blooms to bees,
than dear to me is poesy—Poliziano's.[5]

Farewell, and love me, by whom you are loved best.   3
Venice, June 8, 1485

: XII :

Girolamo Donà to his dear Angelo Poliziano

Hello, my dear Poliziano. I have put off for such a long time re- 1
sponding to your very kind letter that I suppose that, rather than
writing you back, I'm now just writing you, period. Please ascribe
this either to public responsibilities or to private laziness, as long

Imputabis sive occupationes publicas sive privatam desidiam, modo abdices omnem aut oblivionis aut arrogantiae suspitionem. Equidem, Politiane mi, nullum ego thesaurum comparari[1] posse censeo amico qui et probus et doctus sit. Nec aliunde homini locupletior felicitatis proventus accedit quam ex vera incorruptaque amicitia quam virtus probitasque conciliat. Quo fit ut ego saepissime vestram istam, sub parente patriae Laurentio, Academiam absens mirari et amare maxime soleam, in qua praeclara simul optimarum artium morumque pretia contra pertinacissimas animi sordes, vitium atque inscitiam, conspiraverunt. Quorsum haec?[2] Ut facile tibi persuadeas me, quanquam tardius rescripserim, summopere tamen delectatum esse humanissimis et eruditissimis literis tuis. In iis praeclarum istud vestrum ocium intueri licet, et doctrinarum quietem vobis invidere. Nam nos et publica et privata distringunt, et nostra fere sunt temporis furta, non studia. Gratulor vobis amoenissimas Musas, literatissimum ocium, quibus absens impense faveo, subscribo et bene opto, cum vestra, tum bonarum artium causa. Sed haec satis.

2   Scio istic apud vos esse conplura Alexandri Aphrodisei volumina in variis generibus doctrinarum, praecipue vero in philosophia naturali. Sunt item apud me hic nonnulla illius opera, mire erudita et gravia. In his habentur duo volumina Περὶ ψυχῆς, quae per hos dies perlegi. Alterum ex his voluminibus principium habet eiusmodi: Περὶ ψυχῆς τί τ᾽ ἐστὶ καὶ τίς αὐτῆς ἡ οὐσία. Is libellus apud me fere post principium mutilus est. Cupio me certiorem reddas numquid apud vos in delectissima ista Medicum bibliotheca totius atque incolumis sit. Quod si, ut spero, illaesus et

as you forswear any suspicion of either forgetfulness or disrespect. For my part, my dear Poliziano, I think one should compare no treasure to a friend who is a man of integrity and learning. Nor does a richer supply of good fortune accrue to a person from any other source than genuine, unadulterated friendship which virtue and integrity have secured. Thus it happens that I, from afar, have the constant habit of admiring and loving, to the greatest possible extent, that Academy you have under Lorenzo, father of his country, in which the magnificent rewards of the finest arts and the finest morals act together in harmony against the most stubborn stains of the mind: vice and ignorance. In short, I am hoping that you will easily convince yourself that, although I have been rather late in writing back, I nevertheless took tremendous pleasure in your most kind and erudite letter. In it one could observe that magnificently tranquil existence you all share and envy you the serene setting of your studies. Here, both public and private matters pull us in every direction, and what we have are basically stolen moments, not studies. I congratulate you all for your most delightful poetry and most literary leisure, which, from afar but without restraint, I support, endorse, and lend my best hopes, not only for your sake, but also for that of the liberal arts. But enough about this.

I know that, in your house, there are numerous volumes of Alexander of Aphrodisias,[1] on various kinds of learned subjects, but especially on natural philosophy. Here where I am[2] there are several works of his which are wonderfully erudite and substantial. Among these are two volumes *On the Soul* which I read through over the course of the past few days. One of these volumes begins like this: "Regarding the soul, what it is, and what is its essence . . . ".[3] This booklet, the one I have here, breaks off practically just after the beginning. I want you to let me know whether you have there at home, in that very choice library of the Medici, something more complete and undamaged. But if, as I hope, it is

integer, mihi gratissimum facies si primum eius libri caput trans-
cribi feceris, et ad me mitti curaveris. Si negocium librario commi-
seris, neque praeceleri, vix horam absumet.

3   Vale. Picum meum salvere iube. Cum dico Picum, doctos etiam
omnes intellego.

Iterum vale.

Mediolani, pridie Calendas Apriles MCCCCLXXXX

: XIII :

Angelus Politianus Hieronymo Donato suo s. d.

1   Etsi literarum tuarum semper incredibili desiderio teneor, propterea quod mihi ex eruditione fructus, ex elegantia[1] voluptas, ex auctoritate summus honos conciliatur, facile tamen id ego differri
nonnunquam patior, vel ne te a studiis avocem potioribus, vel
certe ut exemplum mihi tuum, sexcentas iam debenti epistolas, pa-
trocinetur. Roges causas tanti debiti. Non inficior desidiam esse
primam, quae mihi semper, nescio quo pacto, fuit in deliciis. Sed
tamen et occupatiunculae, vel trichae[2] potius ineptae quaedam
molestaeque nimis, ocium omne meum pene inter se scripulatim
partiuntur.

2   Nam si quis breve dictum quod in gladii capulo vel in anuli legatur[3] emblemate, si quis versum lecto aut cubiculo, si quis insigne
aliquod, non argento dixerim, sed fictilibus omnino suis desiderat,
illico ad Politianum cursitat, omnesque iam parietes a me, quasi a

inviolate and intact, you will do me an enormous favor if you will have the first chapter of this book copied and see to it that it is sent to me. If you entrust the job to a professional copyist, even a relatively slow one, it will take him scarcely an hour.

Farewell. Tell my friend Pico to take care. When I say "Pico," I 3
mean, in addition, *all* learned men. Again, farewell.

Milan, March 31, 1490

: XIII :

Angelo Poliziano to his dear Girolamo Donà

Although I am under the constant power of incredible longing for 1
your letters, for the reason that I am granted fruit from their erudition, pleasure from their elegance, supreme honor from their author's prestige, nevertheless I easily tolerate occasional deferral, either because I do not want to distract you from more important pursuits, or because I doubtless want to use your example as an excuse for myself, since by now I too owe people a thousand letters. You may ask what the causes are of such a large debt. I shall not deny that the first of these is laziness, which in one way or another has always been one of my favorite things. Nevertheless, it is also the case that tiny responsibilities — or better still, inane and very irritating bits of nonsense — divide up my free time piecemeal.

For if anyone wants a motto fit to be read on the hilt of a sword 2
or the signet of a ring, if anyone wants a line of verse for a bed or a bedroom, if anyone wants something distinctive (not for silver, mind you, but for pottery pure and simple!), then straightaway he dashes over to Poliziano. And already you can see that every wall has been smeared by me (as if by a snail) with diverse themes and inscriptions. Someone, for example, pesters me for some clever

limace, videas oblitos argumentis variis et titulis. Ecce alius Bac-
chanalibus Fesceninorum argutias, alius conciliabulis sanctas ser-
mocinationes, alius citharae miserabiles naenias, alius pervigilio li-
centiosas cantilenas efflagitat. Ille mihi proprios amores stultus
stultiori narrat, ille symbolum poscit quod suae tantum pateat,
caeterorum frustra coniecturas exerceat. Mitto scholasticorum gar-
ritus intempestivos, versificatorum nugas, seque et sua de more ad-
mirantium, quae cottidie cuncta demissis auriculis perpetior. Quid
plebeculam dicam, vel urbanam vel agrestem, quae me tota urbe
ad suum negocium quasi naso bubalum trahit. Ergo[4] dum proterve
instantibus negare nihil audeo, cogor et amicos vexare caeteros et
(quod molestissimum est) ipsius in primis Laurentii mei Medicis
abuti facilitate. Quare adeo mihi nullus inter haec scribendi restat
aut commentandi locus ut ipsum quoque horarium sacerdotis officium pene (quod vix expiabile credo) minutatim concidatur. Postremo cum nihil faciam, nunquam sum tamen ociosus; immo dum
cuiusvis esse compellor, nec meus esse plane nec cuiusquam possum. Proinde sicubi distulero posthac aut omisero ad te responsum, scito me statim, sicuti soleam, nugas agendo fuisse occupatum.

3   Laurentius Medices noster, vel ex epistolis tuis, quas ei semper
honoris mei causa recito, vel ex huius magni Pici testimonio, qui
tibi plurimum tribuere solet, ita te iam diligit ut nobiscum fere
contendat. Hermolaum vero ipsum Romae, hoc est quam[5] oculatissimo loco, legatum fore mire gavisus est, etiam studiorum nomine, quem sic expectamus avide ut spe iam totum pene contrive-

turns of Fescennine verse to use at a Bacchanal,[1] another, for a pi-
ous script to use at meetings, another, for some tear-jerking dirges
for the cithara, another, for some dirty little tunes for an all-night
party. One fool (but I'm a bigger one) tells me all about his own
love affairs; another requests a cypher which will reveal itself only
to his girlfriend and keep others busy conjecturing in vain. I omit
the ill-timed chatter of the rhetoricians and the nonsense of the
versifiers — in awe of themselves and their own work, as is typi-
cal — all of which I put up with every day, my ears drooping.[2]
Why mention the rabble (from the city or the country, take your
pick), which throughout the city drags me over to its own prob-
lems, like a buffalo by the nose.[3] Thus, as long as I do not dare
deny anything to the people aggressively pressuring me, I am
forced both to bother my other friends and in particular (this is
the really annoying thing) to take advantage of my dear Lorenzo
de' Medici's good nature. As a result, so little space among all
these things is left to me for writing or commenting that even my
hourly priestly office is pared away practically bit by bit — something scarcely forgivable, I think.[4] In short, although I am doing
nothing, all the same I am never at leisure. On the contrary, as
long as I am compelled to belong to everybody, I can never really
belong to myself — or to anyone.[5] So then, if at any point in the
future I put off or skip altogether a response to you, know that, as
usual, I was immediately kept busy doing nonsense.

Our friend Lorenzo de' Medici, as a consequence either of your 3
letters, which I always read to him in the interest of my own good
name, or of the testimony of this great man Pico, who regularly attributes a very great deal to you, so esteems you already that he
nearly competes with me. He was marvelously pleased, also in the
name of scholarship, that Ermolao will be sent on an embassy to
Rome, that is to say, to a place in everyone's eyesight.[6] We so eagerly look forward to seeing him that we have practically worn him
out with our expectation. But if, once he has been given hospital-

rimus. Quod si, semel in itere exceptus, abire a nobis properabit, iam nunc dico atque edico, 'Vae hominis togae, vae laciniis!'

4   Alexandri vero quos ais De anima libros, nullos ipsi prorsus hic habemus. Sed nec extare quidem suspicabamur, quod ex indice quoque ipso quem Seraticus at te misit animadvertes. Quin roga-mus ego et Picus ut, cum Venetias (quod propediem fore nun-tiant) remeaveris, eius describendi copiam Laurentii Medicis li-brario facias.⁶ Equidem nonnullas Alexandri huius peracutas in philosophia quaestiones, anno iam tum superiore, Latinas feci. Sed et te quaepiam scriptoris eiusdem narrat Seraticus interpre-tari. Tum Grimanus proxima aestate missurum se mihi exemplar alterum, quod tibi pridem commodaverat, ultro est pollicitus. Qua de re coniecturam facio potuisse illud accidere ut eundem uterque, forte fortuna, librum converterimus. Hoc si non falso ratiocinor, iam scilicet spongiam cogito,⁷ rogoque mihi de eo quam primum significes, ut ipsum saltem limae laborem lucrifaciam.

5   Vale, meque Iacobis duobus, Volterrano et Antiquario, hoc est humanitatis ac probitatis geminis exemplaribus, commenda.

Florentiae, x Calendas Maias MCCCCLXXXX

: XIV :

Hieronymus Donatus Angelo Politiano suo s. d.

1   Accepi Miscellanea. Percurri. Iucundissima lectio, in qua delectari et iuvari vel doctissimus quisque possit. At, inquies, praeceps iudi-

ity along his way, he will be in a hurry to leave us, well, right now I declare and decree a bad day for the man's robe, a bad day for his hem![7]

As for the books of Alexander which you say are *On the Soul*, we 4 ourselves have absolutely none of them here. But I did not even think they were extant, which you can observe as well from the very list that Seratico sent you.[8] Pico and I instead ask you, when you have returned to Venice (any day now, they tell us), to make it available to Lorenzo de' Medici's copyist for duplication. I myself, already last year, put a number of very sharp philosophical questions by this same Alexander into Latin.[9] But Seratico reports that you too are translating something or other by the same writer. Furthermore, Grimani,[10] without my asking, has promised to send me, this summer, a second manuscript, one which he had earlier lent to you. From all this I am guessing that it could have happened that, by complete chance, both of us have translated the same book. If my reasoning is not wrong then I am of course thinking already about the sponge, and I ask you to let me know about this as soon as possible, so that I can at least save myself the actual work of the file.[11]

Farewell, and put in a good word for me with the two Jacopos, 5 the one from Volterra, and Antiquari,[12] twin paragons of humanity and integrity.

Florence, April 22, 1490

: XIV :

Girolamo Donà to his dear Angelo Poliziano

I have received the *Miscellanea*. I raced through it. Very enjoyable 1 reading, in which anyone even of extraordinary learning would be able to find pleasure and profit. But, you will say, judgment is

cium est quod obiter fertur. Sed cum de re literaria agitur, iudicare de te possumus, abdicatis iuris solemnibus, etiam stantes, adeo cuique securum est de eruditionum controversiis cum Politiano in tenebris quoque dimicare. Mihi autem in eo opere tantum tribuis quantum nec agnosco nec postulo. Perge (quod facis) iuvare bonas artes, neque formides blatteratorum et sciolorum aculeos. Nunquam caruere invidia egregii fortesque conatus. ἀλλ' ὅμως (κρέσσων γὰρ οἰκτιρμῶν φθόνος) μὴ παρίει καλά· νώμα δικαίῳ πηδαλίῳ Latinas literas. Fortasse enim ii maxime ex opere profecturi quibus id magis sordescere videbitur.

Vale.

Mediolani, vi Calendas Novemb. MCCCCLXXXVIIII

: XV :

Angelus Politianus Hieronymo Donato suo s. d.

1   Non est is auctoritatis meae rigor ut invidentium flatus[1] quasi ventorum tuto possit excipere, nisi vestris paucorum testimoniis, velut adminiculis, ipsa per se decidua fulciatur. Equidem multorum accepi literas, ex quo Miscellanea publicavi, laudantium scilicet (ut fit) et gratulantium. Sed nescio quo pacto, de tuo, de Barbari, de Pici, de istiusmodi perpaucorum iudicio, sic ipse me censeo ut tum denique stare videar, cum puncta omnia tulerim suffragii vestri. Quanquam etiam istinc reddita mihi nuper epistola est, Iacobi

hasty if it comes right away. But when the matter before us is a literary one, we can deliver a judgment about you while still on our feet, courtroom formalities set aside. Indeed, no one worries about engaging Poliziano on matters of learned controversy, even when the contest is in the dark.[1] In that work, however, you ascribe to me more than I either recognize or request. Continue (as you are doing) to foster the liberal arts, and do not worry about the stings of windbags and smatterers. Bold and illustrious undertakings have never been spared envy. "All the same (better envy than pity) neglect not fair deeds, but with a just rudder, steer"[2] Latin literature. Indeed, those who will derive the most profit from this work may well be those who will turn their noses up at it.[3]

Farewell.

Milan, October 27, 1489

: XV :

Angelo Poliziano to his dear Girolamo Donà

The strength of my authority is not such that it can endure without damage the gale-force exhalations of envious persons, unless, ready to fall on its own account, it be propped up, as if on struts, by the testimonials of a few of you. Since publishing my *Miscellanea*, I have in fact received letters from many people, offering, as is usual, praise and congratulations, but somehow it is as a result of your judgment and that of Barbaro, of Pico, and of very few others of your caliber that I value myself highly enough to seem then, finally, to stand upright, having swept your votes. Another letter from your parts, however, was recently delivered to me, from Jacopo Antiquari. It was wonderfully substantial and erudite. Although the man was otherwise barely known to me personally,

1

Antiquarii, mire gravis et erudita, quem mihi virum minime alioqui facie notum, saepenumero tamen Laurentius Medices meus a literis, a moribus, a prudentia commendaverat. In ea profecto epistola, nec honestam indolem, nec expressam quandam vetustatis imaginem, nec textum illud operosius, quale vestrum est, nec ullum denique stili cultioris ornamentum requisiveris, ut admitti, ni fallor, in istam quasi praerogativam tribuum iure debeat. Sed de hoc ipsi videritis.

2   Epistolam vero ad me tuam legit idem Laurentius, et quidem non incuriose, lectamque verbis exquisitissimis laudavit sic ut mihi quoque apud illum magna accesserit de tuo felici calamo commendatio. Nam quanquam mihi ille vir plus meritis semper tribuit, tamen ut tuas legit literas, visus est nescio quo pacto favere propensius iudicio de me suo, et pluris aliquanto me post eam diem facere, quam antea consuevisset. Iamne igitur sentis quantopere isto literarum nomine debeam tibi, per quem factum sit ut sibi iam Laurentius ipse placeat, quod ego non displiceam? Quare te rogo, cum tibi a re publica ocium fuerit, scribas aliquando ad Politianum tuum, putesque te non epistolas ad ipsum sed stipendia mittere, sed sacerdotia,[2] sed honoris titulos, omniaque denique vitae humanae commoda. Quorum cum semper auctor ei Laurentius unus extiterit, tanto subinde potiora collaturus videtur, quanto eundem gratiorem vobis, hoc est religiossisimis artium bonarum censoribus, intellexerit.

3   Ioannes Picus Mirandula, lux omnium doctrinarum, salutem tibi adscribit, et ut item Merulae Puteolanoque nunties uterque rogamus.

Vale.

Florentiae, Calendis Decemb. MCCCCLXXXVIIII

nevertheless my dear Lorenzo de' Medici had often recommended him as a man of letters, a man of character, a man of wisdom. And in that letter one certainly does not look hard for noble talent, or images modeled on antiquity, or that elaborate embroidery that is your shared fashion, or, in short, any ornament of the more refined style, with the result that, unless I am mistaken, he should by all rights be inducted into the first rank of electors. But I leave that up to you.

The same Lorenzo read, not without great interest, the letter 2 you sent me,[1] and when he had finished he so praised it for its very choice wording that I too, being there, was treated to a great eulogy of your fortunate pen. Indeed, although that man has always attributed to me more than I deserve, nevertheless, as he read your letter, he seemed more inclined to support his own judgment about me, and from that day on to rate me somewhat higher than had been his custom previously. Do you, therefore, now understand how much I am in your debt on account of your letter, through which it has come to pass that Lorenzo is now pleased with himself because I do not displease? For this reason, I ask you, when you have a break from affairs of state, to write now and then to your Poliziano, and to consider that you are sending him, not letters, but a salary, and benefices, and marks of honor — in short, all the comforts of human life. Although Lorenzo has always been for him[2] the one source of these, he seems from now on ready to grant ones that are greater by the same measure by which he understands the same man to find new favor with you, that is, with the most conscientious censors of the liberal arts.

Giovanni Pico della Mirandola, light of all learning, appends 3 his greetings to you, and we both ask that you communicate the same to Merula and to Puteolano.[3]

Farewell.

Florence, December 1, 1489

LIBER TERTIUS

: I :

Angelus Politianus Callimacho suo s. d.

1 Etsi video quae tu de me sentias praedicesque amicius multo quam verius et sentiri et praedicari, tamen gaudeo ea mihi tribui abs te quae ipse in memet neutiquam agnoscam. Quid enim non gaudeam me, etiam praestigia quadam, sensum istum praedicationemque tuam lucrifacere? Nam haud dubium mihi quidem est quin tu tibi quae scribis etiam vera esse persuaseris, quando neque tu ex ea nota es hominum quos Homericus ille heros tantopere se perosum confirmat, aliud in lingua promptum, aliud clusum habentes in pectore, neque ulla est causa cur Politiano Callimachus palpum obtrudere postulet. Non fallis itaque me, sed ipse abs te magis falleris. Atque adeo non falleris; vera sentis; vera de me praedicas. Gratulare igitur iudicio de nobis tuo, atque istanc opinionem perpetuo obtine, dum amorem, dum benevolentiam obtineas. Quin lauda me quoque, ut coepisti, ut ego ille laudatus vir laudari me cum Naeviano Hectore gaudeam.[1]

2 Fiam autem te laudatore vendibilis, potius quam venalis. Neque enim sum unquam[2] dominum mutaturus. Quare quicquid mihi astruxeris tibi accreverit. Sum quippe in tuo aere, unde et forsitan locellos istinc usque ad me misisti. Gratique sunt scilicet quia fes-

BOOK III

: I :

Angelo Poliziano to his dear Callimachus[1]

Although I see that what you perceive and declare about me is 1
perceived and declared with much more friendship than truth, all
the same I am glad that things are attributed to me by you which,
for my part, I do not in the least recognize in myself. Why would
I not be glad to win that perception and declaration, even as the
result of some kind of illusion? For I hardly have any doubt that
you have convinced yourself that the things you write are true,
since, on the one hand, you do not belong to that class of people
whom that Homeric hero declared he so greatly despised — people
who have one thing ready to say and another locked in their
mind[2] — and, on the other hand, there is no reason why Callimachus would seek to palm one off on Poliziano.[3] And so you do
not fool me but, rather, are fooled by yourself, and to the extent
that you are no fool, regarding me you perceive and profess the
truth. Be pleased, therefore, with your judgment regarding me and
hold on to that opinion forever, so long as you hold on to your
love and good will. Indeed, celebrate me as well, as you have begun
doing, so that I, "that celebrated man," may share with the Hector
of Naevius the same pleasure in being celebrated.[4]

In fact, with you celebrating me I become marketable. Not, 2
however, that I am on the market. For I have no intention ever to
change masters. Thus, whatever you add to me accrues to you,
given that I am on your ledger.[5] And this, perhaps, is why you
have sent treasure-boxes from there all the way to me. They are, of
course, welcome, because they are awfully nice, because they are
yours. But I offer no thanks. For you received a favor by doing

tivi, quia tui. Sed gratias non ago. Tute enim beneficium dando accepisti, non quia digno, sed quia tuo, immo tibi (amicus enim alter
ipse est), atque ob id digno, hoc est Callimacho ipsi, dedisti.
Vale.

: II :

Callimachus Angelo Politiano s. d.

1 Ea quae mihi obiicis in principio literarum tuarum adeo subinde
argute purgas et eleganter ut respondendi facultatem simul et causam mihi interceperis, planeque indicaveris id quod prioribus literis meis asseveravi, divinum ingenium tuum omnia posse. Itaque
omissis illis quae neque melius neque subtilius dici pro me possunt quam dicta sint a te, affirmo amice sed et vere (neque enim illud nisi et hoc) quod nisi iampridem mihi prope unicus visus esses
cuius carmen utile dulci commisceat, nunc certe volentem ad-
duxisset me in eam sententiam Rusticus tuus, sane urbanissimus,
doctrinaque et elegantia plenus, et qui vere ex fumo clarissimam
lucem efferat, atque ob id eo titulo indignissimus. Vidi, et legenti
placuere, multa scriptorum nostri temporis. Sed Rusticum hunc
non satis est vidisse semel. Iuvat usque morari et conferre pedem.
Nihilque in eo non summe placet, nisi quod desinit, cum tamen
desit nihil, ut tam multa nemo alter quam tu afferre potuerit pro
materia.

one, not because the recipient was deserving, but because he is yours; or better still, you yourself were the recipient (for a friend is an *alter ego*), and for this reason you did a favor for a deserving person, i.e., for Callimachus himself.

Farewell.

: II :

Callimachus to Angelo Poliziano

You so artfully and elegantly vindicate me of the objections you 1 raise at the beginning of your letter, that you have deprived me of both the ability and the reason to respond. You have given clear proof of what I asserted in my earlier letter, namely, that your divine talent is capable of anything. Having passed over, therefore, those things which cannot be said on my behalf either better or more finely than they have been said by you, I assert — in friendship, but also in truth (you cannot have the former without the latter) — the following: had you not already well before now seemed to me practically the only writer whose verse mixes profit with pleasure,[1] certainly your *Rusticus*[2] would have led me willingly to such a conclusion. It is extraordinarily urbane, full of learning and elegance. Truly it brings brilliant light out of smoke,[3] and for this reason it scarcely deserves its title. I have seen many things by contemporary writers, and I have liked them when I read them. But "it is not sufficient to have seen" this *Rusticus* "just once; pleasure comes from extended lingering, from sharing its pace."[4] Nothing in it fails to give the highest pleasure, except for the fact that it ends, although it lacks nothing, to the point that no one other than you, given the subject, could have provided so much.

2   Habeo itaque tibi gratias quod locellos meos tanti duxeris. Non poterant[1] vendi carius. Cum donare instituissem, voluisti, ut in caeteris omnibus, etiam liberalitate me superare, in qua, hoc genere compensandi, vinci et cupio et patior.

Vale, literarum decus et doctrinae.

Leopoli, iii Calendas Octob. MXVD

: III :

Ludovicus Odaxius Angelo Politiano suo s. d.

1 Nisi mihi de liberalissimis moribus et humanissimo ingenio tuo constaret, hanc nuper ad te scribendi provinciam non desumerem, potiusque in antiquo silentio persisterem. Mirum enim tibi fortasse videbitur cur ego, tecum exigua admodum et quattuor horarum spatio contracta familiaritate devinctus, qui plurimas tribus abhinc annis ad te scribendi occasiones omiserim, quas undequaque aucupari debueram, nunc ad te potissimum scribere voluerim, meamque (ut opinor) vel temeritatem incusabis, quod nunc scribam, vel negligentiam, quod antehac non scripserim. Caeterum quia, non tam ex aliorum sermone quam ex mea opinione, mihi persuasi te eum esse qui omnes tibi ac virtuti tuae deditos nullo unquam tempore reiiceres, eapropter has nunc ad te literulas amoris duntaxat atque observantiae in te meae testes esse volui, quas ob subitam opportunitatem cuiusdam istuc proficiscentis exaravi. Quanquam igitur me prorsus ab omni vel ignavia vel rusticitate praeteriti silentii non excuso. Spero tamen fore ut reliquum meum

I am, therefore, in your debt, because you think my treasures so   2
valuable. They could not have been sold at a higher price. Although I had determined to give them to you as a gift, you wished
to exceed me in generosity (as in everything else), on which score,
with this kind of profit, I want and allow myself to be outdone.

Farewell, glory of letters and of learning.

Lwów, September 29, 1485

: III :

Ludovico Odasio¹ to his dear Angelo Poliziano

If I were not well-informed regarding your most generous charac-   1
ter and most humane brilliance, I would not be taking on the fresh
responsibility of writing you; on the contrary, I would be sticking
to my former silence. Indeed, you may well wonder why, bound to
you by an acquaintance that is no more than shallow and limited
to the space of four hours, although I missed the opportunities for
writing you three years ago (opportunities I should have been
grabbing right and left), I should especially want to write you now.
You will decry, I suspect, either the effrontery of writing now or
the negligence of not doing so previously. But since, on the basis
not so much of what others say as of my own opinion, I have convinced myself that you are the sort of person who would never
ever reject all the individuals who are dedicated to your talent, I
for this reason wanted this present note to you, which I drafted on
the unexpected occasion of someone departing for your city, to
bear witness to the love, at least, and regard I have for you. I do
not, however, thus absolve myself of the sloth and boorishness of
my past silence, but I nevertheless hope that you will look kindly
on the rest of my devotion to you. For with the exception of the
attention to writing by which I long ago should have ratified the

erga te studium boni consulas. Nam praeter hanc scribendi diligentiam qua ego iam pridem initam Patavii familiaritatem con-
firmare debui, nullum a me cum benivoli tum observantis amici
officium praetermissum puto. Siquidem a superioribus annis, quo
primum tempore tua mihi vel doctrina vel humanitas innotuit, fui
semper honorum ac dignitatis tuae studiosissimus, ac saepissime,
cum apud alios eruditissimos viros Venetiis et Patavii, tum hic
apud principes meos, de te sum honorificentissime locutus, effe-
cique (ut opinor) praeconio meo ut claritati tuae maius quippiam
splendoris adderetur. Quo fit ut non dubitem me abs te in eorum
amicorum numero collocari posse qui (ut Isocrates tuus asserit)
non tam praesentes amicos venerantur quam absentes etiam am-
plectuntur. Principes sane mei, quibuscum de te frequentissimum
sermonem habui, de moribus atque eruditione tua optime ac magnifice sentiunt.

2   Quid ita? Quia ego in eam opinionem adductus sum ut existimem eum te fore qui literarum studiosis emolumentum tibi vero
gloriam immortalem sis allaturus. Cuius rei periculum fecisses, si
una cum praestantissimo discipulo tuo Roma discedens superioribus diebus Urbinum ex condicto[1] venisses. Expectatus enim et
plus quam dici possit desideratus venisses. Quod si me nudius
tertius audire potuisses de te verba facientem una cum Mino
Bononiensi sedecimviro, homine (mea quidem opinione) plurimi
faciendo, si nobilitatem, si divitias, si liberalitatem morum, si literaturam inspicias, profecto intellexisses ea, praeterquam ab aman-
tissimo homine, dici aut excogitari[2] non potuisse. In eam enim
confabulationem veneramus ut de viris hoc tempore doctissimis
loqueremur, in quibus facile tu principatum optinere visus es. Nec
me amor aut adulandi studium fallit, a quo semper tanquam intes-
tino morbo abhorrui.

friendship we began in Padua, I believe that I have overlooked no duty belonging to a friend who admires you and wants the best for you. For, beginning years ago when both your learning and your humanity became known to me, I have always been a champion of your honors and standing, and quite often I have spoken of you in the most glowing terms, not only among other very learned men in Venice and Padua, but specifically here in the presence of my princes. And by my trumpeting I have brought it about, I think, that some extra measure of luster has been added to your fame. The result is that I do not hesitate to think that I can be placed by you in that group of friends who (as your dear Isocrates puts it) do not so much adore friends who are present as embrace even those who are absent.[2] Certainly my princes, with whom I have had very frequent conversations about you, think most highly and magnificently of your character and erudition.

Why do I do all this? Because I have come to an opinion by which I regard you as the sort of person who will confer advantage on students of literature — and immortal glory on yourself. You would have made a test of this if, when you were leaving Rome some days back in the company of your outstanding student, you had come to Urbino as agreed. You would have been a much anticipated visitor, desired more than words can say. But if you could have heard me the day before yesterday, chatting about you with the councilman Mino from Bologna (a man, if you ask me, who should be rated most highly, if you take a look at his nobility, his wealth, his generosity of character), you undoubtedly would have understood that my words could not have been said or imagined except by a person who loves you very much. We had, in fact, undertaken this conversation in order to talk about the most learned men of the present, in whose number you easily were seen to have obtained the leading position. Nor does love or a desire to flatter (from this I have always shrunk, as from a disease of the insides) lead me astray.

3   Sed quorsum haec tam multa de officio erga te meo? Nempe ut intelligas me tibi esse ac fore deditissimum, etsi magno montium ac regionum intervallo secludamur, teque habere neminem a quo maiori vel benivolentia vel observantia fovearis. Quod si ulla unquam mihi occasio evenerit ut quapiam in re tibi morem gerere possim, id vero in primis mihi iucundissimum erit. Quam quidem occasionem abs te actutum perveniri cupio, ne me in pollicendo quam in praestando liberaliorem autumes.

4   Demetrium vero, virum eruditissimum, Petrumque in primis, discipulum tuum, elegantissimae atque amplissimae spei adulescentem, nomine meo salvos facito, cui librum ex Plutarcho traductum, unum ex multis ineptiarum mearum monumentis, dedicavi multos iam menses, misissemque hactenus, si dignum putassem qui in manus vestras eruditissimas perveniret. Mittetur tamen, clementia vestra potius allectus quam iudicio deterritus.

Vale.

: IV :

Angelus Politianus Ludovico Odaxio[1] suo s. d.

1   Deprehenderunt me in actu literae tuae. Ideoque lectas paulum in praesens seposui, diligentius dein per ocium recogniturus, ad easque (ut par erat) cum primum possem responsurus. Id si serius quam aut tu pateris aut ego voluissem contingit, est tamen humanitatis tuae quicquid hoc est quod facimus boni consulere. Neque enim tam opellam aliquam alter ab altero quam ipsum animum requirimus, neque[2] continuo parum amat qui parum officiosus est.

But what is my goal in saying so much about my dutiful service   3
on your behalf? Surely this: so that you will realize that I am and
shall continue to be completely devoted to you, even if we are sep-
arated by a great divide of mountains and territories, and that you
have no one by whom you are supported with greater good will or
admiration. But if any opportunity should ever arise for me to
gratify your wishes on any matter whatsoever, this will bring me
the greatest pleasure of all. Indeed, I want such an opportunity to
arrive from you at once, so that you will not think me more generous in making promises than in fulfilling them.

Extend best wishes on my behalf to Demetrius, that very   4
learned man, and above all to your student Piero, a young man of
most refined and abundant promise, to whom I have dedicated a
book translated from Plutarch,[3] one of the many monuments to
my folly. Already for many months at this point, I would have sent
it—if I had thought it worthy of reaching your most learned
hands. Nevertheless, it shall be sent, enticed by your clemency
rather than terrified of your judgment.

Farewell.

: IV :

Angelo Poliziano to his dear Ludovico Odasio[1]

Your letter caught me on the road, and so, having read it, I put it   1
aside for the moment, planning to go back over it later, when I
was free, and to reply as soon as I could, as was only right. If this
has come to pass later than you would allow or I would have
wished, it is in keeping with your humanity to look favorably on
whatever this is that I have crafted. Indeed, between us, one does
not require the other's petty exertions but, rather, his very heart.

Quare ne illud quidem in epistola tuo valde probo, quod te tam scrupulose excusas, cur aut antea nihil ad me scripseris, aut nunc demum scripseris. Si enim amamus ex animo inter nos, sicuti certe amamus, quicquid alteri commodat profecto utrique commodat. Quare neque dissolvere sed nec lassare[3] voluntates nostras, quasi nodo Herculaneo cohaerentis, aut silentium possit, aut ulla officii, praesertim non necessarii, intermissio. Quo autem amicis ista literarum[4] vicissitudo, cum ad absentis tantum missitentur, amor autem verus etiam absentis praesentis faciat, nisi si vel ipsis testantur, vel aliis ostentat mutuam voluntatem? Sed neque testibus eget amor sincerus, quippe oculeus totus, ac Lynceus, et qui Momi quoque iudicium de positu humani corculi despuat, neque se populo iactat, cum sint amici κατ' Ἐπικούρου satis magnum theatrum, alter alteri. Quin istam quoque pene dicam superstitiosam probationem[5] amoris in me tui totam tibi remitto. Est enim mihi, est est ad manum semper amicitiae examen;[6] est et Hecatonis amatorium, quo te vel ingratis ad amandum compellam. Sed nec te monebo ut principibus me tuis insinues, neque invicem moneri me patiar ut patronus te meis adiungam. Quoquo enim tu irrepseris, ego sequar; ubiubi ego me adglutinavero, inde scilicet tu pendebis. Ut enim militem custodemque eadem catena, ita par legitimum amicorum una tenet copula.

2   Plutarchum Latine iam per te loquentem ego atque adulescens meus avidi expectamus, minime quidem dubitantes quin sit absolutissimus futurus, vel ob id certe, ut alicui ex veteribus Graecis τὰ

Nor is it instantly the case that one who is not dutiful enough does not love enough either. As a result, I do not even especially approve of one aspect of your letter, namely, that you so anxiously apologize either for writing nothing to me previously or for writing only now. For if the love between us is heartfelt, as it undoubtedly is, then whatever suits one, clearly suits both. Silence, therefore, or any other pause in service (especially when service is not required) could neither dissolve nor weaken our sentiments, bound, as it were, by a Herculean knot.[2] What, after all, is the point of this back-and-forth of letters for friends (for they are sent only to people who are absent, while true love makes even absent people present), unless they either provide proof of mutual sentiment for the correspondents or make a show of the same for third parties? But genuine love does not need proof, given that it is all eyes, and a Lynceus, and something that can even spurn the judgment of Momus regarding the position of the human heart, nor does it engage in public boasting, since friends, according to Epicurus, are for one another a sufficiently large theater.[3] In fact, I am also returning to you in its entirety that demonstration (which I might almost call mechanical) of your love for me. For I most assuredly have, always ready at hand, a way to test friendship.[4] I also have that love-potion of Hecaton, by which I can make you love even against your will.[5] But I shall neither instruct you to ingratiate me with your princes nor, in turn, allow myself to be instructed to attach you to my patrons. Wherever you insinuate yourself, I will follow, and anywhere I fasten myself, you of course will perch. For, just as the same chain holds a soldier and his guard, so a single bond holds a proper pair of friends.

My boy and I eagerly await Plutarch, now speaking Latin 2 through your efforts. Indeed, we do not doubt in the least that he will be perfectly fluent, if only so that you may repay one of the ancient Greeks your tuition, since you learned Greek from them

147

δίδακτρα referas, quando ita Graece ab eis didicisti ut novos docere iam omneis possis, et quod dicitur ἀντιπελαργεῖν.[7]
Vale.

: V :

Ludovicus Odaxius Angelo Politiano suo s. d.

1 Plutarchi libellus ad te venit, qui, si ullam potius elegantiam quam benivolentiam profiteretur, erubesceret profecto, nec ad exactissimae eruditionis officinam sese nisi verecunde conferret. Nunc autem laetus et securus accedit, humanitate tua magis quam ullo ornamento suo fretus. Proinde meretur ut eum ad te proficiscentem benigne suscipias, illique primariam amoris operam sedulo impertiaris. Siquidem ego illum, quem alioquin frivolum, abiectum et vile munus existimarem, non indignum tamen putavi qui ad exhibendum studii atque observantiae in vos meae pignus adveniret. Utcunque erit, et quanticunque erit, in bonam accipias partem rogamus obsecramusque.

2 Nudius tertius ab Hermolao Barbaro et Petro Contareno, qui duo vel nobilissimi vel ornatissimi vel eruditissimi viri sunt, Venetiis mihi literae venerunt, in quibus admoneor ut, si unquam ad te scripturus sum, eorum te nomine salvum esse iubeam. Memini me, autumno superiore cum Venetiis essem, una cum his de te, perinde ac doctissimo homine, sermonem habuisse. Illi autem se familiaritatem tuam iniisse asserebant cum triennio aut quadriennio proximo, visendae civitatis gratia, eo concessisses. Digni homines sunt qui a te quoque diligantur.

3 Vale igitur, et me ama.
Igubii, v Calendas Iulias MCCCCLXXXV

so well that you can now teach the modern world and, as they say, return a parent's love.[6]

Farewell.

: V :

Ludovico Odasio to his dear Angelo Poliziano

The little book of Plutarch comes to you. If it avowed any elegance 1
rather than good intentions, it would be bright red and would not betake itself to the workshop of flawless erudition without modesty. But as it stands, it approaches joyfully and without worry, relying more on your humanity than on any distinction of its own. It accordingly deserves that you receive it, a traveler to you, kindly and that you zealously apply to it efforts primarily of love. For, although I would otherwise have regarded it as a silly, insignificant, worthless gift, I did not think it unworthy to make the trip in order to offer a token of my enthusiasm and respect for you both.

The day before yesterday, a letter came to me from the Vene- 2
tians Ermolao Barbaro and Pietro Contarini,[1] both of whom are as highly placed, illustrious, and erudite as men can be, in which they instruct me, should I ever happen to write you, to wish you well on their behalf. I remember that last fall, when I was in Venice, I had a conversation with them about you, the sort one has about a very learned person. They explained that they had begun their friendship with you when, three or four years prior, you retreated there for the purpose of visiting the republic. They are the sort of people who deserve to share in your esteem.

And so, farewell—and love me. 3

Gubbio, June 27, 1485

: VI :

Angelus Politianus Ludovico Odaxio suo s. d.

1   Plutarchi lepidum novum libellum, quem tu scilicet Latine inter-
pretatus adolescenti meo nuncupasti, vidi, cepi, legi, et quidem simul omnia, adeo cupide ut prius pene ad calcem prae studio pervenisse quam ex carceribus promovisse me senserim. Illex[1] mihi
fuit statim suavis odor quidam verborum tuorum plane ambrosius.
Tum sententiarum veluti sapor quidam austerus et dulcis, non se-
cus illecebris orationis tuae quam myrothecii[2] condimentis imbutus, ita (quod dicitur) palatum irritavit ut, quasi helluo aliquis, vix
commansas epulas has, tam lautas, tam opiparas, devoraverim, et
sum profecto miratus sic Latine Plutarchum loqui didicisse iam
mortuum, cui viventi quondam (sic enim scribit ipse) adeo sermo
Romanus repugnabat. Videri enim potest non tam obiisse quo die
obiit quam secessisse ad studium Romanae linguae, ut qui Graecorum Latinorumque vitas illustrium hominum inter se contulerit,
cum quo ipse se conferat non inveniat. Nam sese conferre sibi in
utriusque orationis facultate certe non ausit, quia scilicet in nostra
praeponderat.

2   Quod autem princeps iste tuus, atque adeo noster (noster enim
est profecto qui litterarum studiosus est), quod, inquam, bonas arteis complectitur, atque ad omneis parteis bene audiendi se comparat, parentisque sui absolutissimi hominis vestigiis insistit,[3] dici
non potest ut gaudeam, ut exultem atque triumphem, ut tibi

: VI :

Angelo Poliziano to his dear Ludovico Odasio

All at once I saw, grabbed, read the charming new booklet[1] of Plu-   1
tarch which you translated into Latin and named for my young
man, and I did so with such alacrity that, as a result of my enthusiasm, I crossed the last line before realizing I had left the starting-
block. Immediately enticing to me was a certain sweet perfume of
your words — truly ambrosial. Then a certain kind of dry, sweet[2]
taste of its sentences, steeped in the charms of your prose entirely
as if in the perfumes of a Greek unguent-box,[3] so tickled my taste-
buds (as they say) that, like some extravagant glutton,[4] I barely
chewed these delicacies — so rich, so luxurious! — before gulping
them down. And I was utterly amazed that Plutarch had learned
to speak Latin so well after death, when the Roman tongue so re-
sisted his efforts (so he himself writes[5]) when he used to be alive.
Indeed, he may well seem not so much to have died when he came
to the end of his days as to have withdrawn for the purpose of
studying the Roman language. The result is that he who compared
the lives of famous Greek and Latin men to one another does not
find anyone with whom to compare himself. He certainly did not
dare compare himself to himself in fluency in the two languages,
since he obviously has greater gravity in ours.

As for your prince — yours, and just as much ours, for whoever   2
is devoted to literature is undoubtedly ours — as for the fact that
he, I say, embraces the liberal arts, and trains himself to have a
universally good reputation,[6] and follows in the footsteps of that
perfect man, his father,[7] well, it is impossible to describe how glad
I am, how jubilant and proud, to the point that I congratulate you
too, my dear Ludovico. Our age used to seem to me to have
brought forth two men who might restore the state of literary

quoque gratuler, mi Ludovice. Duos mihi viros tulisse aetas nostra videbatur qui rem literariam, non quidem cunctando ut ille verrucosus, sed multa agendo potius, restituerent, Federicum Urbinatem principem olim tuum et Laurentium Medicem patronum semper meum, utinamque semper. Hi duo (ni fallor) ausi in tantis saeculi[4] huius tenebris lucem sperare, quasique contra torrentem pessimorum morum brachia dirigere. Ergo et librorum pulcherrimam supellectilem sibi compararunt, et doctos iuverunt, et ipsi studia tractarunt.

3   Nam ut de principe tuo taceam, de quo longiore subsellio agendum puto, dicam autem de Laurentio meo. Cave putes quenquam esse ex nostro (ut sic dixerim) seminio, hoc est ex iis qui omnem aetatem in literis consumpserunt, cui cedat hic, vel acumine in disputando, vel prudentia in iudicando, vel in explicando quae sentiat facilitate, copia, varietate, gratia. Acer illi sermo et gravis et, cum res postulat, salibus scatens,[5] sed ex illo mari collectis in quo Venus est orta. Exempla et historiam veterem sic habet ad manum ut eis perinde uti semper atque suis stipatoribus videatur, sic ut ingenium habere in numerato, et esse quasi promum condum (ut Plautino utar verbo) totius antiquitatis facile credas.

4   Extincto igitur duce illo tuo, cum viderem nostras iam artis unica spe niti,[6] fateor, vereri coepi, unius ut hominis vires tanto perferendo oneri pares esse possent. Quare cum ostendis recidivam illam virtutem Federici resurgere in filio, isdemque adulescentem artibus quibus olim clarissimum patrem delectari, reddidisti

affairs, certainly not by postponement, like that warty fellow,[8] but instead by doing a great deal: Federico of Urbino, once your prince,[9] and Lorenzo de' Medici, ever my patron (may he always be so!). Unless I err, these are the two men who, having dared to hope for light in the midst of the vast shadows of this age and, one might say, to stretch out their arms against a torrent[10] of very bad habits, accordingly procured for themselves a dazzling collection of books, came to the aid of the learned, and themselves took up the work of scholarship.

Let me say nothing about your prince,[11] on which subject one would, I think, need to speak from a broader platform,[12] but I will say something about my own Lorenzo. Do not dare think that there is anyone from, so to speak, our stock — that is to say, out of those people who have spent their whole lives on literature — to whom he is inferior with respect either to acuity in debating, or to wisdom in exercising judgment, or to facility, abundance and variety of expression, and charm in setting forth what he thinks. His language is penetrating, authoritative, and, when the situation requires, sparkling with salty wit — distilled, however, from the sea from which Venus arose. He keeps exemplary episodes and ancient history so ready at hand that he seems to employ them as nothing less than his constant attendants, to the point that you readily surmise that he keeps his brilliance in ready cash and is something like a "fetch-and-store" (to use a Plautine expression)[13] for the whole warehouse of antiquity.

After your duke died, therefore, when I saw that our arts now rested on a single hope, I admit that I began to worry whether the strength of one man was equal to the task of bearing such a responsibility. This is why, by reporting that the renascent talent of Federico flows again in his son and that this young man takes pleasure in the same arts in which his most illustrious father once did, you have restored my confidence and, as they say, have splashed water on my face.[14] Rejoice, therefore, in your great good

mihi quidem animum, atque aquam (quod dicitur) aspersisti. Quare gaude tuo tanto bono, gaude tuo labore et diligentia. Et (quod facis) perge protinus exercere principem nostrum in stadio Musarum. Assuescat iam nunc a tenero amare literas, fovere literatos, complecti, et colere. Scis autem messem plerumque respondere sementi, tibique potissimum primitias frugum deberi ab hoc agro, quippe (ut ille inquit) morum quos fecit praemia doctor habet.

5   Sed et Petrus nunc studiis acriter incumbit et humanitati. Habet indolem paternam, habet ingenium. Ludit et ipse nunc versiculis, nunc soluta oratione et libera. Graecis plurimum delectatur. In summa, dignus qui sit principi tuo carus, quia similis, similis autem, qua ratione parva magnis componuntur. Is[7] nunc, scribente hanc epistolam me, alteram seorsum commentatur epistolam. Quae, cuicuimodi erit, etiam si minus apte exierit, mittetur tamen ad te, ut ipsius ingenioli degustationem velut aliquam accipias. Amat autem plurimum te de munere hoc, et cupit sane occasionem sibi aliquam dari qua gratiam reponat.

6   Si ad Hermolaum Petrumque Contarenum Venetos rescripseris, velim utrique agas meo nomine gratias, utrique me commendes non vulgariter.

7   Ad superiores tuas literas nescio an responsum acceperis nostrum. Cupio significes, ut in ratione lati atque accepti possim tecum paria facere.

Vale.

fortune, rejoice in your own efforts and care, and proceed at once (as you are doing) with the training of our prince in the stadium of the Muses. From his present tender age let him already grow accustomed to loving literature and to patronizing, embracing, and promoting literary men. You know that the harvest generally repays the work of sowing, and that from this field, the first fruits are due most especially to you, since, as you-know-who says, "the teacher reaps the reward of the character he has fashioned."[15]

But now Piero too enthusiastically applies himself to his studies 5 and to humane learning. He possesses the qualities of his father—and his intellect. He entertains himself now in verse, now in free prose. He especially enjoys the Greeks. In sum, he is the sort who deserves to be dear to your prince, because he is similar to him—similar, however, by the calculus by which small things are compared to great ones.[16] Right now, while I am writing this letter, he is drafting a second one all by himself. However it is, even if it turns out less than perfect, it shall be sent to you all the same, so that you can have some taste of his fledgling talent. Regarding your gift, he loves you very much, and earnestly hopes that some opportunity will be given to him for repaying his debt of gratitude.

If you write back to Ermolao and to Pietro Contarini in Venice, 6 please say thank you on my behalf and put in an uncommonly good word for me with both.

I do not know whether you have received my reply to your ear- 7 lier letter. I would like you to let me know so that I can record an even balance with you in my ledger of incoming and outgoing accounts.

Farewell.

: VII :

Marcus Antonius Sabellicus Angelo Politiano s. p. d.

1 Eram ego aliunde nostram auspicaturus amicitiam, ni subitus Atlantis conterranei tui hinc digressus nostrum in ea re consilium praevertisset. Fuit is annum et amplius Venetiis, ac quandiu fuit, et domi et foris etiam frequens mecum esse perseveravit. Nullius unquam consuetudine sum magis delectatus, siquidem praeter morum elegantiam singularemque modestiam, patrio sermone Tuscaque illa sua urbanitate brevi consecutus est ut eo uno nemo esset mihi iucundior, nemo in hac urbe gratior. Omnia, praeter tempus, secunda habui in illius amicitia fruenda. Etenim tunc potissimum ei visum est hinc abire cum me[1] maxime in sui erexisset admirationem. Sed in eo visus est mihi omne vetustum amicitiae exemplum aequare, quod in tam tumultuario digressu sine meis ad te literis venire identidem recusavit, ratus certissimum se nostrae futurae amicitiae pignus secum in patriam deferre, si apud te, virum clarissimum, cui quam carissimus esse cupit, ipsius mores et studia commendarentur, quasi ita velit evenire ut, cum uterque nostrum de ipsius moribus idem sentire coeperit, non infirmus ad amicitiam gradus (ut Crispo placet) factus videatur. Sed recte ille. Nos vero scribendi consuetudine maioribusque officiis illam his modicis principiis ortam locupletiorem (ut spero) in dies faciemus.

2 Nunc Atlantem ipsum tuae dignitatis studiossisimum maiorem in modum tibi[2] commendarem, nisi urbanissimus poeta moneret

: VII :

Marcantonio Sabellico¹ to Angelo Poliziano

I would have embarked upon our friendship from a different point   1
of origin, had the sudden departure from here of your fellow-
countryman Atlas not preempted my intention on this score. He
was in Venice for a year or more, and throughout his stay he continued to be at my side quite regularly, both at home and out and
about. I never have been more pleased with anyone's company, for,
in addition to his elegance of manner and remarkable modesty, he
quickly brought it about, by means of his mother-tongue and that
Tuscan urbanity of his, that absolutely no one in this city was to
me more agreeable or more welcome than he. In the enjoyment of
his friendship I had all the conditions in my favor, except for time.
As a matter of fact, he decided to leave us at precisely the moment
when he had raised our esteem for him to its heights. But in the
following he seemed to me to match every ancient exemplary case
of friendship: in the midst of such a chaotic departure, he repeatedly refused to come to you without my letter, having decided that
he would be carrying back home with him an unambiguous token
of our future friendship if his character and scholarship were recommended to you, the most illustrious of men, to whom he wants
to be as dear as possible, as if the outcome he wanted was that,
once both of us began to feel the same way about his character, a
healthy step toward friendship (so pleases Crispus²) would be seen
to have been made. And he is right. But we, by habitual writing
and still greater service, will make what has arisen from these
fairly small beginnings richer (I hope) every day.

I would now be giving Atlas, himself the greatest encourager of   2
your fame, my enthusiastic recommendation, if a most urbane
poet did not warn that to think that someone needs a recommen-

peccare eum qui suos putet cuique commendandos. Gratulor igitur, quod superest, tibi lepidissimi adulescentis restitutam consuetudinem, quam tantisper etiam invidere pergam donec in utriusque complexus venero.

3 Vale, Thusci nominis decus. Et Marcum Antonium iam hinc amare incipe, qui te ob tuas amplissimas virtutes amat, colit, observat.

Venetiis, Idibus Iuliis MCCCCLXXXVIII

: VIII :

Angelus Politianus Marco Antonio Sabellico s. p. d.

1 Solebat Atlas quondam suo mihi nomine redire tam gratus ut, recepto contentus amico, nullum ultra officium desiderarem. Nunc autem tuarum nomine literarum, quas fideliter reddidit, tam mihi iucundus rediit ut eius pene[1] praesentiam non requirerem, atque[2] haberet Atlas quippiam secum quod plane plus a me quam Atlas expeteretur. Nunc idem istuc revertitur cum literis meis, quas tibi arbitror fore gratas, non tam suo quam tabellarii nomine. Noram equidem antea quoque quantum ingenio et literatura, quantum etiam stilo facundiaque polleres. De humanitate nihil sane adhuc inaudieram. Sed eam tua mihi nunc epistola deliniavit, Atlas vero penicillo et coloribus expressit. Aucupabar sane iam pridem occasionem quampiam ineundae abs te gratiae, cum tu scilicet hoc agentem praevenisti, non ob id humanior modo, quod prior, sed

dation of his own people is offensive.³ All that remains is for me
to congratulate you on the restitution of a most charming young
man's company, which I shall even begin to envy until I come into
your joint embrace.

Farewell, glory of the Tuscan name. And from this moment on   3
start loving Marcantonio, who, in light of your most impressive
talents, loves, cherishes, and admires you.

Venice, July 13, 1488

: VIII :

Angelo Poliziano to Marcantonio Sabellico

It used to be, once upon a time, that Atlas's returns were so wel-   1
come to me on his own account that, happy to have my friend
back, I felt the need of no other service. Now however, on account
of your letter, which he has faithfully delivered, he returns as
someone I find so delightful that I hardly require his presence at
all—and indeed, Atlas has something with him which plainly demands my attention more than he. Now the same person returns
to your city with my letter, which, I think, will make you happy,
not so much on its own account as on account of its courier. Of
course, I knew even beforehand how impressive you were with respect to your intelligence and literary learning, your style and eloquence. On the subject of your humanity I had not yet heard anything at all, but your letter has now given me a sketch. Atlas,
however, has rendered the same with brush and paints. For quite
some time I had been on the look-out for any opportunity for
winning your favor, when, of course, you anticipated me in this
endeavor. Yours, therefore, is the greater humanity, not only because you were first, but also because you were offered a lesser

quod minore quoque proposito praemio. Quare danda mihi[3] opera
est ut quemadmodum ineunda tecum amicitia posterioris tuli, sic
eadem tuenda colendaque prioris feram.

Vale.

vi Calendas Septemb. MCCCCLXXXVIII

: IX :

Angelus Politianus Ioanni Laurentio Veneto suo s. d.

1 En ad te revertitur Phaedrus, utriusque nostrum homo studiosissimus, cui tu scilicet aliquot abhinc menses literas ad me dedisti,
plenas amoris erga me, rectas, elegantis, qualesque denique a te
uno poterant proficisici. Respondebo ad eas quam brevissime.
Laudas me, Ioannes, quasi unum ex numero eruditissimorum et
tui similium. Laudas, inquam, tu me, unus omnium quos viderim,
quos audierim longe eruditissimus. Ego igitur, etsi memet haud
ignoro, tamen fero aequissime te aut ipsum decipi amore in nos nimio, aut alios item velle deceptos.

2 Non est autem quod paria coner referre. Nam cum tu mihi, vix
levem umbram assequenti doctrinae humanitatisque tuae, tantum
tamen tribueris laudum quantae demum tibi[1] iure debeantur, si
coner ipse invicem laudes regerere, restituenda erunt et resignanda
tibi illa ipsa verba quae abs te acceperam usuraria, ut iure rideatur
egestatis nostrae sinistra quaedam ambitio, illi ipsi divitias osten-
tans unde scilicet emendicaverit.

prize. As a result, I must see to it that, just as I took second place in beginning a friendship with you, so in preserving and fostering the same, I shall come in first.

Farewell.

August 27, 1488

: IX :

Angelo Poliziano to his dear Giovanni Lorenzi[1] of Venice

Here you have Phaedrus back, a man entirely devoted to both of us, to whom, of course, you gave a letter for me some months ago, full of love toward me, well-constructed, elegant, and, in a word, of the sort that could only come from you. I shall respond to it as briefly as possible. You praise me, Giovanni, as if I figured among those very erudite people who are like yourself. You, I say, by far the most erudite person of all I have seen or heard about, praise me. And so for my part, though I am scarcely in the dark about my own self, I nevertheless accept most cheerfully the fact that you yourself either have been deceived by excessive love for me or else want to deceive others on the same score.

There is, however, no reason for me to try to repay like with like. For since, although I barely manage to be a fleeting shadow of your learning and humanity, you nevertheless ascribe to me precisely as much praise as is rightly due to you, if I myself should try to send praise back in your direction, I shall be obliged to offer back under a new seal those very same words which I received from you for my own use, with the result that the perverse kind of flattery that belongs to my poverty — displaying riches to the very person from whom, of course, they have been obtained by begging — would become the legitimate object of ridicule.

3   Libellos tuos atque item quos ex bibliotheca ista codices habemus remittemus cum primum istuc orator noster[2] Florentinus se
contulerit. Pausaniam vero expectamus, cum tibi erit commodum.
Vale.

Faesulis, Idibus Octobribus MCCCCLXXXVI

: X :

Lucius Phosphorus Pontifex Signinus Alexandro Cortesio s. d.

1   Politianas epistolas legi, Alexander, accuratissime summaque cum
voluptate, quorum utrunque prope necessarium fuit, et quod ad
hominem amicissimum, et quod ab homine eruditissimo erant
scriptae. Video os probum — iam interpellas et obstrepis, Ἄπαγε
tu!' Vis scire quid sentiam. Vide quid agas. An ego iudicare possim? Ne ultra crepidas sutor, ut in Graeco adagio est. Pergis ur-
gere? Respondebo, ne superbus videar. Memento tamen me cum
homine familiari tanquam mecum loqui. Scio invidiosam rem esse
huiuscemodi iudicia etiam recta, nedum mea, qualiacunque sunt.
Accipe igitur in aurem; velut μυστήρια, cave enunties.

2   Ego Politianum nostrum, mi Alexander, summopere amo et
admiror, atque ei omnia summa tribuo. Et ut libere quod sentio
dicam, non magis istum damnandum censeo quam illos laudandos
qui, quadraginta[1] abhinc annis, papyros et chartas, velut maculis

As soon as our Florentine ambassador heads your way, I shall 3
send back your booklets and, likewise, the volumes I have from
your library. I, however, am looking forward to Pausanias, whenever you find it convenient.

Farewell.

Fiesole, October 15, 1486

: X :

Lucio Phosphorus,[1] Bishop of Segni, to Alessandro Cortesi[2]

Alessandro, I have read Poliziano's letters very attentively and with 1
the greatest pleasure, both of these being nearly inevitable, seeing
as they were written to a man who is most dear to me and by a
man who is most erudite. I picture his fine mouth—already you
interrupt me and cry in protest, "Get out of here!" You want to
know what I *think*. Consider what you are looking for. Am I really
capable of judging? "Let the cobbler stick to his soles," as the
Greek proverb has it.[3] You push me to go farther. I shall answer,
to avoid seeming arrogant. Keep in mind, however, that I talk to
an intimate as if I were talking to myself. I know that judgments
of this sort, even when accurate, especially when they are mine
(such as they are), are an invidious matter. Listen closely, therefore,
and as if they were divine mysteries, do not dare divulge them.

I, my dear Alessandro, love and admire our Poliziano enor- 2
mously, and I credit him with everything of importance. And to
state my opinion freely, I no more think that he should be reproached than that those persons should be praised who forty
years ago scorched their papers and parchments, as if they were
fringed with stains and were encaustic tablets, rather than illuminating them with any noble form or image.[4] I would make only

praetextas et encausticas tabellas, inusserunt, potius quam ulla
egregia forma atque imagine illustrarunt, praeter unum aut alterum: Laurentium Vallam, me puero, et nuper Domitium Calderi-
num, quos quidem non laudare ac admirari nefas et plane impium
duco. Caeteros autem, ut apud Ciceronem inquit vel Antonius vel
Crassus, non dubitabo inertiae et prorsus inscitiae condemnare,
tametsi illos quoque excusatos habeo. Sum enim aequus iudex, siquidem id quod poterant praestiterunt. Neque enim omnes Catones aut Scipiones aut Laelii, ut ait Marcus Tullius, possumus esse.
Quamvis nonnulli, ut ait idem, sive felicitate quadam sive bonitate
naturae, rectam vitae secuti sunt viam, praeclare tamen actum cum
eis existimo qui id quoquo modo tentaverunt, etiam si non sunt
consecuti. Adde quod non tam ipsis quam temporibus acceptum
est referendum, bonarum literarum et magistrorum penuria. Quis
enim ignorat, iam inde ab diruta urbe, amisso imperio, Italia a barbaris occupata, Romanam eloquentiam atque adeo omnem literaturam et omnes artes periise? Sic Caesari tuo placuit, qui haec
omnia pessum et plane perditum dedit.²

3   Sed emersit tandem aliquando ingenium, et velut ex cineribus
ac carbonibus redivivus ignis effulxit, unde hi tanquam lumina nobis illuxerunt. Quod cum ita sit, dulcissime Alexander, gratulemur
saeculo nostro, et eo magis quod iam istud par impar factum est.
Αἴνιγμα tibi propono. Ego istos pares impares reddo. Non intel-
ligis? Quin Apollinem, quin vatem Cumaeam, quin Hammonem,
quin Ethruscos, quin quid est ariolorum consulis? At non est
opus. Ecce tibi solutum aenigma. Laurentio Vallae, Domitio Cal-
derino, Angelum Politianum adiicio, et quasi triumviratum creo.
Ego sic sentio, sic censeo, sic iudico, in aurem tuam insusurrans.

one or two exceptions: Lorenzo Valla, who belongs to my boyhood, and more recently, Domizio Calderini.[5] I regard it as sacri-
lege and unambiguous impiety not to praise and marvel at these
two. But the rest, as either Antonius or Crassus says in Cicero, I
shall not hesitate to find guilty of laziness and utter ignorance.[6]
Actually, I let them off the hook too. For I am a fair judge, given
that they offered what they could. After all, we cannot all be
Catones, or Scipiones, or Laelii, as Marcus Tullius says. Although
a few, as the same person says, have followed life's proper path, either by some stroke of luck or by the excellence of their innate disposition,[7] I nevertheless think that things have gone quite well for
those who have attempted this in one way or another, even if they
have not succeeded. In addition, the shortcoming should be assigned not so much to them as to their period, given its shortage
of fine literature and teachers. Who indeed is unaware that, from
the moment when the city was demolished, the empire lost, and
Italy occupied by barbarians, Roman eloquence — and thus all literature and every art — ceased to exist? So pleased your Caesar,
who drove all these things to ruin and utter extinction.[8]

But at long last, intelligence re-emerged, and from, so to speak,   3
ashes and coals, a reborn flame gleamed forth, from which these
men, like lamps, cast light on us. Since this is so, Alessandro my
sweet, I congratulate our age — so much the more so in that what
was even has become odd. I am offering you a riddle: I make the
even odd. You do not understand? Why not consult Apollo, why
not the Cumaean Sibyl, why not Hammon, why not your Etruscans, why not whatever soothsayers there are in existence?[9] But
there's no need. Here's the riddle solved: to Lorenzo Valla and
Domizio Calderini, I add Angelo Poliziano and create what you
might call a triumvirate. Such is my opinion, my estimation, my
judgment, as I whisper into your ear. But I feel like shouting it
out. As a matter of fact, I am announcing my decision officially,
and I broadcast it to all good and learned men — and thus with the

Sed libet exclamare. Sic, inquam, pro tribunali sententiam fero, et omnibus bonis doctisque viris, atque adeo toto orbe terrarum audiente, proclamo: 'Thraces, Sauromatae, Getae, Britanni, possum ostendere literas, venite,' ut ait lepidissimus poeta.

4   Habes meum, Alexander, de Politiano iudicium. Neque hoc adulationi datum quempiam arbitrari velim, quippe qui alteros iam mortuos et sensibus orbatos conciliare mihi nequeo, alterum nondum novi vivum, quanquam fateor me id vehementer optare, et talia iacere fundamenta amicitiae ut ea nulla unquam temporum iniuria possit abolere. Quod ut facias, o noster Alexander, maiorem in modum a te peto, ut insinuatione tua me voti compotem facias, et principi literarum me concilies ac plane dedas. Ipsum vero Politianum (audin' tu vir doctissime? tecum mihi res est) oratum velim ut quod ab aliis beneficii loco accipit a me rogatus non aspernetur, ut in amore ac benivolentia respondeat, simul ut viro clarissimo et civi primario, Laurentio Medici, me commendatum reddat. Aliquot enim aguntur anni ex quo tam magno amico et praepotenti me dicare summopere cupio, et in clientelam ac voluntariam tradere servitutem.

Vale.

iii Idus Martias MCCCCLXXXV

: XI :

Angelus Politianus Lucio Phosphoro Pontifici[1] *Signino s. d.*

1   Misit ad me Alexander Cortesius, homo utrique nostrum amicissimus, epistolam quandam tuam ad ipsum scriptam, in qua tu mihi multa tribuens, cupere postremo affirmas per eum ipsum[2]

whole world listening. "Come Thracians and Sarmatians, come Getae and Britons: I can show you a letter," as a most elegant poet puts it.[10]

Here you have, Alessandro, my judgment regarding Poliziano. 4 Nor would I want anyone to think that this was attributable to flattery, given that I cannot ingratiate myself with the two who are already dead and insensate, and I have not yet met the one who is alive. I admit, however, that I very much want to meet him and to lay the foundations of such a friendship that no damage ever wrought by time can efface. Oh my dear Alessandro! I emphatically request you to do this, so that by your subtle influence you enable me to get my wish, attaching me and utterly dedicating me to the Prince of Letters. I would like, however, that Poliziano himself be asked (are you listening, most learned man? this is a transaction between you and me!) first not to disdain what, on my request, he receives as a favor from others, so that he may reciprocate in measures of love and affection, and second, to procure for me favored status with that illustrious man and leading citizen, Lorenzo de' Medici. Indeed, some years have now passed since I began wanting to dedicate myself to such a great and powerful friend and to offer myself as his protégé and voluntary servant.

Farewell.

March 13, 1485

: XI :

Angelo Poliziano to Lucio Phosphorus, Bishop of Segni

Alessandro Cortesi, a dear friend to both of us, sent me a letter of 1 yours written to him, in which, crediting me with many things, you end by asserting that you want to be attached by him to me, and by me to Lorenzo de' Medici. It is impossible to say how

nobis, per me autem Laurentio Medici conciliari. Eam epistolam cum legerem, dici non potest quantopere sim delectatus.[3] Nam ita et verbis et sententiis et concinnitate erat absoluta ut plane appareret Musis eam[4] dictantibus fuisse exceptam. Cogita igitur tu quam mihi nunc placeam, quamque ipse me mirer, qui sim Musarum καπυρῷ στόματι laudatus. Sed tamen vereor ne ita me tuae istae puellae ornandum susceperint ut Isocrates[5] Busirin, Thersiten Libanius, Muscam Lucianus, Favorinus etiam quartanam febrim ad ingenii modo periclitandas vires artemque ostentandam laudaverunt. Sunt enim in fabulis totae, sunt in mendaciis atque praestigiis. Mihi tamen libet hoc loco verum locutas. Quis enim damnet sua vota libenter? Quod si in hoc erro, libenter, ut Cicero inquit, erro. Est enim id ipsum lucro apponendum, quod decipimur, quippe voluptatem certe aliquam falsa quoque opinio nobis conciliat. Scis Stratoclem illum oratorem, devictis praelio Atheniensibus suamque fortunam ignorantibus, victoriam nuntiasse, re autem postmodum sic ut erat intellecta, ita indignantibus popularibus respondisse: 'Qui vobis, cives mei,' inquit 'iniurius fui, si bidui tristitiam me auctore lucrifecistis?' Quare ego quidem falli me sinam, et quod esse verum maxime cupio, verum esse facillime patiar.

2   De te autem, amoto ioco, sic sentio, mi Phosphore (malo enim te Phosphorum, homo in literis agens, quam, ut vulgus, Reverendum Patrem appellare; hoc enim literarum atque humanitatis, illud nomen dignitatis est; nos autem ex literis te et humanitate, si pateris, magis quam ex dignitate pendimus), sed ita, mi Phos-

pleased I was when I read this letter.[1] For with respect to its language, expression, and composition, it was so finely finished that it plainly appeared to have been written down to the Muses' dictation. Consider, therefore, how pleased I am with myself now and how I myself admire myself, since I have been praised "by the clear-sounding mouthpiece" of the Muses.[2] Nevertheless, I worry that those girls of yours have taken me up, for embellishment, just as Isocrates praised Busiris, Libanius praised Thersites, Lucian praised the fly, and Favorinus even praised malaria, all solely for the purpose of testing their powers and demonstrating their artistry.[3] The Muses are all about storytelling, fiction, and deception. Nevertheless, I am willing to think that, this time, they have spoken the truth. "For who would willingly denounce his own fond hopes?"[4] But if I err on this score, I err willingly, as Cicero says.[5] Indeed, the very fact that I am deceived should count as profit, since certainly even an incorrect opinion affords me some pleasure. You know that the orator Stratocles, when the Athenians had been defeated in battle but were still unaware of their misfortune, reported a victory, and when the actual situation eventually became known, he answered his indignant countrymen by asking, "How have I done you any harm, my citizens, if on my guarantee you have earned two days on your sorrow?"[6] Naturally, therefore, I permit myself to be deceived, and what I most especially want to be true, I quite readily allow to be true.

But joking aside, my opinion about you is this, my dear Phosphorus (being myself a person engaged in literary endeavors, I prefer to call you Phosphorus rather than the "Reverend Father" used by the crowd, since the former pertains to letters and humanity and the latter to an office, for if you do not mind, I value you more for your letters and humanity than I do for your office) — anyway, my opinion about you is as follows: you are a person full of humanity. When I say "humanity," I intend learning no less than kindness. For to people who know Latin it clearly means both.[7]

2

phore, sentio, te esse hominem plenum humanitatis. Humanitatem cum dico, non magis φιλανθρωπίαν quam παιδείαν intellego. Utrunque enim Latine quidem scientibus significat. Itaque ne cornu quidem copiae aut virgulam divinam pluris quam tuam amicitiam fecerim. Esque tu iam nunc meo infixus[6] cordi, et quidem trabali clavo, daboque operam, quantum quidem praestare potuero, ne tu avidius quam prudentius me tibi ascivisse amicum videare. Et quando longius abs te agitare contingit quam ut subservire usibus tuis queam, favebo certe laudibus, omnique, ut aiunt, pede in te honestando consistam.

3   Epistolam certe ipsam tuam, non tam epistolam quam Venerium illud cingulum amoribus medicatum, nunquam a me amittam. Quin potius, quasi imaginem animi tui identidem contemplans, ita meum desiderium consolabor. Caeterum nunc demum intellego quantum iacturae fecerim, quod te prius haud cognoverim, cum tanta mihi te cognito voluptas arriserit.

4   Nos ad Laurentium Medicem, qui nunc balneis dat operam, exemplum epistolae tuae mittemus, simul ut animum erga se tuum ex ea perpendat, simul ut nos ex tuo testimonio pluris aliquanto faciat quam fortasse facit, quamvis multo iam pluris[7] faciat quam digni ipsi nobis videmur.

Vale.

: XII :

Lucius Phosphorus Pontifex Signinus
Angelo Politiano suo s. d.

1   Officiose quidem et amice fecit Alexander, qui nescioquas literulas meas ad te misit. Sed hominem certe nimium amantem mei fefellit

As a result, I would not regard a cornucopia or a magic wand as more valuable than your friendship. You already have been nailed to my heart—with a spike,[8] no less—and I shall make every effort to prevent you from seeming to have adopted me as your friend more enthusiastically than wisely. And since circumstances place my activities too far away from you for me to be able to serve your needs, I shall definitely lend my support with words of praise and, in honoring you, shall stand my ground, as the saying goes, "on every foot."[9]

Certainly I shall never allow your letter itself—not so much a   3
letter as that strap of Venus, treated with potions for love[10]—out of my possession. On the contrary, as if gazing again and again at a picture of your heart, I shall thus soothe my sense of loss. Now at last I understand, however, how much it cost me not to know you at all before now, since, having come to know you, so much pleasure smiles upon me.

I shall send a copy of your letter to Lorenzo de' Medici, who is   4
now seeking relief at the baths, so that by it he may measure your feeling for him, and likewise so that, by virtue of your testimony, he may esteem me a little more than perhaps he does, although he already esteems me much more than, in my own eyes, I think I deserve.

Farewell.

: XII :

Lucio Phosphorus, Bishop of Segni,
to his dear Angelo Poliziano

Alessandro was dutiful and kind to send you some note or other   1
of mine to him. But clearly what deceives lovers has deceived this

id quod amatores fallit. Solent enim aliqui prae nimio amore zelotypia laborare (sic enim appellant quandam nimii amoris sive sedulitatem sive suspitionem). Quod ideo accidit quoniam ea quae sibi ipsis tantopere placent, eadem omnibus placere credunt, ac vix tutum hominum intuitum arbitrantur. Simile aliquid Alexander noster fecit, qui dum mea extollit, praedicat, amat, admiratur, eadem aliis placere putat. Quod fortasse cum Tarentinis et Consentinis, aut cum Laelio Decimo, ut ille inquit, optime factum esset. Sed cum Persio, omnium doctissimo, hoc est cum Politiano, vereor ne imprudens fuerit et inconsideratum. Feliciter tamen cecidit quando illae meae (ut scribis) puellae, pro uno amatore, duos sortitae sunt, et ego ex usura (inquit Plinius) sortem feci. Vellem illas easdem non quidem fucatas aut unguentis delibutas, tanquam ad moechos, sed quasi ornatas matronas, cum muliebri mundo et dote, ad viros ivisse. Nam quis aut repudium aut certe repulsam non formidaret?

2   Sed, mehercule, extra iocum nec μεταφορικῶς, Politiane, non minus horrui quam laetatus sum, cum illas literas ad manus tuas pervenisse audivi. Me potius recta oratione ac praeparata et conperendinata ad te scripsisse oportuit ac decuit, et ita amicitiam petere. Sed illas literas ad Alexandrum dedi, ut eo veluti legato et caduceatore uterer, cum quo tibi veterem amicitiam intercedere sciebam et hospitalitatem. Tu pro tua sapientia ac facilitate, si quid illic obiurgandum et parum aut te aut me dignum offendisti, condonabis amori nostro et nimiae familiaritati. Est enim Alexander plane alter ego, et ego alter Alexander. Quod si tu condicionem non reiicis, tertius accedes. Et ne unquam a triumviratus magistratu discedas, quando proximis comitiis te triumvirum lite-

person who loves me too much. Some people, as a result of excessive love, tend to suffer from jealousy (for this is the name given to a kind of officiousness or suspiciousness belonging to excessive love). This occurs because they believe that everyone likes the same things that they themselves most especially like, and they think it risky if people even look. Our dear Alessandro has done something analogous, for while he celebrates, proclaims, loves, admires things about me, he assumes that the same things please others. This might work quite well with people from Taranto or Cosenza, or with Laelius Decimus. But I worry that it was rash and unwise to do so with Persius, the most learned of all — that is, with Poliziano.[1] Nevertheless, it was a lucky accident when those girls of mine (as you write) drew out two lovers in the place of one and I myself (as Pliny says) made capital out of interest.[2] I would have liked for them to have approached their husbands not, of course, heavily made-up and dripping with perfume, as if on their way to their paramours, but in the guise of well-dressed married ladies, with wifely charms and a dowry. For who would not have dreaded, if not a divorce, then at least a rejection?

But, Poliziano, jokes and metaphors aside, I swear I was no less   2 terrified than pleased when I heard that the letter in question was in your hands. I should instead have written to you in language that was direct, well thought-out, long-pondered, and in such a way request your friendship. But I gave that letter to Alessandro, with whom I knew you were joined by hospitality and an old friendship, in order to use him as an ambassador and go-between. If you have come across anything in it which merits criticism or is too little worthy either of yourself or of me, then in accord with your wisdom and gentle nature, please pardon our love and tremendous intimacy. For Alessandro clearly is another I, and I, another Alessandro. If you do not reject the terms, you shall join us as a third. And to keep you from ever leaving the office of the triumvirate, since in the most recent election we made you Triumvir

rarum creavimus, comitiis futuris te triumvirum amicitiarum crea-
bimus. Sustulisti digitum. Bene habet. Non perhorrescam posthac.

3   Nunc volo te aliquantulum vellicare. Cur tandiu nobis ignotus
fuisti? Parum pie, mi Politiane, et plane crudeliter fecisti. Nunc
demum post tot annos ad nos venis? Me miserum, tam longo
tempore Politiano caruisse, sine eius literis egisse, non scripsisse,
non legisse, non recitasse, praesertim quando et Romae fuisti, et
ad multos istinc saepe scripsisti. Sed quid ago? Quasi vero ego
quoque non eandem navim conscenderim et in eadem culpa sim,
qui de te non sciscitarim. Hernicis meis refero acceptum. Nam
postquam his sacris initiatus fui, in illa saxa me conieci, ubi ne nomen quidem clarorum virorum audiebam. Sed nec literis vacabam.
Cum pecoribus et glebis res gerebatur. Tanta erat satietas vel potius fastidium curiae et fori. Rursus nunc, mutata voluntate, consilium nostrum totum est Ciceronianum, qui ad Rufum scribens,
'Urbem,' inquit, 'mi Rufe, cole,' et ex Sicilia reversus statuit ab
oculis civium non discedere. Sed quid dico Ciceronianum? Immo
Alexandrinum. Alexander enim est qui me retinere nunquam de-
sistit. 'Hic fiunt homines.' Et ut est in quadam eius, 'Hic caput,
hic sedes, hic fortunarum alea.' Quid quaeris? Vehementer his verbis sum incensus et plane confirmatus.

4   Quare, iucundissime Politiane, demum operam ut tam diuturni
temporis iacturam resarciamus, et tanto impensius recentem amicitiam colamus, quanto serius est coepta. Ego tuas expecto singulis
hebdomadibus per tabellarios qui trapezitis Medicibus tuis ratio-

of Letters, in the next we shall make you Triumvir of Friendships. You have raised your finger.[3] Wonderful. From now on, I won't be terrified of you.

Now I want to needle you a bit. Why did you remain a stranger 3 to me for so long? You did so, my dear Poliziano, with precious little kindness and obvious cruelty. You come to me now, at last, after so many years. What terrible luck, to have gone without Poliziano for such a long time, to have lived without a letter from him, not to have written one, not to have read one, silently, aloud. Especially given that you have been in Rome and often write many people there. But what am I saying? As if, in fact, I had not boarded the same boat as well and share the same fault for not making inquiries about you. I blame this on my Hernicans.[4] For after I was initiated into these rites, I planted myself on those rocks, where I did not hear even the name of any famous men. Nor did I have time for literature. Sheep and soil were my business. Of Curia and Forum[5] I'd had enough — indeed, more than I could bear. Now, by contrast, my intention is entirely Ciceronian, who, writing to Rufus, said, "Live in the City, my dear Rufus," and who, upon his return from Sicily, decided never to step out of sight of the citizenry.[6] But why do I call it "Ciceronian"? It is instead Alexandrine. For Alessandro is the one who never stopped holding on to me. "This is where real people are made."[7] And as he says in something of his own, "Here is the summit; here is the center; here fortunes are made and unmade."[8] What more can I say? By these words my enthusiasm has been fueled and my resolve unquestionably strengthened.

Most agreeable Poliziano, let us therefore make every effort to 4 mend the loss of such a long stretch of time, and to the extent that our new friendship had a late start, let us cultivate it that much more extravagantly. I look forward to a letter from you every week by way of the couriers who deliver accounts for your money-changing Medici. It will not be the kind of letter that is about the

nes afferunt. Genus literarum erit non de re publica, quae nulla
est, non de imperio, quod iam diu amisimus, quo dolore maxime
crucior infelix, sed de philosophia, de bene beateque vivendi ratione, de studiis artibusque nostris praeclarissimis, et de illorum
felicissimorum temporum contemplatione. Nam in his nihil est
quod pro magnitudine animi nostri spectare possimus, nisi forte te
Samarobrinae et Batavi delectant. En quo discordia cives perduxit
miseros. An hoc ita fato datum erat, et de nihilo nihilum? Nollem
potius unquam factum. Quamvis tanta nobis monumenta relique-
rint illi viri literarum, rei militaris, artificiorum, aedificiorum, virtutum denique omnium, tamen nescio quo modo desiderium illud
ferre non possumus, et fuisse felicem miserius est quam semper in-
felicem, et orbum esse quam nunquam patrem,[1] et mori quam non
nasci. De his igitur velim ad me scribas accurate, ut soles, ac ele-
gantissime.

5   Cum Laurentio nava mihi operam, per fortunas, Politiane. Admiror istum principem civitatis et amo plane, ut eum saepe cum
magno Pompeio comparare sim solitus, etsi feliciorem exitum et
opto et spero.

Vale.

Romae, xii Calendas Maias MCCCCLXXXV

Republic, as there is none, or about the Empire, which we lost long ago (I suffer terribly from that grief, given my bad luck!), but about philosophy, about the methods for living well and joyfully, about our glorious studies and arts, and about meditating on those most happy times. For in these nearer ones, there is nothing to look at in keeping with the nobility of our thought, unless by chance Burgundians and Dutchmen entertain you.[9] Look where conflict has led its unhappy citizens! Can it really have been assigned to such a fate, starting and ending with nothing? I would instead have preferred that it never have existed. Despite the fact that those men left us such massive monuments of literature, military science, artistic technique, architecture, and in short, every talent, nevertheless I am unable, for some reason or another, to bear that sense of loss. It is a worse condition to have been happy than always to have been unhappy, to have lost a child than never to have been a parent, to die than never to have been born. Please therefore write to me about them in your usual meticulous and extremely elegant way.

For heaven's sake, Poliziano, spare no effort on my behalf with 5 Lorenzo. I admire your leading citizen and love him completely, to the point that I have the frequent habit of comparing him to Pompey the Great, although I hope and pray for a happier outcome![10]

Farewell.

Rome, April 20, 1485

: XIII :

Angelus Politianus Lucio Phosphoro
Signino suo s. d.

1 Nihil peccavit Alexander meus, qui mihi epistolam miserit quae mihi debebatur. Peccasset magis, nulla expiandus victima, si meas mihi laudes invidisset, quanquam non meae illae sed tuae potius laudes sunt, atque ob id etiam meae. Κοινὰ γὰρ τὰ τῶν φίλων. Sed tu, personam ex nobis mutuatus, te ipsum scilicet in scaenam detulisti. Nam ut ego libenter hunc amicorum, ita tu iure illum literarum[1] expleveris triumviratum. Quod autem conquereris parum scriptas diligenter eas fuisse literas, aut me ludis, aut omnium es homo felicissimus, qui promas de summo quod vix quispiam de imo pectore. Non est autem quod aut ruri urbem aut rus in urbe desideres, si ipse habitas tecum, si quocunque is, te sequeris, magnum tibi in quavis solitudine theatrum, magnam solutudinem in quovis theatro facturus.

2 Officium porro epistolarum, quod requiris, hac lege polliceor, ut tu invicem pollicearis, illo etiam, cum res tulerit, intermisso, nullam tamen amoris inter nos iacturam factum iri. Ita enim sum aliquando districtus et occupatus ut non liceat, ita tristis et nauseabundus ut non libeat scribere. Tu igitur, ut vetus est dictum, 'amici vitia noveris, non oderis.'

Vale.

: XIII :

Angelo Poliziano to his dear Lucio Phosphorus,
Bishop of Segni

Alessandro did nothing wrong by sending me a letter which was   1
due to me. He would have done something worse, for which he
would not atone by any sacrifice, if he had begrudged me my
praise. That praise, however, is not mine, but rather yours — and
therefore mine too. "Friends hold all things in common."[1] But
you, needless to say, having borrowed a mask from me, put yourself on stage.[2] For just as I gladly complete this Triumvirate of
Friends, so too you can rightly complete the Triumvirate of Letters. As for the fact that you complain, however, that your letter
was written with insufficient care, either you are making fun of
me, or else you are the most blessed of all men, since you offer off
the top of your head what hardly anyone can from their deepest
thoughts. There is, however, no reason for you to miss the city in
the country or the country in the city, if you live with yourself,[3] if,
wherever you go, you follow yourself, ready to create an audience
in any solitude, and a great solitude before any audience.

Next, regarding the obligation to correspond that you are seek-   2
ing, I promise, but on this condition: that you promise in turn
that, should there be an interruption under certain circumstances,
there nevertheless will be no detriment to the love between us. For
sometimes I am so busy and distracted that writing is impossible,
so sad and sick to my stomach that it is not pleasurable. Therefore, as the old saying goes, "Take note of a friend's faults, but do
not despise them."[4]
Farewell.

: XIV :

Lucius Phosphorus Pontifex Signinus
Angelo Politiano suo s. d.

1 Ubi sunt isti qui obloquuntur et allatrant? En quo redacti sumus,
o Politiane, ut imperiti iudicent? Mihi Miscellanea tua atque adeo
quaecunque scribis magnopere placent. Garriant isti quid velint,
quod portenta verborum loquaris;[1] ego te plane Latinum esse iudico. Nam illud ne inimici quidem negant, te supra quam dici
possit curiosissimum ac diligentissimum esse, et omnes forulos ex-
cussisse, teque doctrinae quidem singularis hominem fatentur, eloquentiae vero[2] nullius, quasi possit aliquis eloquens esse, nisi idem
sit doctus. Ridiculi aestimatores et critici nostrorum temporum!
Quid quod et de Pico tuo, vel nostro potius, tot laudes quot scribis cum audiunt, stomachantur, et (si dis placet) faceti esse volunt,
asserentes illud Aesopeum, nihil reliqui aliis esse. Quibus quid potest esse verius? Is enim unus est in quo natura omnia bona
congessisse, et ubi omnes suas vires exercuisse videtur.

2 Sed tu ridere debes. Volo tibi narrare quo erga illos adagio utor.
'Videte,' inquam, 'quid agatis, boni viri. Nam iste piscis paucorum
hominum est,' ut ille Scipioni dixisse fertur. Quod ita transfero:
Politianus paucorum, id est doctissimorum est, non turbae litera-
tulorum ac paedagogorum et vulgi. Ergo omnes docti te unum admirantur, et fatentur te omnes qui sexcentis abhinc annis scripserunt facile superare (hoc est, te illos, non illos te, ne quis me
reciprocis argumentis uti, aut amphibologice loqui credat) et doc-

: XIV :

Lucio Phosphorus, Bishop of Segni, to his dear Angelo Poliziano

Where are these people who rail and bark? Look at what we are 1
reduced to, Poliziano: the ignorant sit in judgment. I very much
like your *Miscellanea*, as I do whatever you write. Let those people
jabber as they wish, saying that you pronounce "linguistic monstrosities"; in my judgment, you are absolutely Latin. Indeed, even
your enemies do not deny that you are extremely painstaking and
meticulous (more so than words can say) and have emptied every
shelf, and they acknowledge that you unquestionably are a person
of unparalleled learning—but of no eloquence at all. As if anyone
could be eloquent if he were not also learned! These appraisers
and critics of our era are laughable. What of the fact that, even
about your (or better, our) Pico, when they hear each and every
word of praise you write, they start complaining and, heaven forbid, want to be funny, saying after Aesop, "That leaves nothing for
everyone else."[1] But what could be truer than what you write? He
is the one person in whom Nature seems to have amassed all its
gifts and to have exercised all its powers.

But you ought to be laughing. I want to relate to you the prov- 2
erb I use regarding them. "Gentlemen," I say, "watch what you're
doing, for that's a fish for just a few," as someone reportedly said to
Scipio.[2] I apply this as follows: Poliziano is for a few, i.e., for the
most learned, not for a crowd of literary amateurs, schoolteachers,
and members of the general public. All learned persons, therefore,
admire you alone and acknowledge that you easily surpass everyone who wrote countless years ago (to clarify, lest anyone think I
am using reversible arguments or speaking equivocally: you surpass them, not they you[3]) and that both learning and eloquence

trinam ac eloquentiam in te esse coniunctas. Non enim quis non eloquens dici debet, si suo quodam modo utitur stilo, cum conplura[3] et varia sint genera dicendi.

3   Sed epistolam plicabo, quoniam festinat tabellarius. Mox plura audies. Haec scripsi tumultuarie, cum in Pauli Cortesii domum divertissem, qui est plane tuus, et omnem impetum adversariorum sustinet. Tuum erit scuto et parma tela suscipere, et in eosdem retorquere, nisi mavis, ut supradixi, ridere.

Vale.

pridie Idus Februarias

: XV :

Angelus Politianus Lucio Phosphoro Pontifici[1] Signino s. d.

1   Irasceris obtrectatoribus nostris, eruditissime Phosphore, quod in Miscellaneis portenta me loqui verborum dicant, et ut hominum (quod ais) doctum fateantur, ita negent eloquentem, tum quod illud etiam criminentur, tantas me in unum Picum laudes contulisse ut aliis omnino nullas fecerim reliquas. Me vero ista, Phosphore, nihil movent, neque enim ulla sermonum talium 'nova mi facies inopinave surgit. Omnia praecepi[2] atque animo mecum ante peregi.' Quin ad ea ne responderem quidem, nisi te ita velle sentirem, cui negare nihil possum.

2   Portenta igitur verborum quae vocent isti, fateor, ignoro, nisi si portenta credunt quae ipsi nova nunc primum vocabula vel au-

are united in you. Indeed, no one should be said not to be eloquent for using in one way or another his own particular style, since there exist numerous diverse rhetorical modes.

But I shall fold the letter, since the courier is in a hurry. You 3
will hear more soon. I wrote the above in a disorganized way, when I had stopped off at Paolo Cortesi's[4] house. He is utterly yours and resists every push by your adversaries. Your task will be to take their barbs on your shield and then turn these against them — unless you prefer, as I said before, to laugh.

Farewell.

February 12

: XV :

Angelo Poliziano to Lucio Phosphorus, Bishop of Segni

You are angry at my detractors, most erudite Phosphorus, because 1
they say that in my *Miscellanea* I pronounce "linguistic monstrosities," and because, even as they acknowledge that a person is (as you say) learned, they likewise deny that he is eloquent, and, furthermore, because they even denounce the fact that I have heaped such considerable words of praise on Pico alone, with the result that I have left behind nothing at all for anyone else. But their criticisms, Phosphorus, have no effect on me, and of such talk "no form either new or unexpected rises to greet me: I foresaw and quietly thought through everything."[1] In fact, I would not even offer any response were I not sensing that you, to whom I can never say no, want me to.

I confess that I have no idea what it is that these people call 2
"linguistic monstrosities," unless it's the case that they consider words which they themselves now hear or understand for the first

diunt vel intellegunt. Nam ego nec verba ulla peperi 'cinctutis non exaudita Cethegis,' nec ullos habeo nisi receptissimos auctores. Non tamen ex eorum sum numero qui cessare Latinam linguam magna ex parte patiuntur, dum quisque illa reformidat quae vulgo hactenus ignorata sunt, siquidem eo res rediit ut ne magnorum quidem auctorum lingua tuto loquamur, quoniam vulgo minus innotuerit, itaque barbaris uti malumus quam Romanis vocibus, et cum siligineus domi sit panis, emendicato furfure magis vescimur.

3   Quod autem mihi eloquentiam sic adimunt ut doctrinam concedant, non modo equidem non succenseo, sed et gratias ago. Noli, quaeso, amori erga me tuo nimis indulgere, Phosphore, nec parum laudari putes, si Marci Varronis exemplo lauder, quem et ipsum veteres scientiae multae, nullius eloquentiae esse crediderunt.[3] Ego sane, mi Phosphore, nec eloquentiam mihi vindico, nec doctrinam agnosco. Si cui tamen in Miscellaneis, etiam citra eloquentiam, sciolus videor, bene habet. Vici. Nam istuc ipsum quaerebam. Quo enim eloquentia mihi in hoc opere, non ad persuadendum, sed ad docendum parato?

4   Quod autem de stilo scribis, utique verum puto, non continuo peius esse quod variet, cum sit ipsius eloquentiae non vultus, non color unus.[4] Quapropter nec adhuc quisquam suffragiis est omnibus habitus[5] eloquens, sive quod sibi quisque prae ceteris placet, sive quod alios alia dicendi forma plus capit. Demosthenem[6] cogita et Ciceronem. Illius quibusdam sicca oratio, Demadi lucernam olere, Aeschini etiam (si dis placet) barbara videbatur. Hunc Cal-

time "monstrosities." For I have spawned not one word "unheard by the belted Cethegi,"[2] nor do I rely on the authority of any but the most standard writers. I am not, however, to be counted among those who allow the Latin language to come largely to a standstill while each of them trembles before things which, until now, have been the object of general ignorance. Indeed, the situation has become so bad that we cannot safely speak even the language of major authors, because less familiar to the general public. We thus prefer to use foreign words in place of Roman ones, and although we have the best white bread at home, we feed primarily on hand-outs of bran.

As for the fact that they strip me of eloquence even as they grant me learning, not only am I by no means incensed, but I even say, "Thank you." Please do not indulge in excessive love for me, Phosphorus, nor should you think me inadequately praised if I am praised on the model of Marcus Varro, whom the ancients likewise considered to be someone of great knowledge, but no eloquence. Certainly I myself, my dear Phosphorus, neither claim eloquence nor acknowledge learning. If, however, in my *Miscellanea*, even leaving aside eloquence, I impress anyone as having a smattering of knowledge,[3] then that's wonderful, I win, for this was exactly my goal. What, indeed, would have been the point of eloquence in this work, put together not to persuade, but to teach? 3

I regard what you write about style as being particularly true: something is not instantly worse just because it varies, since eloquence itself has no single face,[4] no single color. This is why, hitherto, no one has been held to be eloquent by every voter, either because people like themselves more than anyone else, or because different rhetorical styles move different people more than others. Think of Demosthenes and Cicero. To some people's taste, the former's language is dry; to Demades it "smells of the lamp"[5]; to Aeschines it is, heaven forbid, barbaric. Calvus thought the latter bloodless and predictable; Brutus, fragmented and dislocated; cer- 4

vus exanguem et tritum, Brutus fractum et elumbem, quidam ieiunum atque aridum, contra alii tumentem et inflatum, nec satis
pressum, exultantemque supramodum et superfluentem, alii frigidum in iocis, alii parum antiquum, quidam etiam in dicendo viro
molliorem superstitiosumque,[7] et peregrinis quasi legibus nimis
addictum putaverunt. Neque vero haec ideo refero quo me putem
cum talibus conferendum. Non enim sic insanio, Phosphore. Sed
utendum magnis nominibus fuit, ut stomacho isti tuo fortius[8] oc-
currerem.

5   Nam quid ego de Pico Mirandula dicam? Hi sunt invidiae nimirum, Phosphore, mores. Sed vivat ille! Vivat modo nec eat alio
deinceps quam quo pede iam coepit, etiam livor ipse fatebitur non
modo eum non supra modum, sed longe etiam infra modum fuisse
a nobis laudatum. Cuius tamen praeconium non video quid aliorum titulis offecerit, quos in hoc ipso Miscellaneorum libro conce-
lebramus.

6   Reliquum est ut tibi agam, Phosphore, gratias, qui me hominem tenuissimae fortunae, neque multae admodum literaturae, ne
visum quidem tibi adhuc, ita diligas ipse, et pontifex et doctissimus, ut etiam contentiones, honoris dignitatisque meae causa,
suscipias. Sed et Picus debere se tibi plurimum sentit, salutemque
tibi et Curtesio suo nomine iussit adscribi. Laurentius quoque
Medices noster visus est epistola tua magnopere delectari, quem
scito esse hominem tui studiosissimum. Quod esse verum tum denique agnosces,[9] cum periculum feceris.

Vale.

Florentiae, pridie Calendas Martias MCCCCLXXXXI

tain others, feeble and withered; others still, swollen and inflated, insufficiently concise, too unbridled and overflowing; others, bland in his humor; others, not traditional enough; and certain people even thought him rather effeminate in speaking, and superstitious, and too subservient to what could be considered foreign rules.[6] I do not recount all this, however, because I think I should be compared to such men. I am not *that* crazy, Phosphorus. But big names needed to be used in order that I might more effectively attempt to soothe your irritation.

What, on the other hand, can I say regarding Pico della Miran- 5 dola? This is, of course, the customary behavior of envy, Phosphorus. But long may he live! If he just keeps living and takes no further steps other than the ones he has already begun taking, even Spite itself will admit that he was praised by me not only not too much, but even far too little.[7] Nevertheless, I fail to see any shouted praise of him that could drown out the achievements of the other people whom I celebrate in these very *Miscellanea*.

All that remains is for me to thank you, Phosphorus, because 6 you yourself, both bishop and consummate scholar, feel such affection for me, a man of slenderest fortune and not very much linguistic skill, someone you have not yet laid eyes on, that you take on disputes for the sake of my reputation and prestige. But Pico too understands that he is greatly in your debt and has instructed me to append a hello from him to you and to his dear Cortesi. Our dear Lorenzo de' Medici as well clearly derived great pleasure from your letter. Know that he is a very great supporter of yours. You will realize that this is true when the day comes that you put it to the test.

Farewell.

Florence, March 28, 1491

: XVI :

Angelus Politianus Lucio Phosphoro Pontifici Signino s. d.

1 Accepta epistola tua statim ad Laurentium cucurri. Exposui quid optares. Grata voluntas, gratus illi tuus animus. Denique pro munere accipit quod pro munere poscis. Quam ad eum dedisti epistolam, nondum mihi quidem legendam dedit. Sed tamen ut et doctam laudavit et amoris erga se plenissimam, ac si per occupationes liceat, responsurum se tibi, vel hodie, promisit.
Vale.
Florentiae, pridie Idus Maias MCCCCLXXXXI

: XVII :

Angelus Politianus Cassandrae Fedeli Venetae,
puellae doctissimae, s. d.

1 'O decus Italiae virgo, quas dicere grates,[1] quasve referre parem,' quod etiam honore me tuarum literarum non dedignaris? Mira profecto fides, tales proficisci a foemina (quid autem a foemina dico? immo vero a puella et virgine) potuisse. Non igitur iam Musas, non Sibyllas, non Pythias obiiciant vetusta nobis saecula, non suas Pythagorei[2] philosophantes foeminas, non Diotimam Socratici nec Aspasiam. Sed nec poetrias illas Graeca iactent moni-

: XVI :

Angelo Poliziano to Lucio Phosphorus, Bishop of Segni

The moment your letter arrived, I ran to Lorenzo. I explained 1
what you were hoping for. Your wish and your intention found his
favor. As a matter of fact, what you request as a gift he regards as
a gift. He has not yet given me to read the letter you sent him. He
praised it, however, as both learned and replete with love toward
himself. And he promised that, if it his schedule permits, he will
send you a reply, even today.

Farewell.

Florence, May 14, 1491

: XVII :

Angelo Poliziano to Cassandra Fedele[1] of Venice,
Most Learned Girl

"O maiden, Italy's glory, what words of gratitude or grateful rec- 1
ompense can I devise"[2] for the fact that you did not deem me unworthy of the honor of a letter from you? It staggers the mind that
such a letter could have come from a woman. But why am I saying
"woman"? A child, rather, and a maiden. No longer, therefore, will
the ages of antiquity taunt us with its Muses, or its Sibyls, or its
Pythian priestesses, nor the Socratics with Diotima or Aspasia.[3]
Nor will the Greek classics vaunt those poetesses: Telesilla, Corinna, Sappho, Anyte, Erinna, Praxilla, Cleobulina, and the rest.[4]
And we now can readily trust the Romans when they say that the
daughters of Laelius and Hortensius, along with Cornelia, mother

menta, Telesillam, Corinnam, Sappho, Anyten, Erinnen, Praxillam, Cleobulinam, caeteras, credamusque facile Romanis iam Laeli et Hortensi filias, et Corneliam Gracchorum matrem fuisse matronas quantumlibet eloquentissimas. Scimus hoc profecto, scimus nec eum sexum fuisse a natura tarditatis aut hebetudinis damnatum. Sed enim veterum saeculorum talis ista pene publica laus fuit ut in quibus etiam vilissimos servos ad extremum pervenisse quondam vel literarum vel philosophiae fastigium reperiamus. At vero aetate nostra, qua pauci quoque virorum caput altius in literis extulerunt, unicam te tamen existere puellam quae pro lana librum, pro fuso calamum, stilum pro acu tractes, et quae non cutem cerussa, sed atramento papyrum linas. Id vero non magis usitatum, nec minus rarum aut novum, quam si de glacie media nascantur violae, si de nivibus rosae, si de pruinis lilia.

2   Quod si conatus ipse pro miraculo iam cernitur, quid de profectu studiorum tanto dicemus? Scribis epistolas, Cassandra, subtiles, acutas, eleganteis, Latinas, et quanquam puellari quadam gratia, virginali quadam simplicitate dulcissimas, tamen etiam mire gravis et concordatas. Orationem quoque tuam legimus, eruditam, locupletem, sonoram, illustrem, plenamque laetae indolis. Sed nec extemporalem tibi deesse facultatem accepimus, quae magnos etiam oratores aliquando destituit. Iam vero in dialectis implicare nodos inenodabiles, explicare ab aliis nunquam solutos, nunquam solvendos diceris. Philosophiam vero sic tenes ut et defendas acriter quaestiones praepositas et impugnes vehementer, 'audesque viris concurrere virgo,' sic scilicet in doctrinarum stadio pulcherrimo ut non sexus animo, non animus pudori, non ingenio pudor officiat. Et cum te laudibus nemo non attollat, summittis ipsam te tamen, et temperas nec minus ad humum modeste cunc-

of the Gracchi, were ladies who were every bit as eloquent as you could want.[5] This, I tell you, we know for sure: this sex was not condemned by Nature either to slowness or to dullness. As a matter of fact, merit in antiquity was assigned so nearly without discrimination that we find that, back then, even the lowliest slaves occasionally reached the highest pinnacle of letters or philosophy. But in our own day, in which a few men have also held their heads up, to some extent, in letters, you nevertheless are the only girl in evidence who works with a book instead of wool, a pen instead of a spindle, a stylus instead of a needle, and who does not smear her skin with makeup but, instead, her paper with ink. This truly is no more common or less extraordinary or strange than if violets were to sprout straight from ice, if roses from snow, if lilies from frost.

But if the very fact that you tried is already regarded as miraculous, what can I say about the considerable progress of your studies? You write letters, Cassandra, that are pure, penetrating, elegant, and Latin. And although a certain girlish charm and maidenly simplicity makes them extremely pleasant, they are at the same time impressively serious and judicious. I have also read your oration — erudite, copious, melodious, distinct, and full of rich talent. But I have heard that you do not lack extemporaneous ability, something that has sometimes failed even great orators. And you are now said to tie knots in dialectical questions that cannot be loosed and to untie those never loosed (and never to be loosed) by others. Furthermore, you have such a grasp of philosophy that, on disputed questions, you can mount both a fierce defense and an energetic assault, and you "dare, though a maiden, to join battle with men"[6] — in such a way, of course, in learning's magnificent race, that sex does not oppose spirit; nor spirit, modesty; nor modesty, genius. And although no one does not exalt you with words of praise, you humble yourself, and you discreetly try to bring the universal high opinion of you down to earth, no less

2

torum de te opinionem, quam verecunde virgineos oculos reveren-
terque deiicis.

3   O qui me igitur statim sistat istic, ut faciem, virgo, tuam castis-
simam contempler, ut habitum, cultum, gestumque mirer, ut dictata instillataque tibi a Musis tuis verba, quasi sitientibus auribus
perbibam, denique ut afflatu, instinctu tuo consummatissimus repente poeta evadam,

> nec me carminibus vincant aut Thracius Orpheus,
> aut Linus, huic mater quamvis atque huic pater adsit,
> Orphei[3] Calliopea, Lino formosus Apollo.

4   Mirari equidem antehac Ioannem Picum Mirandulam solebam,
quo nec pulchrior alter mortalium, nec in omnibus (arbitror) doctrinis excellentior. Ecce nunc etiam te, Cassandra, post illum protinus coepi, fortasse iam cum illo, quoque venerari. Tibi vero tanta
incepta Deus Optimus Maximus secundet, et cum recesseris a pa-
rentibus, is auctor contingat et consors, qui sit ista virtute non in-
dignus, ut quae nunc propemodum sua sponte naturalis ingenii
flamma semel emicuit, ita crebris deinceps aut adiuta flatibus, aut
enutrita fomitibus effulgeat, ut a nostrorum hominum praecordiis
animoque nox omnis geluque penitus et languoris[4] in literis et inscitiae discutiatur.

Vale.

than, out of modesty and respect, you cast your maidenly eyes in the same direction.

O for someone to put me at once where you are,[7] so that I might gaze upon your very chaste countenance, maiden, so that I might admire your bearing, your style, your gestures, so that I might drink and drink with thirsty ears, so to speak, the words that were dictated to you and poured into you by your Muses, so that, finally, by your inspiration and impulse, I might walk away an instant poet of consummate skill, and

> in verse shall surpass me not Thracian Orpheus, nor Linus,
> though mother give aid to the one, to the other, the father:
> Calliope to Orpheus, handsome Apollo to Linus.[8]

Before now, to tell the truth, my custom was to admire Giovanni Pico della Mirandola, than whom no other mortal is more beautiful or more eminent in all branches of learning, in my estimation. But see how now I have begun to adore you too, Cassandra, right behind him — or maybe already even alongside him. May the Supreme Deity smile upon your undertakings. And when you leave your parents' home, may the sort of guide and companion come your way who is not unworthy of your talent, so that the flame of innate genius that now, almost entirely of its own accord, has first glimmered may subsequently blaze forth, either helped by constant blowing, or fed by constant fuel, so that all night and penetrating chill of ignorance and literary torpor may be dispelled from the hearts and minds of our contemporaries.

Farewell.

: XVIII :

Iacobus Antiquarius[1] *Angelo Politiano s. d.*

1 Pergens nuper, ex vitae instituto, ad scribarum Mediolanensium decuriam, conpluris adulescentes qui ibi versantur, remisso aliquantisper principis negocio, certatim intentos offendi ad legendum dispertitum quem in manibus habebant inter se librum. Roganti, quidnam operis novi emersisset, 'Miscellanea,' inquiunt, 'Politiani.' Conscendo, ac inter eos sedeo. Tum una incipio avidissime legere. Quippe delector ingeniis aetatis nostrae, quae non solum manca non sit, sed iam plane in Romanae antiquitatis vestigia abeat. Verum cum parum temporis impendere liceret, ex bibliopolae taberna codicem requiro. Affertur a puero meo. Statim cum domi essem, eum intentius evolvo. In primis verbis, immo in ipsa inscriptione, quod in Laurentii Medicis nomine liber apparuerit, animus valde coepit delectari. Tum ipsa praefatio multam literis spem ostendere specimenque quoddam pulcherrimum prae se ferre visa est. Capita subinde libri excurro. Ubique summa eruditio, ubique fastidii expultrix blanditur varietas, et quod plurimum ingenii ac laboris postulavit, tot tantorumque auctorum testimonio res agitur ut quicunque sugillare aliquid ex istis lucubrationibus tuis tentaverit canis latrator haberi possit, non demorsor.

2 Nollem cum Domitio tanquam cum larva, quando olim inter mortales desiit esse, pedem te saepius conferre. Iuvit enim quantum potuit rem literariam. Inter primos situm et pulverem veteri-

: XVIII :

Jacopo Antiquari[1] to Angelo Poliziano

Recently making my way, as is my routine, to the office of the Mil-   1
anese secretaries, I ran into a large number of young men attached
to the place who, during a brief pause in the prince's business, vied
keenly with one another to read a book they had in their hands,
its pieces distributed among them. When I ask, "What new work,
pray tell, has come out?" they reply, "Poliziano's *Miscellanea*." I
walk down and take a seat among them. Then in their company I
begin to read most eagerly. I delight, of course, in the talented intellects of our era, since not only is it not crippled, but already it
sets out unmistakably in the footsteps of Roman antiquity. But as
soon as I can spare a moment of time, I request the volume from
the bookseller's shop. It is brought by my servant. As soon as I am
home, I flip through it eagerly. My heart begins to fill with delight
over its first words, or rather, over its very dedication, in that the
book has appeared in the name of Lorenzo de' Medici. Then the
very preface visibly offers literature great cause for optimism and
holds out a kind of magnificent model. At once I skim the book's
chapters. Everywhere maximum erudition, everywhere variation,
banisher of boredom, lure you in. And something that demands a
very great deal of talent and effort: each case is made on the basis
of the evidence of so many writers, and ones of such authority,
that whoever tries to bully any products of your all-night efforts
can be regarded as a dog with a bark, but no bite.

I would have preferred for you not to have squared off so often   2
with Domizio,[2] as if with a ghost, since he long ago left the world
of the living. To the extent of his ability, he assisted literary affairs.
He was among the first to strive to shake the mold and dust off
the ancients, and, had he lived, he would have turned out ever

bus excutere studuit, politiora in dies, Politiani emulatione vel exemplo, praestiturus, si vixisset. Non tamen aliter eum abs te peti arbitror, quam primi pili hominem. Mors illum, ut scis, immatura praeripuit, emendaturum fortasse, si quid inconsideratius excide-rat. Satius est, ut tu inquis, candidatum, ut autem ego, philo-sophiae virum consularem aliorum errata notatis locis coarguere, nomini autem parcere. Verum in hanc ipsam sententiam ambiguus tendo, quia pugnis aerem creditur verberare aut commenticia nu-gamenta sectare, extantem qui nullum habet in quem suscepta vi-deatur oratio. In hac tamen opinionis ambiguitate vacillantem, certum in ea parte me esse sentio: qui prodesse voluerunt, diem capitis illis dicendum non esse. Fuit inter nos Domitius, et moni-menta reliquit famae non poenitendae.

3   Te aeternitas manet. Sincipitio capillo eam praehendisti. Cupio, et pro humano iure abs te peto, ut cum in his Miscellaneis quae edisti centurionem te esse volueris, iam in reliquo opere, quod in-ter manus (ut arbitror, multiplex et eruditum) est, tribunum, aut plane positis castris legatum te facias et imperatorem. Nam quibus centum capita placuerunt, ii longe maiore numero delectabuntur.

Idibus[2] *Novemb.* MCCCCLXXXVIII[3]

more polished products by emulating or imitating Poliziano. Nevertheless, I suppose you go after him simply as the leader of the pack.[3] As you know, an untimely death overtook him, before, perhaps, he had time to correct whatever had left his desk without due consideration. Preferably, what you call a candidate for Philosophy and what I call one of its senior statesmen refutes others' errors once the relevant passages have been pointed out—but spares their good name. On this very question, however, I am somewhat torn, since anyone who has no evident opponent against whom his discourse may seem to have been undertaken is thought to shadow box or to chase figments of his imagination. Nevertheless, although I waver back and forth over this question of opinion, I know that I am decidedly of this view: people who want to be useful should not be accused of a capital crime. Domizio was part of our world, and he left behind lasting evidence of a reputation that needs no apology.

Your destiny is immortality. You have grabbed it by the hair on its brow.[4] I want and by human right request from you that, whereas in the *Miscellanea* that you have published you wanted to be a centurion, now in the remaining work which is in your hands (and which, I expect, is intricate and erudite) you make yourself a colonel or, having pitched your camp definitively, a brigadier and a major general.[5] For whoever likes a hundred chapters will find a far larger number thrilling.

November 13, 1489[6]

: XIX :

Angelus Politianus Iacobo Antiquario suo s. d.

1 Utinam quas in me confers epistola tua laudes ita veras esse, nec ab humanitate magis quam a iudicio profectas, aliis mihique persuaderes, ut ego statim de hac ipsa epistola tua iudicium semper gravissimum Laurentii Medicis agnovi. Nam cum tibi ille summus hominum in omni usu plurimum sermonibus tuis deferat, tum se videre ait neminem cui tu literis probitate prudentiaque concedas. Crederem vero facile quae sic ex animo, quasique dicam vero vultu de me scribis, ac propriis[1] omnino laudibus faverem, nisi testimonio isti, praeter conscientiam meam, fama quoque ipsa publice in omnes tuae humanitatis obstreperet.[2] Quare tota equidem sic accipio laudationem, non ut illam meis meritis, sed ut tuis moribus assignem, tanto plus tibi me debere sentiens, quanto ipse minus mihi debeam.[3]

2 Quod autem ad Miscellanea nostra attinet, aut ego fallor, aut nihil in eis aeque fructuosum quam libertas illa et simplicitas, incauta fortasse, sed et ingenua tamen, ac si minus a prudentia, certe a charitate profecta communium studiorum, quae prima videlicet in huius saeculi scriptoribus desideratur. Nam quod me pedem conferre cum Domitio nolles, equidem quid spectes intellego, nec ego non aliquid istiusmodi iam tum videbam cum personam mihi illam censoris odiosissimam imponebam, diligentiamque pene improbam, iactationi verborum cantilenaeque cuilibet[4] expositam,

: XIX :

Angelo Poliziano to his dear Jacopo Antiquari

Would that you were convincing others (and me too) that the 1
praise you bestow on me in your letter were true and not the consequence of your kindness rather than your settled opinion—just
as I immediately recognized the truth of the always weighty judgment of Lorenzo de' Medici with regard to your letter. For although that man, preeminent in every category, gives the highest
credit to your conversation, he also says that he sees no one to
whom, in letters, you take second place with respect to quality and
wisdom. I would readily believe, however, what you write about
me in such a heartfelt way—with an honest face, I might say—
and would lend full support to my own praise, if, besides my conscience, the very reputation of your kindness toward everyone did
not also cry out against your testimony. And so I accept your
whole eulogy in such a way as to attribute it not to my merits but
to your character, aware that I owe you more in proportion to how
much less I owe myself.

As for what regards my *Miscellanea*, either I am mistaken, or 2
they contain nothing equally productive as that freedom and ear-
nestness (imprudent perhaps, but genuine all the same, and if less
a product of judiciousness, then certainly one of the camaraderie
of shared studies) which was of course the first goal among the
writers of this century. Indeed, in that you would have preferred
me not to square off with Domizio, I of course understand what
you mean, nor did I myself fail to see something along these lines
back when I donned that role of censor that is most abhorrent to
me and, throwing caution to the wind and feigning an almost un-
principled meticulousness, susceptible to any and all repetitiveness
and pomposity, I, to the best of my abilities, applied all my inge-

neglectis cautionibus, affectans, ad sarcienda literarum damna, so-
lertiam omnem, pro virili parte, dirigebam. Semper autem sum veritus quam denique in partem meum tale consilium, non dico ab
obtrectatoribus raperetur, sed a prudentissimis etiam hominibus,
iisdemque cautissimis acciperetur. Quanquam autem omnino[5]
convenire mihi tecum, id est cum viro amicissimo doctissimoque,
necesse est, tamen quia suo cuique corde quaedam pervidentur, dicam ad ea nonnihil quae mihi in hac epistolae tuae parte sapienter
obiciis et amice.

3   Cum mortuo negas, quasi cum larva, decertandum. Mihi vero
contra videri solet. Etenim quod adversus mortuos pronuntiamus
pro vero accipi tam solet quam debet, ut item quod adversus vi-
ventis plerunque odii vel invidiae suspitione laborat. 'At iuvit ille
rem literariam.' Quis neget? An non isto nomine sic a me laudatur
ut a nemine magis, et quidem in eadem ipsa pagina qua et reprehenditur? 'Sed erat,' inquies, 'emendaturus ea si diutius vixisset.'
Qui sciam vero istuc? An usquequaque de ingeniorum profectu
bene sperare est? Aut non huius ipsius[6] postrema quaeque mendo-
siora? Quid quod futurus in dies ambitu honorum minus ociosus,
opinione quoque sui magis inflatus. Sed fac emendaturus fuisse.
Nunc igitur ob id, inter scriptores omneis, unus a censoria virgula
Domitius asseretur, unus erit iste (si dis placet) gallinae filius
albae? Iam cur dissimulari quoque nomen oporteat, cuius in auctoritate venenum (si quod est ipsius commentariorum), velut an-
guis in herba, delitescat?

4   Ego vero sic Domitium studiosis, quasi foveam viatoribus, ostendo, nec autem oblivisci videor humanitatis. Quin potius, ut iam

nuity to patching the damage done to literature. I worried constantly, not about the ultimate interpretation with which such an intention on my part would be seized upon by my detractors, but how it would be received by very wise and, at the same time, very conservative individuals. Although it is essential that I be in full accord with you, that is to say, with a very dear and very learned man, nevertheless, since particular things seem especially precious to each individual, I shall say a word or two in reply to the objections you raise, wisely and affably, in this part of your letter.

You say that one should not contend with a dead man, as if with a ghost. I tend to take the opposite view, since, in fact, what we say against the dead tends to be taken as true to the proper degree, whereas what we say against the living suffers from the constant suspicion of malice or envy. "But he assisted literary affairs." Who can deny it? On this score, was he not praised by me in terms matched by no one—indeed, on the very same page on which he also is criticized? "But," you will say, "he was going to correct his mistakes, had he only lived longer." How should I know this? Are you really saying that it is always and everywhere a good idea to expect intellectual progress? Were not all of this particular person's final contributions even *more* inaccurate? What of the fact that, day by day, he would have become less free for study, as a result of his canvassing for honors, and, worse still, swollen with increasing self-satisfaction. But let us suppose he was going to make corrections. Is Domizio, alone among all writers, really to be released from the censor's mark on this account?[1] Will he alone, so please the gods, be "a son of a white hen"?[2] What need should there be now to hide the name, since under its authority any poison belonging to his commentaries lurks like a snake in the grass?

I show Domizio to scholars in this light, however, as one would point out a hazard to travelers. Nor do I seem to have forgotten my humanity. On the contrary, as already I seem to be able not

non sperare modo, sed etiam explorate videor iudicare posse, melius aliquanto de vita merebor censura ista mea, quam forsan alius indulgentia. Adde quod illustribus factum id quoque exemplis, nisi cui tamen levis est auctor Horatius, Ennium, Plautum, Lucilium, Dossenium, totamque illam cohortem poetarum veterum semel iugulans, et quidem reclamante populo. Quid, non in Senecam quoque Gellius[7] magna libertate verborum incurrit? Non eundem Quintilianus atro notat calculo? Non Marino Ptolemaeus diem dicit, Eratostheni Strabo, Thessalo Galenus, Hermagorae Cicero? Non omnes denique philosophorum scholae maxime cum prioribus digladiantur? Nec cuiusquam sane parcitur nomini, dum pro se quisque certat publico bono.[8] 'Sed ista,' inquies, 'graviora.' Fateor. At idem cur non liceat in levioribus? Certe Plato philosophorum princeps, etiam sine praefatione honoris, nugari dicit Aeschylum, tragoediae summum (siquidem Aristophani credamus) auctorem, quod in levicula re dissenserit ab Homero.

5   Nec ego tamen causam Domitii damnavi totam. Sed ut iam decuriatus hominem,[9] sic ipsum neutiquam negligenter expendi critica lance, dissimulaturus in plenum si non aliquo certe habendum numero credidissem. Et videbatur ita mihi rectum sane tum cum illa meditabar,[10] qui tamen idem facile iam libenterque muto factum te dissentiente, cuius mihi, protinus ut debet, etiam pro magnis rationibus est auctoritas. Caeterum quoniam de eo nobis integrum non est, ubique divulgatis exemplaribus, et quidem plu-

only to hope but even to judge first-hand, I shall do a somewhat greater service to his memory by way of my censure than someone else perhaps will by means of indulgence. Add the fact that this was done on the basis of famous precedents — unless someone finds Horace to be an inconsequential authority, the Horace who cuts the throats of Ennius, Plautus, Lucilius, Dossennius, and that whole cadre of ancient poets, once and for all, while the public cries out in protest.[3] What, did not Gellius also attack Seneca in uncensored terms?[4] Did not Quintilian designate the same with a black pebble?[5] Did not Ptolemy indict Marinus? Strabo, Eratosthenes? Galen, Thessalus? Cicero, Hermagoras?[6] In sum, don't all philosophical schools lock swords most especially with their predecessors? Nor was anyone's reputation shown any mercy while each individual struggled on his own behalf for the sake of the public good. "But those are more serious subjects," you will say. Fine. But why should the same thing not be allowed regarding less consequential ones? Certainly Plato, prince of philosophers, says, without any respectful preamble, that Aeschylus — the greatest of tragedians (assuming we trust Aristophanes) — is full of nonsense, because on a trivial point he departed from Homer.[7]

All the same, I have not ruled against Domizio's entire case. 5 But given that he is already a member of the bench,[8] I weighed him fairly carefully on the critical balance, ready to repress the truth entirely, had I not been confident that he surely was to be regarded as being of some appreciable value. And this seemed to me to be very much the right thing to do back when I was thinking everything through. Nevertheless, I readily and willingly alter my position, given that you disagree, for your authority carries weight with me that is equal even to that of strong reasons, as of course it should. But since, on this subject, matters are beyond my control, since copies have been distributed everywhere, copies too numerous to be retracted by any means, I kindly ask you, from now on, in accordance with your remaining good will, to adopt the oppos-

ribus quam ut ullo modo retexi[11] queant, velim tu tibi de caetero, secundum reliquum candorem tuum, contrarias parteis in me gratiam sumas, et, ut homo doctus homini non indoctissimo favens, eloquentiae tuae blanditiis impetres ut hanc adversus Domitium (quando ita vis) pugnam tam caeteris videar non ab insectandi studio proterviter aut malevole, quam me scio a certo sensu et vero simpliciter et sedulo suscepisse. Quod si feceris maximo mihi fueris invitamento ad caetera quoque edenda, quae domi cottidie, nec (ut quidem spero) minus elaborata proximis, excuduntur.

6   Vale. Ioannes Picus Mirandula, nullius homo magis quam sui simillimus, salutem tibi a me suo quoque nomine iussit adscribi.

Florentiae, pridie Calendas Decemb. MCCCCLXXXVIIII

: XX :

Iacobus Antiquarius Angelo Politiano suo s. d.[1]

1   Scripsi ad te optima fide, sciens fore ut literae meae pari candore animi acciperentur. Quod factum non muto, et ita contigisse sicut optabam valde laetor. Supervacua est in Domitium excusatio, in quem omnes (sic enim dixerim) vehellas utilitate publica discentium a te susceptas fuisse arbitror. Neque eas a me vel minimo verbo repunctas esse velim, vel notatas contraria censura. Sed op-

ing faction, in order to please me, and to obtain by the charms of your eloquence, as a learned person supporting one not entirely unlearned, that, when you so wish, I may appear just as much to everyone else to have undertaken this fight against Domizio not out of an eagerness to go after him in a violent and malicious way, a fight which I know I undertook on the basis of a fixed intention and with, indeed, both integrity and painstaking care. If you do this you will be a tremendous incentive for me publish as well the rest of the things that, here at home, are subjected to hammering every day, and which are (I hope!) no less finely finished than my most recent ones.

Farewell. Giovanni Pico della Mirandola, who resembles no one 6 more completely than he does himself, has instructed me to append a hello to you in his own name as well.

Florence, November 30, 1489

: XX :

Jacopo Antiquari to his dear Angelo Poliziano

I wrote you without a worry, knowing that my letter would be re- 1 ceived with corresponding good will. I do not regret having done so, and I am exceedingly pleased that things turned out just as I hoped. Justification regarding Domizio is superfluous. I regard all your mild invective[1] against him (for this is what I would call it) as having been undertaken by you for the general good of students, and I would not want this to have been marked in turn as wrong[2] by the least little thing I said, or to have been blotted with an opposing censure. I would have preferred, while you were aggressively pursuing the problem, more restraint from personal attacks, though this is no longer an option after publication. All the same,

tassem, quod amplius opere edito liberum non est, temperatum esse frequentius a persona, dum rem incesseres. Utcunque tamen id studium susceperis, more optimi agricolae, quicquid sentium occurebat sulcis tuis penitus cum radicibus extirpatum iri te voluisse non dubito. Nec vetus adhiberi exemplum oportuit, ubi negocium praesens non caret laude. Equidem scriptis tuis deesse id tantum sentio, quod priscam aetatem non vixeris, cum qua memoriam omnium saeculorum consecutus esse videris industriae ac laboris similitudine. Hoc testimonium qui non dederint, infelici nothi sunt Musarum partu et adulterino.

2   Noli igitur longi incubatus fetura nos in expectatione macerare, sed accepto etiam in tui nominis securitatem sponsore Pico, cuius tota vita gloriarum plena est, a quo in amicorum gregem per te receptum iri omnibus votis expeto, cuius vestigia semper adoro, quicquid ex altilium cohorte domi nascitur, spectandum, legendum, ediscendum emittas, detenturus eos omnis in fidibus tuis, qui aliquo virtutum simulacro aut harmonia ducuntur.

3   Vale. Chalcus tibi salutem dicit. Tuus est. Et Antiquarius tuus est. Uterque velut dexterae tuae digitus haberi cupit.

Mediolani, quinto Idus Decembris MCCCCLXXXVIIII

: XXI :

Iacobus Antiquarius Angelo Politiano s. d.[1]

1   Pudorem nuper mihi fecit Hieronymus Donatus, qui receptam a re publica personam magno apud hunc principem aestimatu agens, officium meum singulari humanitate praevertit. Sed tu

I do not doubt that, in whatever spirit you undertook this task, you wanted, in the way of a very good farmer, whatever brushwood came your way to be ripped out of your furrows entirely, along with its roots. Nor was it necessary to resort to ancient precedent, when the present business is not lacking in acclaim. My personal opinion is that the only thing missing from your writings is the fact that you did not actually live in that long-ago age, along with which you seem to have won, by the similarity of your diligence and efforts, an eternal place in history. All who do not attest to this are the bastard products of an unpromising (and adulterous) delivery by the Muses.

Do not, therefore, steep us in anticipation by sitting on your eggs for extended incubating. But having received, to vouch for your worth, Pico too as sponsor—whose entire life is full of accomplishments, by whom (through you) I ask in all my prayers to be admitted into that cluster of friends whose footsteps I always worship—release for inspection, reading, learning whatever is born domestically from that flock of fatted fowl. For you are sure to leave hanging on your strings all who are guided by any image or harmony of the virtues.[3]

Farewell. Calco[4] says hello. He is yours. Antiquari is yours too. Both want to be regarded as fingers of your right hand.

Milan, December 9, 1489

: XXI :

Jacopo Antiquari to Angelo Poliziano

Girolamo Donà recently gave me cause for embarrassment when, fulfilling a role he had accepted from the Republic to great approval on the part of our prince, he anticipated, with uncommon humanity, my own responsibility. But you too are to blame. Writ-

quoque in causa, nam ad eum simul et ad me scribens ita inter sese utranque epistolam commisisiti ut, maiorem meritis de me opinionem tuam apud illum testatus, plus pignoris (quod aiunt) deposueris quam mea pecunia possit[2] redimi. Unde statim legendum misit quod (pace tua) falso praedicabas. In mea itidem epistola demonstrasti[3] illum esse dignum quem veneremur, cumulata optimarum artium laude. Equidem institueram ad eum quod scripseras deferre. Sed mei ingenii remissa natura, quasi perendinandi ius usurpans, spatium dedi homini praestantissimo, ut istiusmodi verecundia me conspergeret, quam longe tamen aequiore animo fero quam testimonium tuum, quod magnis verbis, nullo alioquin ad veritatem confinio pertinentibus, ita confercis ut nihil potius agere coneris quam ut inter dulce resonantes tibias carmen aliquod demeruisse videar.

2   Equidem prolutos digitos me habere non sentio, quibus mysterium philosophiae ab istis sanctissime ac penitus tractatum contingere liceat. Profanus sum, et procul limen adoro. Satis est tale arcanum inter eorum manus versari quos idoneos perspeximus ad restituenda humana et divina animorum exercitamenta, quae paulo ante ex disciplinis 'displicinae'[4] censebantur, congesta barbarice terra in oculos miserae et toto orbe in unam sepulturam redactae philosophiae. Mihi certe in partem felicitatis tribuo quod hoc saeculo nasci contigit, in quo velut e coelo delapsi homines expultricem immunditiarum curam literis adhibentes effecerunt ut, ubi picus, phoenix et id avium genus auspicatissimum est, obstrepere anser amplius non debeat.

3   Licuit Hermolaum de facie cognoscere, licuit eum disserentem audire de fato, de fortuna, de casu. Quae res, ut populari captu

ing him and me at the same time, you so jumbled the two letters that, having sworn to your opinion of me (a higher one than I deserve) in his presence, you offered a richer pledge, as they say, than can be redeemed with my cash. Right away, he sent along for me to read what you profess—I say to you with all due respect—falsely. In exactly the same way, in the letter to me, you demonstrated that he deserved my adoration by the excellence he had accumulated in the finest arts. I in turn had decided to forward him what you had written. But given the casual nature of my temperament, and invoking, you might say, the right of procrastination, I put this most excellent individual off, resulting in shame of this kind showering me. This, however, I accept far more serenely than I do your testimony, which you so cram with big words (which otherwise have no connection to the truth) that you attempt to do nothing other than to make me seem to have earned some lyrics amidst sweetly sounding pipes.

For my part, I do not believe I have the kind of clean fingers by 2 which it is permissible to touch the mystery of Philosophy, handled piously and thoroughly by your people. I am uninitiated, and I worship the threshold from a safe distance. It is sufficient that such a ritual object is handled by men we fully recognize to be equipped to restore the human and divine exercises of the mind, which not long ago were listed as "displicines" rather than disciplines,[1] since, barbarically, dirt had been scooped onto the eyes of Philosophy, pitifully reduced, driven from the entire world into a single grave. Certainly I chalk it up to my good fortune that I happened to be born in this age, in which individuals who seem to have floated down from heaven apply trash-clearing efforts to literature and achieve this: wherever the Pico, the Phoenix,[2] and that most auspicious race of birds may be, the goose should honk no longer.

One was allowed to know all about Ermolao from his outward 3 appearance; one was allowed to hear him discussing fate, fortune,

difficilis est, et in primis a Peripateticis operose tractata, ita ab eo reddebatur perspicua ut omnem illam caelestium causarum seriem, velut catenam quandam, ante oculos ponere videretur. Saepe ad pacem, saepe ad gratiam, in quae templa uterque nostrum divinae rei causa pergebat, convenimus. Mira in eo comitas, lepor multus. Totam mentem ad afflatum divinum refert cuidam terrestri numini similis.

4   Cum Hieronymo nondum frequens congressus, quoniam etsi cultura literarum in eo eminentium plurimum invitat ut ei fiam quam familiarissimus, quod tam facile futurum perspicio quam cum viro in officium semper exposito et obvio, negocii tamen publici ratio, quae nusquam suspitione vacavit, me deterret, et ab eius honestissima ac frugifera consuetudine retrahit, unde dolor, ira et indignatio frequenter macerant animum meum, ut in singulari ac diu alioquin multisque rebus perspecta fide, alienam delationem[5] cavere oporteat, iucundissimi[6] in vita fructus amissione atque iactura. Verum proprius eum intueor quotiens in regiam venit, delectorque amoenitatibus ingenii, quas prudentia et gravitate condivit, qualem in amplissima re publica opportuna ad honores subsellia sortitum esse decet.

5   Sed sollicitudine quadam pungor (id scilicet curat homuncio) ne, per quos linguae Latinae ornamenta restituuntur, per eosdem aliquando Italicum imperium in unam rem publicam cedat. Veneti enim in omni tempestate sapientes viri, quod superbiam suam nimis infensam omnibus esse intelligerent (ampullosa nanque quorundam imperitia et ostentatione id accidebat), novato nuper in

chance. This material, considering how difficult it is for the average person to understand, and above all, how elaborately it was treated by the Peripatetics, was rendered so transparent by him that he seemed to put before your eyes that entire sequence of celestial causes, like some kind of chain. We often came together for peace, for grace, into which temples each of us made his way for religious purposes. He possessed remarkable taste, considerable charm. Like some kind of earthly spirit, he traces his whole mind back to divine inspiration.

I have not yet had much contact with Girolamo since, although his cultivation of outstanding literature emphatically urges me to be joined to him by the greatest possible intimacy (this, I am fully aware, would be as easy as is possible with any man constantly subject to the call of duty), nevertheless, the attitude of public responsibility — which has never been short on suspicion — discourages me and draws me away from his most noble and profitable company. Regret, therefore, anger and frustration constantly vex my thoughts, asking how, when his fidelity has long been plain to see in other circumstances, it should be necessary to fear the report of a third party, with the resulting loss and waste of life's most agreeable fruit. I inspect him rather closely, however, as often as he enters the palace, and I revel in the charms of his intellect, which he has seasoned with wisdom and authority — the proper sort of man, in a flourishing republic, to have been blessed with timely steps to public office.

But I am vexed by a kind of anxiety (this, of course, is the worry of one of the little people) that, by the offices of those same men who have restored splendor to the Latin language, control of Italy should one day pass to a single republic. Wise whatever comes their way, the Venetians, since they realized that their arrogance was too threatening to everyone (and this, of course, was happening as the result of certain individuals' overblown boasting and lack of experience), having changed their attitude for the

melius more, eos legatos circummittunt qui et molliant[7] animos quibuscum agunt, et familiarius commercia misceant, atque patefacto quod prius senioribus tantum licebat etiam iuventuti, et gliscenti philosophiae aditu honoribus et praemiis ornant. Incredibile est quantum isti proficiant.

6   Sed quoniam imperium non nisi fato dari cernimus, quod sit eventurum, alii viderint. Nos interea communibus studiis gratulamur, quae assertores vos[8] habent maximos et primae classis viros. Bene profecto nobiscum agitur quod lucernam a vobis anteferri contigit. Cottidie aliquid excuditur posteritate dignum. Id magnopere ad mei animi laetitias pertinet. Illud tantum mea interesse ut putes velim: quod quam operam praestare nequeo, in aliorum industria libenter intuear. Ultra onerari non patior quam hominem postremae tribus, sine praerogativa ferentis suffragia.

7   Vale, et Pico, omnium qui vivunt laudem supergresso, me saepius et iterum commenda.

Mediolani, xvi Calendas Ianuarias MCCCCLXXXVIIII[9]

: XXII :

Angelus Politianus Iacobo Antiquario suo s. d.

1   Arguis me[1] mendacem quod in epistola mea proxima stilum literasque tuas apud eruditissimum virum quasi plus nimio laudaverim. Sed hoc ita docte facis tamen ut, quibus me verbis accusas, isdem prorsus absolvas, quo fit ut non alio magis iudicii mei ratio

better, send around envoys who are supposed to calm the thoughts of those with whom they have dealings and make commercial arrangements in a more friendly way. And since the way to the expanding realm of Philosophy, once open only to their elders, is now open to youth as well, they adorn her with honors and prizes. It is hard to believe how much progress they have made.

But since we see that power is not granted except in accord 6 with destiny, let others worry about what will happen. In the meantime, I congratulate myself on our shared studies, which have as their principal champions you and men of the first rank. I am truly lucky in that you happen to go first with a lamp. Something worthy of posterity emerges from the anvil every day. This is of considerable relevance to my intellectual pleasures. Please consider that this alone matters to me, for in the activity of others I gladly contemplate the effort I myself am unable to provide: I cannot bear being burdened more than a man of the least important tribe, casting its votes without the right to go first.[3]

Farewell, and put in a good word for me, again and again, with 7 Pico, who has surpassed the praiseworthiness of all living persons.

Milan, December 17, 1489[4]

: XXII :

Angelo Poliziano to his dear Jacopo Antiquari

You call me a liar because, in my most recent letter, you say that I 1 praised, on the part of a most erudite man, your style and literary learning almost beyond excess. You do this in such a learned way, however, that you fully prove my innocence by the very same words with which you accuse me, with the result that the logic of my judgment stands on nothing more firmly than the fact that it

mihi constet quam quod abs te sic reprehenditur eloquenter, nisi forte parum verus ob id ego testis (testis enim plane, non laudator) quod attigi testimonium de te, nec implevi. Verum cogita quam sit arduum verbis exaequare laudes, quae fidem sic excedant ut eis nec tu quidem protinus assentias, qui iam pridem satisfeceris.

2   Quod autem me Ioanni Pico Mirandulae Hieronymoque Donato et Hermolao Barbaro, tantis in omni literatura viris quantos olim non meminimus, adnumeras, equidem irrideri me putarem, nisi persuasissimum haberem falli te duntaxat amore nimio, quem solere ait Plato in iudiciis caecutire. Caeterum ego tam me scio cum talibus nec ingenio nec doctrina, qui nec natalibus nec fortuna debere conferri.

3   De imperio vero quod ais, Fors ipsa viderit. Aut si quis est in magnis rebus meae quoque preci et voto locus, utinam denique apud eos residat qui sint illo quam dignissimi.

4   Picus noster unice te[2] diligit, nec autem plus de meis verbis quam de tuis epistolis, quin eas nunc me tibi dictante cum maxime legit curatque describendas. Sed et mire gaudet quod Hieronymum Donatum iuxta secum probes, tum quod inter vos cohaeseritis tu et Barbarus, non invicem modo, sed et in commune consultum putat. Idem pene me quoque provocat in te redamando, nulli scilicet hominum concedentem. Quare velim mihi pro meo in te studio Chalcum perpetuo vel patronum, si patitur, vel, si hoc mavult, amicum magnum, quibus potes machinis, retineas.

Vale.

Florentiae, quarto Calendas Ianuarias MCCCCLXXXVIIII

was criticized by you so eloquently. Unless, perhaps, I am too in-accurate a witness for this reason: I cited testimony regarding you, but I did not complete it. Consider, however, how arduous a task it is to match your merits with words, since these would pass so beyond the limits of credibility that not even you would immedi-ately agree with them, even though you already have given ample evidence of their truth.

As for the fact that you count me along with Giovanni Pico 2 della Mirandola, Girolamo Donà, and Ermolao Barbaro, men whose magnitude in every pursuit was formerly beyond my ac-quaintance, well, I would think I was being made fun of if I were not entirely convinced that you err only as a result of excessive love, which, Plato says, tends to be blind in its judgment.[1] I know, however, that I should be compared to such men no more in terms of talent or learning than of birth or position.

Chance herself, however, will see to what you say about ruling 3 power. Or if there is any place in great affairs for my hopes and prayers too, may it devolve in the end upon those who are as wor-thy as possible of it.

My dear Pico admires you in singular fashion, not, however, on 4 the basis more of my words than of your letters. Right now, as a matter of fact, even as I am addressing my response to you, he is reading your letters and arranging for their transcription! But he is also wonderfully pleased that you share his good opinion of Girolamo Donà and, furthermore, that you and Barbaro have formed a bond, one directed not only reciprocally, in his view, but toward a common cause. This same Pico nearly lures me into a contest over loving you back, a contest in which I yield to nobody. Please, therefore, in return for my devotion to you, keep — by whatever means at your disposal — Calco permanently mine, either as a patron, if he allows this, or if he prefers, as a friend.

Farewell.

Florence, December 29, 1489

: XXIII :

Iacobus Antiquarius Angelo Politiano suo s. d.

1 Perferuntur cottidie ad te manipulatim ex toto doctissimorum hominum coetu literae, quae tuae laudi multum videntur afferre.
Qua eas fronte accipias ignoro, opinor tamen indissimulata et familiari. Quod[1] vero scribunt, saeculo gratulantur et tibi. Inter eas[2]
Pomponii epistola plurimum me delectavit, quam mihi legendam
nuper tradidit Bernardus noster, adulescens in tua schola tornatim
expolitus. Cupio tamen ex te scire an tibi ex tam referta multorum
laudatione quicquam vindices. Nam sapientes viri, in quorum sententia te esse arbitror, quicquid inspexerint in se boni, non sua
opera id partum paratumve, sed naturae et Dei beneficio tributum
esse credunt. At vero qui illud sibi acceptum referunt, ii procul du-
bio lenae purpurissatae comparandi sunt aut Poggianae fabulae,
'Et nos poma natamus.'

2 Saepe eas cogitationes immigrare in te (sic enim puto) quae ad
alicuius rei vestigium iam tenendum spectent, sed extrarias et tuae
menti quasi quibusdam igniculis collucentes, haud dubie sentis.
Itaque cum te alicuius humani decoris conscium cernis esse, supra
hominem te ne uno quidem digito efferre debes. Ego enim is sum[3]
qui te amem atque etiam colam virtutem tuam, sed rursus qui do-
num caelitus datum in te agnoscam, quo et vetera illustres longae-
vitate rubiginata, et surgenti atque ad aemulationem laudis adni-
tenti saeculo manum porrigas.

Vale.

Mediolani, Calendibus Septemb. MVIIIID

: XXIII :

Jacopo Antiquari to his dear Angelo Poliziano

Handfuls of letters which seem to add much to your glory are de- 1
livered to you daily from the whole assembly of most learned persons. I do not know your reaction when you receive these, but I
assume that it is frank and ordinary. Indeed, by writing they are
congratulating our age as well as you. Among these, Pomponio's
letter brought me the most pleasure. (Our friend Bernardo,[1] a
young man finished in your school as if on the lathe, passed it on
to me to read.) I want to hear from your own lips, however,
whether you claim anything as your own out of such well-stuffed
praise from many people. For wise men, to whose way of thinking
I believe you subscribe, believe that whatever of value they observe
in themselves was not born or fashioned there by their own exertions but was instead granted to them by the generosity of Nature
and the Divine. Those, however, who regard this as due to themselves are surely to be compared to a rouged madam, or to that fable in the style of Poggio, "We apples float too!"[2]

Unquestionably you feel that those thoughts which already aim 2
at grasping the trace of this or that move into you (this is my
view), but from outside, illuminating your mind as if with tiny
flames. And so, when you perceive that you are privy to some
splendid human achievement, do not elevate yourself even one
inch beyond human stature. I am disposed to love you and even
adore your talent, but at the same time, to recognize in you a
heaven-sent gift that will enable you to polish antiquities, rusty
with old age, and to extend a hand to an age rising to its feet and
striving to match others in merit.

Farewell.

Milan, September 1, 1491

: XXIV :

Angelus Politianus Iacobo Antiquario suo s. d.

1 Quaeris ex me per epistolam qua tandem fronte doctissimorum
hominum tam crebras literas, meis refertas laudibus, accipiam, et
an quippiam mihi ex illorum testimonio plus vindicem, pruden-
terque me admones et benivole, ne meum esse putem quod divini
beneficii sit, neve supra hominem efferar. Denique sic epistolam
claudis ut esse in magna spe vel expectatione potius studiorum li-
terarumque nostrarum videaris. Equidem, ut planissime dicam,
sentio me tibi in suspitionem venisse quasi plus nimio sim gloriae
avidus, quod ut, quas a doctis hominibus proximis aliquot mensibus acceperim literas, earum exemplum statim istuc Bernardo Riccio miserim, quo tibi protinus ostenderentur.

2 Ut autem sic ineptirem, non mea me voluntas, verum ipsius
Bernardi, optimi quidem iuvenis, sed mei nimium amantis, as-
siduae prope obsecrationes[1] inpulerunt, praesertim qui te quoque
ipsum magnopere id velle atque etiam contendere assereret.[2] Non
igitur ut auras quasi captarem, quod a meis moribus procul abest,
sed ut amicis obsequerer, quorum me semper iudicio permiserim,
crebras istuc epistolas illas missitabam, quas tamen probe[3] memi-
neram non iuratorum testium, sed blandientium esse amicorum.
Quod igitur rogas qua eas denique fronte suscipiam, plane fateor

: XXIV :

Angelo Poliziano to his dear Jacopo Antiquari

You ask me in a letter what my ultimate reaction is when I receive 1
such frequent letters from most learned individuals, filled with my
praises, and whether I make any greater claim for myself as a result of their testimony. And you wisely and kindly caution me not
to think mine what belongs to divine generosity, nor to be elevated
above human stature. Finally, you close your letter in such a way
that you seem to be given to great hope for—or rather, anticipation of—my scholarly and literary efforts. To be perfectly clear
from my point of view, I feel as if I have fallen under suspicion, in
your eyes, of being more than excessively hungry for glory, given
that, whatever letters I have received from learned persons in the
past few months, I have immediately sent a copy to Bernardo
Ricci over there, as though to have it shown at once to you.

To be so silly, however, was not my wish; rather, the almost 2
constant entreaties of Bernardo himself (an excellent young man,
though too devoted to me) were the driving cause, especially since
he claimed that you yourself very much wanted this as well and
even were pressing him for it. It was not, therefore, in order to
catch the wind of popular favor (so to speak)—something far out
of keeping with my character—but in order to oblige my friends,
to whose judgment I always have entrusted myself, that I was
sending frequent letters your way. At any rate, I kept properly in
mind that these came not from sworn witnesses, but from flattering friends. As for your question about my ultimate reaction to
them, I admit that it is utterly joyful, for this is my usual response
to whatever comes from men who are my friends, and learned.
But I tend to think the following to myself: If someone who
praises me is mistaken, I must make sure that he is not mistaken a

laeta, sic enim soleo quaecunque a viris et amicis et doctis proficis-
cuntur. Caeterum sic ipsemet mecum cogitare soleo: si fallitur qui
me laudat, danda mihi opera est ne iterum fallatur, atque interim
habenda gratia, sin autem minime fallitur, aut idem nec etiam
fallit atque ita maior sum quam mihi fortasse videor, aut si fallit,
animandi mei vel conciliandi vel irridendi gratia fallit, quorum primum mihi expedit, alterum non displicet, tertium cadere in amicum non solet. Itaque ratiocinationem sic colligo ut aut ego ne
doctus[4] quidem sim quod isti vel opinantur vel dictitant, aut sim
certe qualem praedicant. Sed quoniam vir esse nemo doctus potest
quin sibi ipse quoque videatur (prima enim docti hominis condi-
cio est ut ipse se norit), ego vero mihi doctus non videor, sequitur
omnino ne sim doctus. Sed hoc ipsum tamen non falli me in eo
quo plerique, opinor, falluntur, nisi divini esse muneris intellege-
rem, etiam plus caeteris fallerer.

3   Ibi vero fateor risi mediocriter cum me admones ne supra hominem efferar, scilicet periculum est hoc in me, qui quidem adhuc
in primis literulis haesitem. Quasdam vero arteis ex iis ne attige-
rim quidem quae philosophiae studio famulantur, cum sit eorum
quoque qui disciplinas omneis omnemque sapientiam prohibuis-
sent celebris illa sententia: sic ad ea quae natura in promptu haberet nostrae mentis aciem, sicut ad solem noctuae oculos caligare.
Procul haec a nobis insania sit, ut quantum absimus adhuc, non
dico a summis, sed vel a mediocribus viris ignoremus. Assenta-
tiunculis autem quorundam aut item obtrectatiunculis, et ineptis
et levibus, non magis equidem aut attolor aut deprimor quam umbra ipsa mei corporis.[5] Non enim quia longior illa et extentior
mane ac vesperi sit, meridie vero brevior et contractior, ob id ego

second time, and in the meanwhile, I should be grateful. If, however, he really is not mistaken, then either not even is he himself
deceitful, and thus I am greater than perhaps I seem to myself, or,
if he is deceitful, then he deceives for the sake of energizing me, or
of winning my favor, or of making fun of me. Of these, the first
does me good, the second does not bother me, and the third is not
usually the case in a friend. And so I synthesize my reasoning as
follows: Either I am not even learned, because this is what they either think or repeatedly say I am, or else I unambiguously am the
sort of person they pronounce me to be. But since no one can be a
learned man without seeming such to himself as well (for the principal requirement of a learned man is that he know himself¹), but
I do not seem to myself learned, it absolutely follows that I am not
learned. But if I were not aware that this very thing—the fact that
I am not mistaken on the matter by which most people, I think,
are deceived—is part of a divine gift, I would be even more mistaken than everyone else.

I had a bit of a laugh, I admit, when I came to the part where   3
you caution me not to be elevated above human stature—in other
words, there is this risk in me, although I am still feeling my way,
of course, through my ABCs. As a matter of fact, I have not even
dabbled in various arts ancillary to the study of philosophy, since
even those people who block all learning and all wisdom possess
that often-heard saying: thus does our mind's vision grow cloudy
at those things which nature keeps in full view, like the eyes of a
night-bird at the sight of the sun.² Keep far from me the madness
by which I might be unaware of how far I still am, not, I tell you,
from men at the top, but even from those in the middle. I am no
more raised or lowered by foolish and frivolous notes of praise or
criticism by this or that person than I am by the very shadow of
my own body. For just because it is longer and more distended in
the morning and evening, but shorter and squatter at midday, I

quoque statim maior proceriorque mihi mane ac vesperi quam meridie ipso videri debeo.

4   Quod autem fore suspicaris opera, studio industriaque mea ut et vetustati squalor abstergatur et ad frugem iuniores perveniant, vide, quaeso, ne tibi verba det amor erga me nimius. Ego certe (nescio autem vitione mentis captus, an consilio magis adductus) magnum quiddam omnino molior facturusque operae pretium videor, modo vires, animum subsequantur.

Vale.

Faesulae, ante vii Calendas Septemb. MCCCCLXXXXI[6]

should not therefore seem to myself to be suddenly bigger and taller in the morning and evening than I am at noon.

As for the fact that you suspect that, by my efforts, enthusiasm, 4 and diligence, the dirt will be cleared from antiquity and persons of a younger age will mature, please be careful not to let too much love for me beguile you. Whether under the influence of a mental defect or, rather, induced by sound judgment (I know not which), I definitely am planning something big indeed, and I appear ready to do something well worth the trouble, provided that my capabilities and courage follow suit.

Farewell.

Fiesole, August 26, 1491

LIBER QUARTUS

: I :

Iacobus Antiquarius Angelo Politiano s. d.

1 Ante diem quintum Idus Aprilis secesseram Ticinum. Postridie eius diei, cum officii causa praefectum arcis, humanissimum virum, Iacobum Pusterlam convenissem, perbenigne me exosculatus, 'Secunda,' inquit, 'noctis vigilia, de Laurentii Medicis obitu praevolens tabellarius ad principem contendit.' Hoc nuncio attonitus, oculos cum in terram defixissem, 'Estne,' inquam, 'nobis iratus Deus, ut in illo omnium sapientissimo viro tot spes, tot virtutum imagines et signa, tanquam ad vasa conclamans, sustulerit?' Sed de Italiae calamitatibus mox. Quae enim ab eminentissimis locis mala ingruunt, nivibus cum in montium cacuminibus liquescentes ingentia efficiunt flumina simillima esse solent.

2 Biduo post, Mediolanum regressus, offendi sermonem varium. Ea nanque de moestissima re iam populus erat certior. Alii de caelo aedem Liberatae paulo ante quam Laurentius decederet tactam, alii desperata eiusdem salute, Petrum Leonem medicum, qui aegrotanti assederat, sese in puteum praecipitasse affirmabant. Dedi conplusculos dies dolori meo, neque possum, mi Politiane, magnopere non torqueri, et ut me ipsum assidue magis urgeam, tum mea tum aliorum causa facit. Scis qua illum veneratione prosequebar, quove, quasi restituta vice, me ipse complectabatur animo non ignoras, qui unus omnium vitae meae praesidium in pleraque fortuna a me censeretur constantissimum. Sed in communi rerum acervo plura sunt. Saepe enim inter Scyllam et Caryb-

BOOK IV

: I :

Jacopo Antiquari to his dear Angelo Poliziano

On April 9 I left for Ticino. On the following day, when I went   1
to see, as a courtesy, the prefect of the citadel, Jacopo Pusterla, a
really decent fellow, he, after kissing me kindly, said, "In the
hours before midnight, a courier bearing news of the death of
Lorenzo de' Medici made his way to the prince at breakneck
speed." Stunned by this announcement and staring at the ground,
I said, "Is God angry at us, even to the point of uprooting as many
hopes and signs and standards of virtue as were in that wisest man
of all, as if He were crying, 'Strike camp!'?" But more about Italy's
calamities in a moment. Evils that descend on us from lofty places
tend to be like snowfalls melting on mountaintops, producing
massive rivers.

When I returned to Milan two days later, I encountered vary-   2
ing reports. For the populace had already been informed on the
dismal subject, and some affirmed that, shortly before Lorenzo
passed away, the church of the Liberata was struck by lightning;
others, that Pierleone,[1] the doctor who had attended to him in his
illness, had hurled himself down a well. I have devoted several
days to my grief, and I cannot, my dear Poliziano, not be greatly
tormented. First my own situation, then that of others causes me
to distress myself ever more relentlessly. You know the reverence
with which I did him homage, and with what feeling, as if by
reciprocity, he himself embraced me. You are not unaware how
he alone of all men was considered by me to be my own life's
most reliable safeguard under nearly all conditions. But there are
more things in our shared lot. Often set between a Scylla and a

dim positus, Italiam non minus temperabat quam Isthmus ille qui inter Ionium et Aegeum, ne inter se concurrentia maria confundantur, natura constitutus esse videtur.

3   Scio in clarissimo iuvene Petro Medice ab universa civitate, quod nostrum dolorem plurimum extenuat, patris auctoritatem prorsus confirmatam esse, idque decretum publicum, quoniam in unius familiae incolumitate totius rei publicae salus versatur, perpetuo mansurum et speramus et cupimus. Laurentii tamen desiderium lenire nequeo, et quod recenti vulneri accidere solet (quo magis frigescit, eo gravius dolet) in me sentio. In ista vero tua ingenti studiorum calamitate atque iactura, quid abs te optem, video; quid impetrare possim, ambigo. Faciam tamen quod in communi luctu assolet, ac per ipsius Laurentii felicem memoriam, ut abstersis aliquantisper lachrymis, quo ille emigraverit animi terrore, quive antea ad suos sit praefatus (in utriusque nostrorum consolationem totam illius vitam splendoris et laudis plenam, tuis aliquando lucubrationibus ad posteritatem perventuram non dubito), quibus honoribus sit elatus, cui quoque monumento et quibus eulogiis intulerint, perscribas, et rogo et obsecro.

Vale.

Mediolani, xviii Calendas Maias[1] MCCCCLXXXXII

: II :

Angelus Politianus Iacobo Antiquario suo salutem

1   Vulgare est ut qui serius paulo ad amicorum literas respondeant nimias suas occupationes excusent. Ego vero, quo minus mature

Charybdis, he moderated Italy no less than the Isthmus between the Ionian and the Aegean seems to have been designed by nature to prevent the clashing seas from mixing.

I know that his father's authority has been ratified in that out- 3
standing young man, Piero de' Medici, by the unanimous citizenry, something that very much mitigates the grief of people here, and we hope and pray that the public decree, [stating] that the health of the entire republic lies in that family's safety, lasts forever. All the same, I am unable to miss Lorenzo any less acutely, and I experience what tends to happen to a fresh wound: the more it stops bleeding, the deeper the pain. In this immense catastrophe and loss for scholarship that you have sustained, however, I see what I would like from you, but I am unsure what I can get. Nevertheless, I shall do what is customary in a case of public mourning and ask and beseech you, in the name of Lorenzo's own blessed memory, to wipe away your tears a little bit and record with what fear for his soul he left this world, and what he said beforehand to his intimates (I have no doubt that, as a consolation to us both, his entire life, full of radiance and glory, will reach future generations by way of your eventual lucubrations), with what honors his funeral was conducted, and also to what monument he was conveyed, and with what eulogies.

Farewell.

Milan, April 14, 1492

: II :

Angelo Poliziano to his dear Jacopo Antiquari[1]

It is common custom for anyone who replies to a friend's letter 1
with something of a delay to make the excuse of having too many

ad te rescripserim, non tam culpam confero in occupationes, quanquam ne ipsae quidem defuerunt, quam in acerbissimum potius hunc dolorem, quem mihi eius viri obitus adtulit, cuius patrocinio nuper unus ex omnibus literarum professoribus et eram fortunatissimus et habebar. Illo igitur nunc extincto, qui fuerat unicus auctor eruditi laboris videlicet, ardor etiam scribendi noster extinctus est, omnisque prope veterum studiorum alacritas elanguit.

2   'Sed si tantus amor casus cognoscere nostros' et qualem se ille vir in extremo quasi vitae actu gesserit audire, quanquam et fletu impedior et a recordatione ipsa quasique retractatione doloris abhorret animus ac resilit, obtemperabo tamen tuae tantae ac tam honestae voluntati, cui deesse pro instituta inter nos amicitia neque volo neque possum. Nam profecto ipsemet mihi nimium et incivilis viderer et inhumanus, si tibi, et tali viro et mei tam studioso, rem ausim prorsus ullam denegare. Caeterum quoniam, de quo tibi a nobis scribi postulas, id eiusmodi est ut facilius sensu quodam animi tacito et cogitatione comprehendatur quam aut verbis aut literis exprimi possit, hac lege tibi iam nunc obsequium nostrum astringimus, ut neque id polliceamur quod implere non possumus, et si quid tamen possimus,[1] tua certe causa non recusemus.

3   Laboraverat igitur circiter menses duos Laurentius Medices e doloribus iis qui, quoniam viscerum cartilagini inhaereant, ex argumento hypochondrii appellantur. Hi, tametsi neminem sua quidem vi iugulant, quoniam tamen acutissimi sunt, etiam iure molestissimi perhibentur. Sed enim in Laurentio, fatone dixerim an

things to do. I, however, for writing you back in a less than timely fashion, do not put the blame so much on my responsibilities — though not even these have been lacking — as on, instead, this most bitter grief, instilled in me by the death of that man under whose patronage I was not long ago the luckiest of all professors of literature — and was regarded as such, too. Hence, now that he who clearly had been the sole source of learned effort has been extinguished, my warmth for writing has been extinguished too, and nearly all my enthusiasm for my old studies has flagged.

"But if there is so much desire to learn our misfortunes"[2] and to hear what this man's demeanor was during, as it were, his life's final act, then, although weeping and the very act of remembering get in my way, and my heart shrivels and recoils, as if from a repetition of pain, I nevertheless shall respect your wish, so strong and so honorable, which I neither want nor am able to disappoint, given the friendship that has been established between us. Indeed, I myself unquestionably would seem unjust and unkind in my own eyes if I were to dare to withhold anything at all from you, such are both your character and your devotion to me. Given, however, that the subject on which you ask me to write you is of a nature that it is more easily apprehended by a kind of unspoken intuition than it can be expressed in either oral or written form, I now restrict my compliance with your wish by this same condition, so that I neither make a promise I cannot fulfill, and at the same time, should anything be within my power, I do not, for your sake of course, refuse to do it.

Lorenzo de' Medici had suffered for roughly two months from those pains which, since they settle into the cartilage deep in the body, are called, on that basis, hypochondrian. Although these, in fact, never prove fatal to anyone in and of themselves, nevertheless, since they are extremely painful, they quite rightly are regarded as especially bothersome. But in Lorenzo's case — due, I might say, either to fate or to the inexperience and inattentiveness of those re-

inscitia incuriaque medentium, id evenit ut, dum curatio doloribus adhibetur, febris una omnium insidiosissima contracta sit, quae sensim illapsa, non quidem in arterias aut venas, sicuti caeterae solent, sed in artus, in viscera, in nervos, in ossa quoque et medullas incubuerit. Ea vero, quod subtiliter ac latenter quasique lenibus vestigiis irrepserat, parum primo animadversa, dein vero, cum satis magnam sui significationem dedisset, non tamen pro eo ac debuit diligenter curata, sic hominem debilitaverat prorsus atque afflixerat ut non viribus modo sed corpore etiam pene omni amisso et consumpto distabesceret. Quare pridie quam naturae satisfaceret, cum quidem in villa Caregia cubaret aeger, ita repente concidit totus nullam ut iam suae salutis spem reliquam ostenderet. Quod homo, ut semper cautissimus, intellegens nihil prius habuit quam ut animae medicum accerseret cui de contractis tota vita noxiis Christiano ritu confiteretur. Quem ego hominem postea mirabundum sic prope audivi narrantem: nihil sibi unquam neque maius neque incredibilius visum quam quomodo Laurentius constans, paratusque adversus mortem, atque imperterritus et praeteritorum meminisset, et praesentia dispensasset, et de futuris item religiosissime prudentissimeque cavisset.

4   Nocte dein media quiescenti meditantique sacerdos adesse cum sacramento nuntiatur. Ibi vero excussus, 'Procul,' inquit, 'a me hoc absit, patiar ut Iesum meum, qui me finxit, qui me redemit, adusque cubiculum hoc venire. Tollite hinc, obsecro, me quam primum, tollite, ut domino occurram.' Et cum dicto sublevans ipse se quantum poterat, atque animo corporis imbecillitatem sustentans,

sponsible for his care — the consequence was that, during the administration of treatment for the pain, a fever — the most insidious of all — was contracted, and this, having gradually spread downward, settled not, in fact, into his arteries or veins, as others tend to do, but into his frame, his vital organs, his muscles, his bones too, and their marrow. But since it spread subtlely and invisibly, as if on tip-toe, it was little noticed at first. When, however, it finally gave fairly extensive evidence of itself — still, though, not treated as carefully as it should have been — it so precipitously weakened the man and wore him down that, since not only his strength had slipped away and been consumed, but practically his entire body too, he wasted away to nothing. Thus, on the final day before he paid nature its inevitable due, as he lay sick in bed in his villa at Careggi, a complete collapse came so instantaneously that he no longer offered any residual hope of recovery. When the man, scrupulous as ever, realized this, his first priority was to summon a doctor of the soul so that he could, by the Christian sacrament, make confession regarding the wrongdoings he had accumulated over the course of a lifetime. I later had occasion to hear this person relate, full of wonder, that nothing had ever appeared to him greater or more incredible than the way in which Lorenzo, steadfast, ready for death, and unafraid, had recalled past events, had set present affairs in order, and likewise had taken extremely wise and conscientious precautions regarding the future.

In the middle of the ensuing night, as he rested and reflected, a 4 priest was announced to have arrived with the sacrament, and thereupon roused, he said, "Far be it from me to suffer that my dear Jesus, who made me, who redeemed me, should come all the way to this bedroom. Lift me out of here, I beg you, lift me out of here at once, so that I may go to greet the Lord." Even as he spoke, he raised himself as much as he could by himself and supported the fragility of his body on his spirit, and then he proceeded, surrounded by the hands of his friends, all the way to the hall to meet

inter familiarium manus obviam seniori ad aulam usque procedit.
Cuius ad genua prorepens, supplexque ac lacrimans, 'Tune,' inquit, 'mitissime Iesu, tu nequissimum hunc servum tuum dignaris
invisere? At quod dixi servum? Immo vero hostem potius, et quidem ingratissimum, qui, tantis abs te cumulatus beneficiis, nec tibi
dicto unquam audiens fuerim et tuam toties maiestatem laeserim,
quod ego te per illam qua genus omne hominum complecteris charitatem quaeque te caelitus ad nos in terram deduxit, nostraeque
humanitatis induit involucris, quae famem, quae sitim, quae frigus, aestum, labores, irrisus, contumelias, flagella et verbera, quae
postremo etiam mortem crucemque subire te compulit, per hanc
ego te, salutifer Iesu, quaeso obtestorque: avertas faciem a peccatis
meis, ut cum ante tribunal tuum constitero, quo me iandudum citari plane sentio, non mea fraus, non culpa plectatur, sed tuae crucis meritis condonetur. Valeat, valeat in causa mea sanguis ille
tuus, Iesu, pretiosissimus, quem, pro afferendis in libertatem hominibus, in ara illa sublimi nostrae redemptionis effudisti.' Haec
atque alia cum diceret lacrymans ipse, lacrymantibusque qui aderant universis, iubet eum tandem sacerdos attoli atque in lectulum suum, quo sacramentum commodius administraretur, referri.
Quod ille, cum aliquandiu facturum negasset, tamen ne seniori
suo foret minus obsequens, exorari se passus, iteratis eiusdem
ferme sententiae verbis, corpus ac sanguinem Dominicum, plenus
iam sanctitatis, et divina quadam maiestate verendus, accepit.

5   Tum consolari Petrum filium (nam reliqui aberant) exorsus,
ferret aequo animo vim necessitatis admonebat, non defuturum

his elder.[3] He crawled to the man's knees and, kneeling and weeping, said, "Have you, most gentle Jesus, have you deigned to visit this your most worthless servant? Did I say 'servant'? More like 'enemy' — indeed, an ingrate, since, though showered with such great blessings by you, I never paid attention to what you said, and again and again I undermined your authority. But now, by that charity with which you take the whole human race into your arms, and which led you down from heaven to us on earth and dressed you in the wrappings of our human nature, and which compelled you to endure hunger, and thirst, and cold, heat, toil, mockery, insults, whips and blows, and finally, even death and the cross, by that charity, I ask you, salvation-bringing Jesus, I ask and implore you to turn your face away from my sins, so that, when I stand before your tribunal, to which I have plainly felt myself being summoned for a while now, my guilt and responsibility will be not punished but pardoned, on the grounds of your crucifixion. May it count, may that most precious blood of yours count in my case, Jesus, the blood you poured out on that sublime altar of our redemption as the price for delivering humankind to freedom." When he, weeping, as was everyone present, had said these and other things, the priest finally gave instructions to lift him up and carry him back to his own bed, so that the sacrament could be administered with greater ease. Although he insisted for a while that he would not do this, nevertheless, in order to avoid being less deferential to his elder, he allowed himself to be won over and, having repeated words roughly to the same effect, full now of sanctity, and made venerable by a kind of divine grandeur, he received the Lord's body and blood.

Then, having undertaken to console his son Piero (for his other 5 sons were away), he admonished him to bear the power of the inevitable with equanimity; that protection from on high would not be lacking, something which not even he himself had ever lacked amid sweeping vicissitudes of politics and finance; that he should

caelitus patrocinium, quod ne sibi quidem unquam in tantis rerum fortunaeque varietatibus defuisset, virtutem modo et bonam
mentem coleret, bene consulta bonos eventus paritura. Post illa,
contemplabundus aliquandiu quievit. Exclusis dein caeteris, eundem ad se natum vocat. Multa monet, multa praecipit, multa edo-
cet, quae nondum foras emanarunt, plena omnia tamen (sicuti au-
divimus²) et sapientiae singularis et sanctimoniae. Quorum tamen
unum quod nobis scire quidem licuerit adscribam. 'Cives,' inquit,
'mi Petre, successorem te meum haud dubie agnoscent. Nec autem
vereor ne non eadem futurus auctoritate in hac re publica sis, qua
nos ipsi ad hanc diem fuerimus. Sed quoniam civitas omnis corpus est (quod aiunt) multorum capitum, neque mos geri singulis
potest, memento in eiusmodi varietatibus id consilium sequi semper: quod esse quam honestissimum intelleges, magisque universi-
tatis quam seorsum cuiusque, rationem habeto.' Mandavit et de
funere, ut scilicet avi Cosmi exemplo iusta sibi fierent, intra modum videlicet eum qui privato conveniat.

6   Venit dein Ticino Lazarus vester, medicus, ut quidem visum
est, experientissimus, qui tamen sero advocatus, ne quid inexpertum relinqueret, pretiosissima quaedam, gemmis omne genus mar-
garitisque conterendis, medicamenta temptabat. Quaerit ibi tum
ex familiaribus Laurentius (iam enim admissi aliquot fueramus)
quid ille agitaret medicus, quid moliretur, cui cum ego respondis-
sem, epithema eum concinnare, quo praecordia foverentur, agnita
ille statim voce, ac me hilare intuens, ut semper solitus, 'Heus,'
inquit, 'heus Angele,' simul brachia iam exhausta viribus aegre at-
tolens, manus ambas arctissime prehendit. Me vero singultus la-

simply cultivate virtue and a sound mind; that well-laid plans would yield good results. After this, he sank for a while into a reverie. Then, once everyone else had been sent out of the room, he called this same son over to himself. He gave him much advice, many recommendations, much instruction—knowledge of which has not yet spread beyond the household—all, nevertheless, full (according to what I heard) of singular wisdom and piety. However, I shall record one thing he said which, in fact, I was permitted to know. "The citizens," he said, "my dear Piero, will recognize you, no doubt, as my successor. Nor am I worried that you will not enjoy the same position of authority in this republic as we have to the present day. But since every political unity is, as they say, a body with many heads, and it is not possible to make each of them happy, remember, among such conflicting interests, to follow this advice: take account of what you understand to be the most honorable thing to do—and this more in terms of the whole community than of each individual member." He also gave instructions regarding his funeral—namely, that his obsequies be performed on the model of his grandfather, i.e., within the limits appropriate for a private citizen.

Next, your Lazzaro, a very creative[4] physician, as indeed became apparent, arrived from Ticino. Although he had been summoned too late, in order to avoid leaving anything untested, he tried a very expensive kind of remedy by grinding pearls and precious stones of all sorts. Lorenzo thereupon asked his friends (for a few of us had been let in) to tell him what that physician was busy about, what he was fussing over. When I replied that he was concocting an epithem[5] to provide internal relief, he, having recognized my voice at once, and looking at me in the light-hearted way that had been his custom, said, "Hey! Hey there, Angelo!" At the same time, painfully lifting arms now drained of strength, he clutched both my hands tightly. But although I was overcome by sobs and tears—which, all the same, I tried to hide, my neck bent

6

crymaeque cum occupavissent, quas celare tamen reiecta cervice conabar, nihilo ille commotior etiam atque etiam manus retentabat. Ubi autem persensit fletu adhuc praepediri me quominus ei operam darem, sensim scilicet eas quasique dissimulanter omisit. Ego me autem continuo in penetrale thalami coniicio flentem, atque habenas, ut ita dicam, dolori et lacrymis laxo.

7 Mox tamen revertor eodem, siccatis quantum licebat oculis. Ille ubi me vidit (vidit autem statim)[3] vocat ad se rursum, quaeritque perblande quid Picus Mirandula suus ageret. Respondeo manere eum in urbe, quod vereatur ne illo, si veniat, molestior sit. 'At ego,' inquit, 'vicissim ni verear ne molestum sit ei hoc iter, videre atque alloqui extremum exoptem, priusquam plane a vobis emigro.' 'Vin' tu,' inquam, 'accersatur?' 'Ego vero,' ait ille, 'quam primum.' Ita sane facio.

8 Venerat iam,[4] assederat, atque ego quoque iuxta genibus incubueram, quo loquentem patronum facilius, utpote defecta iam vocula, exaudirem. Bone Deus, qua ille hunc hominem comitate, qua humanitate, quibus etiam quasi blanditiis excepit. Rogavit primo ignosceret quod ei laborem hunc iniunxisset, amori hoc tamen et benevolentiae in illum suae adscriberet, libentius sese animam editurum, si prius amicissimi hominis aspectu morientes oculos satiasset. Tum sermones iniecit urbanos, ut solebat, et familiares. Nonnihil etiam tunc quoque iocatus nobiscum: quin utrosque intuens nos, 'Vellem,' ait, 'distulisset me saltem mors haec ad eum diem, quo vestram plane bibliothecam absolvissem.'

9 Ne multis: abierat vixdum Picus, cum Ferrariensis Hieronymus, insignis et doctrina et sanctimonia vir, caelestisque doctrinae

back—he, his anxiety not at all increased, just kept on holding my hands. When, however, he fully realized how hindered I was by weeping even from paying attention to him, he gradually let them go, as if disguising the real reason. For my part, I threw myself at once into the apartment's innermost room and gave free rein, so to speak, to my grief and tears.

Soon, however, I retraced my steps, my eyes dried as much as possible. When he saw me—for he saw me right away—he called me back to his side and asked very amiably what his friend Pico della Mirandola was up to. I replied that he was staying in town because he was worried that he would be something of a nuisance to him if he came. "But," he said, "if I myself in turn did not worry that the journey would be annoying for him, I would very much like to see and speak to him one last time, before I leave you once and for all." "Do you want him to be sent for?" I asked. "Yes," he said, "as soon as possible." I did so, of course.

He had now arrived and had sat down by the bed, and I too had settled on my knees close by, so that I might hear our patron more easily, given that his thin voice had now given out. Dear God, with what courtesy, what humanity, what blandishments, even, did he receive his guest! He first asked that he forgive him for having imposed this task on him and that he nevertheless attribute to his love and goodwill toward him the fact that he was prepared to give up the ghost more willingly if first he would have sated his dying eyes on the sight of a very dear friend. He then introduced witty and intimate topics of conversation, as was his wont. He joked with us some too, even then. "I would have preferred," he said, "for death to have put me off till that day when I had fully completed your library."[6]

To make a long story short: Pico had barely left when Girolamo of Ferrara,[7] a man eminent both in learning and in sanctity, and a superb preacher of heavenly doctrine, entered the bedroom. He exhorted him to keep the faith (Lorenzo, however, said that he

7

8

9

praedicator egregius, cubiculum ingreditur. Hortatur ut fidem te-
neat (ille vero tenere se ait inconcussam), ut quam emendatissime
posthac vivere destinet (scilicet facturum obnixe respondet), ut
mortem denique si necesse sit, aequo animo toleret. 'Nihil vero,'
inquit ille, 'iucundius, siquidem ita Deo decretum sit.' Recedebat
homo iam, cum Laurentius, 'Heus,' inquit, 'benedictionem, pater,
priusquam a nobis proficisceris.' Simul demisso capite vultuque et
in omnem piae religionis imaginem formatus, subinde ad verba illius et preces rite ac memoriter responsitabat, ne tantillum quidem
familiarium luctu, aperto iam neque se ulterius dissimulante, com-
motus. Diceres indictam caeteris, uno excepto Laurentio, mortem,
sic scilicet unus ex omnibus ipse nullam doloris, nullam perturba-
tionis, nullam tristitiae significationem dabat, consuetumque
animi rigorem, constantiam, aequabilitatem, magnitudinem, ad
extremum usque spiritum producebat.

10   Instabant medici adhuc tamen, et ne nihil agere viderentur, offi-
ciosissime hominem vexabant. Nihil ille tamen aspernari, nihil
aversari quod illi modo obtulissent, non quidem quoniam spe vitae
blandientis illiceretur, sed ne quem forte moriens vel levissime
perstringeret, adeoque fortis ad extremum perstitit ut de sua quoque ipsius morte nonnihil cavillaretur, sicuti cum porrigenti cuidam cibum rogantique mox quam placuisset respondit, 'Quam solet morienti.'

11   Post id, blande singulos amplexatus, petitaque suppliciter venia
si cui gravior forte, si molestior morbi vitio fuisset, totum se post
illa perunctioni summae demigrantisque animae commendationi
dedidit. Recitari dein evangelica historia coepta est, qua scilicet ir-

held it unshaken), to be determined to live as blamelessly as possible from now on (he resolutely replied that this was of course what he would do), to endure death, if this in the end should prove necessary, with equanimity. "Nothing, in fact, would be more pleasant," he replied, "should this be in God's plan." The man was already making his exit when Lorenzo said, "Father! A benediction, before you leave us." And having simultaneously bent his head and molded his face into every feature of religious piety, he gave a chain of responses, correct and from memory, to the preacher's words and prayers, not even minimally disturbed by the grieving of his intimates, which was now open and beyond disguising itself. You might have said that death had been imposed on everyone else, Lorenzo being the only exception, given, that is to say, the way in which he alone of everyone gave no evidence of pain, of anxiety, of sorrow and preserved his customary mental steadiness, self-possession, balance, dignity, all the way to his very last breath.

The doctors, despite everything, were still hovering around, and in order to avoid seeming to do nothing, they bothered the patient in the most importunate ways. He, nevertheless, did not resist or refuse anything once they had put it in front of him, not, obviously, because he was tempted by hope for alluring life, but in order to avoid hurting anyone's feelings even slightly while he was dying. To the end he remained so brave that he even made some fun of his own death, such as when someone who offered him food and, a bit later, asked how he had liked it, he replied, "As much as any dying man would!" 10

After this, he embraced each and every person gently, and having humbly asked forgiveness if by any chance he had been something of a burden or nuisance to anyone through the fault of his illness, he finally devoted his full attention to his extreme unction and to the recommendation of his departing soul. The gospel story then began to be read aloud — the one in which the torments 11

rogati Christo cruciatus explicantur, cuius ille agnoscere se verba et sententias prope omneis, modo labra tacitus movens, modo languenteis oculos erigens, interdum etiam digitorum gestu, significabat. Postremo sigillum crucifixi argenteum margaritis gemmisque magnifice adornatum defixis usquequaque oculis intuens identidemque deosculans expiravit.

12   Vir ad omnia summa natus, et qui flantem reflantemque toties fortunam usque adeo sit alterna velificatione moderatus ut nescias utrum secundis rebus constantior an adversis aequior ac temperantior apparuerit. Ingenio vero tanto ac tam facili et perspicaci ut quibus in singulis excellere alii magnum putant, ille in[5] universis pariter emineret. Nam probitatem, iustitiam, fidem[6] nemo (arbitror) nescit ita sibi Laurenti Medicis pectus atque animum, quasi gratissimum aliquod domicilium templumque, delegisse. Iam comitas, humanitas, affabilitas quanta fuerit eximia quadam in eum totius populi atque omnium plane ordinum benevolentia declaratur, sed enim inter haec omnia, liberalitas tamen et magnificentia explendescebat, quae illum pene immortali quadam gloria ad deos usque provexerat, cum interim nihil ille famae duntaxat causa et nominis, omnia vero virtutis amore persequebatur. Quanto autem literatos homines studio complectabatur, quantum honoris, quantum etiam reverentiae omnibus exhibebat, quantum denique operae industriaeque suae conquirendis toto orbe terrarum coemendisque linguae utriusque voluminibus posuit, quantosque in ea re, quam immanes sumptus fecit, ut non aetas modo haec aut hoc saeculum sed posteritas etiam ipsa maximam in huius hominis interitu iacturam fecerit.

inflicted on Christ are recounted—the words and practically every line of which he indicated he already knew, sometimes by silently moving his lips, sometimes by lifting his dimming eyes, occasionally even by a gesture of his fingers. Finally, contemplating with uninterrupted focus and repeatedly kissing a silver statuette of a crucifix, magnificently decorated with pearls and precious stones, he breathed his last.

This was a man born for every excellence, the sort who, by shifting his sails, regulated the winds of fortune—at his back, in his face, over and over—to such a degree that you would not know whether he presented himself more determined in favorable conditions or calmer and more self-controlled in adverse ones. His talent was so great, so natural, so penetrating, that where others think excellence in a single field a great accomplishment, he rose to the top in all, equally. Indeed, no one, I think, is unaware that integrity, justice, loyalty[8] singled out for themselves the heart and mind of Lorenzo de' Medici, like some very charming apartment and shrine. The measure of his graciousness, kindness, courtesy is made plain by the good will toward him on the part of the combined populace and of each and every civic rank. But indeed, amidst all these things, his generosity and magnificence nevertheless outshone the rest, raising him nearly even to divine status by a kind of immortal glory, even as, all the while, he himself pursued nothing solely for the sake of fame and renown but, rather, all out of love of virtue. How great was the devotion with which he embraced literary men! How abundant was the honor, how abundant the deference he exhibited to everyone! How much, finally, of his own effort and attention did he place in searching the world over for books in both languages, and buying them up! How lavish were the expenditures he made in this pursuit, so that not only this generation, or this age, but posterity itself has endured a tremendous loss in the passing of this man!

13   Caeterum consolantur nos, maximo in luctu, liberi eius, tanto patre dignissimi, quorum qui maximus natu, Petrus, vixdum primum et vigesimum ingressus annum, tanta iam et gravitate et prudentia et auctoritate molem totius rei publicae sustentat ut in eo statim revixisse genitor Laurentius existimetur; alter, annorum duodeviginti, Ioannes, et cardinalis amplissimus (quod nunquam cuiquam id aetatis contigerit) et idem pontifici maximo, non in ecclesiae patrimonio duntaxat sed in patriae quoque suae dicione, legatus, talem tantumque se iam tam arduis negotiis gerit et praestat ut omnium in se mortalium oculos converterit, atque incredibilem quandam, cui responsurus planissime est, expectationem concitaverit; tertius porro, Iulianus, impubes adhuc, pudore tamen ac venustate neque non probitatis et ingenii mirifica quadam suavissimaque indole, totius sibi iam⁷ civitatis animos devinxit.

14   Verum, ut de aliis in praesenti taceam, de Petro certe ipso cohibere me non possum quin, recenti re, testimonium hoc loco paternum adscribam. Duobus circiter ante obitum mensibus, cum in suo cubiculo sedens, ut solebat, Laurentius de philosophia et literis nobiscum fabularetur, ac se destinasse diceret reliquam aetatem in his studiis mecum et cum Ficino Picoque ipso Mirandula consumere, procul scilicet ab urbe et strepitu, negabam equidem hoc ei per suos cives licere, qui quidem in dies viderentur magis magisque ipsius et consilium et auctoritatem desideraturi. Tum subridens ille, 'Atqui iam,' inquit, 'vices nostras alumno tuo delegabi-

But his children, most worthy of so great a father, offer us   13
enormous consolation in our grief. The eldest, Piero, barely
twenty-one, already bears the load of the entire republic with such
gravity and wisdom and authority, that his father Lorenzo is considered to have been reincarnated immediately in him. The second, eighteen years old, Giovanni, both as a most eminent cardinal (something that has never happened to anyone of his age) and,
at the same time, as an ambassador for the pope, not only in the
States of the Church but also in the jurisdiction of his own native
land, conducts and presents himself, with respect to responsibilities so challenging, already as a man of such quality and greatness
that he has turned the gaze of every living person onto himself
and has aroused an incredible degree of expectation, which he pa-
tently is going to meet. The third, Giuliano, though not yet ado-
lescent, nevertheless has already bound the hearts of the whole citizen body to himself by his modesty and grace, as well as by
astonishing and delightful innate qualities of integrity and intellectual ability.

However, on the subject of Piero (to leave aside the others for   14
the time being) I certainly cannot restrain myself from recording,
while it is fresh in my mind, paternal testimony on this topic. Ap-
proximately two months before his death, when Lorenzo, sitting
in his bedroom (as was his habit), was chatting with me about
philosophy and literature, and he was saying that he had decided
to spend the rest of his life on these scholarly pursuits, in my company and in that of Ficino and Pico della Mirandola, far, that is to
say, from the city and its noise, I for my part was denying that this
was possible for him with the citizens' consent, since they seemed
sure to require his counsel and influence more and more each day.
Then, smiling, he replied, "Well, in that case, I shall pass my responsibilities on to your student and unload this baggage and every burden onto him." And when I asked whether he had detected
so much strength in one who was still a young man that already

mus, atque in eum sarcinam hanc et onus omne reclinabimus.'
Cumque ego rogassem an adhuc in adulescente tantum virium de-
prehendisset ut eis bona fide incumbere iam possemus, 'Ego vero,'
ait ille, 'quanta eius et quam solida video esse fundamenta, latu-
rum spero haud dubie quidquid inedificavero. Cave autem putes,
Angele, quenquam adhuc ex nostris indole fuisse tanta, quantam
iam Petrus ostendit, ut sperem fore, atque adeo augurer, nisi me
ipsius ingenii aliquot iam experimenta fefellerint, ne cui sit maio-
rum suorum concessurus.'

15   Atque huius quidem iudicii praesagiique paterni magnum profecto et clarum specimen hoc nuper dedit, quod aegrotanti praesto
fuit semper, omniaque per se, pene etiam sordida ministeria obivit,
vigiliarum patientissimus et inediae, nunquamque a lectulo ipso
patris, nisi cum maxime res publica urgeret, avelli passus, et cum
mirifica pietas extaret in vultu, tamen ne morbum aut sollicitudi-
nem paternam moerore suo adaugeret, gemitus omneis et lacrymas
incredibili virtute quasi devorabat. Porro autem, quod unum tris-
tissima in re pulcherrimum ceu spectaculum videbamus, invicem
pater quoque ipse, ne tristiorem filium tristitia sua redderet, frontem sibi ex tempore velut aliam fingebat, ac fluentes oculos in illius
gratiam continebat, nunquam aut consternatus animo aut fractus,
donec ante ora natus obversaretur. Ita uterque certatim vim facere
affectibus suis ac dissimulare pietatem pietatis studio nitebatur.

16   Ut autem Laurentius e vita decessit, dici vix potest quanta et
humanitate et gravitate cives omneis suos Petrus noster ad se domum confluentes exceperit, quam et apposite et varie et blande
etiam dolentibus consolantibusque pro tempore suamque operam

we could lean on it with confidence, he replied, "On the contrary, given how deep and solid I see his foundations to be, I confidently expect him to bear whatever I shall have built upon them. Do not dare think, Angelo, that anyone of ours[9] before now has been possessed of innate ability commensurate with that which Piero already displays, with the result that I hope and, indeed, predict (assuming that the several tests of his talent I already have made have not been deceptive) that he will not take second place to any of his ancestors."

And, in fact, Piero recently gave the following unmistakable   15
confirmation of this paternal assessment and premonition: he was always at the sick man's side, and he took on everything by himself, practically even degrading tasks. Being entirely willing to go without sleep or food, he never allowed himself to be torn from his father's bedside, except when affairs of state were most urgent. And although filial devotion was evident in his face, nevertheless, in order to avoid adding to his father's illness or worry with his own grief, he swallowed every sob and tear with unbelievable courage. Furthermore — and this alone was like a gorgeous spectacle amidst tragic circumstances — his father too, in turn, in order to avoid rendering his son sadder by his own sorrow, fashioned for the occasion something like an artificial face for himself, and restrained his streaming eyes to keep him happy, neither upset nor dejected as long as the boy was in view. Each thus strove, in competition, to do violence to his own feelings and, out of devotion, to conceal his devotion to the other.

When, however, Lorenzo left life behind, it is barely possible to   16
relate the degree of kindness and solemnity with which our dear Piero received all his citizens as they flocked to him at home, and with what aptness, variety and charm he replied even to those in grief, to those offering the customary condolences, and to those pledging their support, and then how extensive and precise was the care he devoted to setting family affairs in order, so that he

pollicentibus responderit, quantam deinde et quam solertem rei
constituendae familiari curam impenderit, ut necessitudines suas
omneis, gravissimo casu perculsas sublevarit, ut vel minutissimum
quenque ex familiaribus deiectum diffidentemque sibi adversis rebus collegerit, erexerit, animaverit, ut in obeunda quoque re publica nulli unquam aut loco aut tempore aut muneri aut homini
defuerit, nulla denique in parte cessaverit, sic ut eam plane insti-
tisse iam viam atque ita pleno gradu iter ingressus videatur, brevi
ut putetur parentem quoque ipsum vestigiis consecuturus.

17   De funere autem nihil est quod dicam. Tantum ad avi exemplum ex praescripto celebratum est, quemadmodum ipse, ut dixi,
moriens mandaverat. Tam magno autem omnis generis mortalium
concursu quam magnum nunquam antea meminerimus.

18   Prodigia vero mortem ferme haec antecesserunt, quanquam alia
quoque vulgo feruntur. Nonis Aprilibus, hora ferme diei tertia,
triduo antequam animam edidit Laurentius, mulier nescioquae,
dum in aede sacra Mariae Novellae quae dicitur declamitanti e
pulpito dat operam, repente, inter confertam populi multitudi-
nem, expavefacta consternataque consurgit, lymphatoque cursu et
terrificis clamoribus, 'Heus heus,' inquit, 'cives: an hunc non cerni-
tis ferocientem taurum, qui templum hoc ingens flammatis corni-
bus ad terram deiicit?'

19   Prima porro vigilia, cum coelum nubibus de improviso foedaretur,[8] continuo basilicae ipsius maximae fastigium, quod opere
miro singularem toto terrarum orbe testudinem supereminet, tac-
tum de caelo est, ita ut vastae quaepiam deiicerentur moles, atque
in ea potissimum partem qua Medicae convisuntur aedes, vi quadam horrenda et impetu, marmora immania torquerentur, in quo
illud etiam praescito non caruit, quod inaurata una pila, quales

might raise all his relatives to their feet from the grave catastrophe that had flattened them; so that he might pull together, stand up straight, and revitalize even each and every most insignificant member of his household who was downcast and despondent under these trying circumstances; so that in taking on public responsibilities he might not ever come up short with respect to any place or occasion or responsibility or individual and, finally, not be remiss in any role. The result is that he is seen already to have set a firm foot on the road and to have commenced his journey with such long strides that in no time he is expected to be following even in his father's footsteps.

I have nothing really to say about the funeral. It was conducted as planned along the lines of his grandfather's, just as he himself, as I have said, instructed on his death-bed, with, however, a concourse of all manner of persons greater than any I remember from ever before. 17

More or less the following prodigies anticipated his death, though others too are commonly reported. On April 13, around mid-morning, three days before Lorenzo gave up the ghost, some woman, as she was listening to someone preaching from the pulpit in the church of Maria Novella (as it is called), suddenly, in the middle of a thick crowd of people, leapt up, frightened and agitated, and amidst frenzied running and terrifying shouts cried, "Look! Look! Citizens! Don't you see the raging bull that knocks this massive temple to the ground with his flaming horns?" 18

Then, early that night, as the sky grew unexpectedly dark, the main cathedral's own lantern, which rises above the dome which through its wondrous engineering is unique in all the world,[10] was rapidly struck by lightning, with the result that several vast chunks were toppled, and gigantic marbles — especially toward the side from which the Medici palace is visible — were twisted out of shape by some awesome power and force. In this, the following too was not without future significance, for a single gilded ball, 19

aliae quae[9] in eodem fastigio conspiciuntur, excussa fulmine est, ne non ex ipso quoque insigni proprium[10] eius familiae detrimentum portenderetur. Sed et illud memorabile, quod ut primum detonuit, statim quoque serenitas reddita.

20   Qua autem nocte obiit Laurentius, stella solito clarior ac grandior, suburbano imminens in quo is animam agebat, illo ipso temporis articulo decidere extinguique visa quo compertum deinde est eum vita demigrasse. Quin excurrisse etiam faces trinoctio perpetuo de Faesulanis montibus, supraque id templum quo reliquiae conduntur Medicae gentis scintillasse nonnihil, moxque evanuisse feruntur. Quid quod et leonum quoque nobilissimum par, in ipsa qua publice continentur cavea, sic in pugnam ferociter concurrit, ut alter pessime acceptus, alter etiam leto sit datus? Arreti quoque, supra arcem ipsam, geminae perdiu arsisse flammae, quasi Castores, feruntur, ac lupa identidem sub moenibus ululatus terrificos edidisse. Quidam illud etiam (ut sunt ingenia) pro monstro interpretantur, quod excellentissimus (ita enim habebatur) huius aetatis medicus, quando ars eum praescitaque fefellerant, animum desponderit, puteoque se sponte demerserit, ac principi ipsi Medicae (si vocabulum spectes) familiae sua nece parentaverit.

21   Sed video me, cum quidem multa et magna reticuerim, ne forte in speciem adulationis inciderem, longius tamen provectum quam a principio institueram. Quod ut facerem, partim cupiditas ipsa obsequendi obtemperandique tibi, optimo, doctissimo, prudentissimoque homini, mihique amicissimo, cuius quidem studio satisfacere brevitas ipsa in transcursu non poterat, partim etiam amara

like others visible on the same lantern, was knocked off by light-ning, to insure that, given this particular sign as well, harm spe-cific to this family was portended.[11] But it is also worth mention-ing that no sooner had it thundered than calm skies were restored.

On the night of Lorenzo's passing, a star brighter and larger 20 than usual, hanging over the suburban villa in which he was breathing his last, was seen to fall and be extinguished at the very moment in time at which it was subsequently discovered that he had left this life. Furthermore, three nights in a row, torches were reported to have raced down from the hills around Fiesole, all night long, and to have flickered for a while and then vanished over the sanctuary where the mortal remains of the Medici family are interred. And what is more, a most noble pair of lions too, in the very cage in which they are kept on public display, so fero-ciously attacked one another that one was badly hurt, and the other was even put to death.[12] In Arezzo too, right over the cas-tle, twin flames are said to have burned like the Dioscuri.[13] And a she-wolf, just outside the city walls, repeatedly emitted terrifying howls. Some people (such is human ingenuity) even gave a porten-tous interpretation to the fact that the most excellent medical doc-tor of our day (for this was his reputation), when his method and his prognostications failed him, gave in to despair and, of his own free will,[14] drowned himself in a well, and so, by his self-slaughter, performed a relative's sacrifice (if you consider the name) to the very prince of the Medical family.

But I see that, although I have left many things, important 21 things unsaid, in order to avoid slipping into apparent flattery, I nevertheless have been made to go on longer than originally planned. Driving me to do so have been, in part, the desire to gratify and oblige you, an excellent, very learned, and very wise person — and a very dear friend to me — whose curiosity the brev-ity of a cursory treatment could not have satisfied, and in part, as well, a kind of bittersweet pleasure (almost a thrill) found in recol-

quaedam dulcedo quasique titillatio impulit recolendae frequen-
tandaeque eius viri memoriae, cui si parem similemque nostra aetas unum, forte, atque alterum tulit, potest audacter iam de splen-
dore nominis et gloria cum vetustate quoque ipsa contendere.
Vale.

xv Calendas Iunias MCCCCLXXXXII, *in Faesulano rusculo*

: III :

Caesar Carmentus Angelo Politiano s. d.

1 Politias tuas, hoc est Miscellaneorum librum, ostendit nuper mihi
Iacobus Rufinus, amoenissimi homo ingenii, tibique amicissimi.
Nihil, mehercules, illis mundius, nihil acutius, nihil doctius. Ista
una centuria, ut equidem sentio, non modo Gellium et id genus
alios aemularis, sed longe superas. Fama quanquam magnus es,
scriptis certe maior, quare aetati huic nostrae gratulor. Est enim,
praesenti in saeculo, quod admirari possimus, ne semper veterum
ingenia suspiciamus.

2 Ego per te cum multa didicerim, tibi me debere fateor, cunc-
taque mea polliceor. Amicos habes supremae fortunae viros; nos
humili de plebe sumus, qui quasi fores amicitiae tuae pulsamus.
Quid, tu tenuis hominem sortis despicies? Inter ganeatas dapes,
vilis quandoque iuvat atque appetitur oliva. Porro, quod et ipse literas istas profitear, nihil velim carum me tibi reddat. Nam profes-
sio adeo ieiuna est, in hoc laude dignus, quod ad studia ista anhe-
lem, non quod profitear. Quali enim simus doctrina, ipsi probe
scimus. Iter in densis tentamus tenebris.

lecting and revisiting the memory of that man. For if our age has produced an equal to match him, or maybe even two, then already it too can boldly compete with antiquity in glory and the brilliance of its fame.

Farewell.

May 18, 1492, in the country house at Fiesole

: III :

Cesare Carmento[1] to his dear Angelo Poliziano

Jacopo Ruffini,[2] a man of a most agreeable temperament, and very devoted to you, recently showed me your *Politeia*, that is to say, the book of your *Miscellanea*.[3] Nothing, I swear, is more refined, more penetrating, more learned than these. By that one set of a hundred, in my opinion, you not only rival Gellius and others of his kind, but you even far surpass them. Although everyone says you are great, your written works clearly prove you greater. As a result, I congratulate this age of ours. For there is in the present day something for us to admire, lest we always be looking up to the abilities of the ancients, from below.

Having learned many things through you, I confess that I am in your debt, and I promise you everything I have. You have as friends men of the highest class; I who am banging at the doors of your friendship come from the lowly masses. What, will you look down on a fellow of slender means? Among the offerings of a vulgar buffet, sometimes an inexpensive olive is pleasant and appetizing. Besides, I would not want the fact that I lecture on your same literature to render me at all dearer to you. For my lecturing is pretty uninteresting. I earn praise for panting after those studies of yours, not for lecturing on them. I myself know full well the quality of my education. I feel my way along in thick darkness.

3 Lucella sectamur, quamdiu tantum congesserimus, quantum sit satis pro victu annorum aliquot. Mox Athenas, id est Florentiam, ad capiendum abs te cultum ingenii proficiscemur. Absentem, quaeso, et incognitum, si potes, dilige interea.

Et vale.

: IV :

Angelus Politianus Caesari Carmento suo s. d.

1 Ignosce occupationibus, Caesar, neque me vel superbum crede vel inofficiosum, quod ad tuas hactenus literas non rescripserim. Melior diei pars lectionibus variis mihi teritur; reliqua datur amicis opera; noctem sibi quies et somnus cum precibus, horario, et stilo dividunt. Ac (ne manifesta dissimulem) recrastinator quoque natura sum maximus, nec ad diem facile solvo, quanquam omnino aliquando solvo quod debui, quorum alterum dum redditur (ut verum fatear) nonnihil dolet ob ignaviam, alterum me, quoniam redditum non est, semper excruciat.

2 Venio nunc ad epistolas tuas, quas equidem, quoniam sunt elegantissimae plenaeque mearum laudum, cupiebam sic invicem ferre laudibus, ut par pari relatum cognosceres. Atenim si fecero, credet aliquis me forsitan huius denique spe mercedis abs te antea fuisse laudatum. Quare malo equidem tibi hoc officium debere quam meas laudes adducere in suspitionem, praesertim sic abs te rhetorice dictas, ut ob eas ipse quoque mihi placeam, qui scio veras[1] non esse. Sine igitur quae de me scripsisti mora aliqua tempo-

I am trying to make some money until I shall have accumulated 3
enough to live on for a few years. Then I shall set out for Athens — that is to say, Florence — to receive intellectual training from
you. In the meantime, please, if you can, hold me dear, though absent and a stranger.

And please, farewell.

: IV :

Angelo Poliziano to his dear Cesare Carmento

Forgive my responsibilities, Cesare, and do not think me arrogant 1
or negligent for not yet replying to your letter. The better part
of my day is consumed by various lectures. The rest of my attention is given to friends. Peace and quiet partition the night with
prayers, the hourly offices and the pen. And besides — there is no
point in hiding what is obvious — I am also by nature an enormous procrastinator. Nor do I easily pay off my debts on time,
though sooner or later I pay absolutely everything I owe. To tell
the truth, while one of these is being discharged, it causes me no
insignificant grief over my neglect; the next, since it has not been
discharged, inevitably tortures me.

I come now to your letters, which, since they are most elegant 2
and full of my praises, I in turn wanted to lavish with such praise
that you might acknowledge exact compensation. Yes, but if I do
this, someone will believe that perhaps I was earlier praised by you
in expectation of this eventual reward. Thus I actually prefer to
owe you this service rather than to subject my own praises to suspicion, especially when they were pronounced by you so persua-
sively that, because of them, I too (who know they are untruths)
please myself. Permit, therefore, what you wrote about me to

ris roborari, talionemque tum denique a nobis expecta. Nunc usuram laudationis tuae gratuitam, quaeso, permitte dies aliquot, ne quis argutulus dicat, nos inter nos (ut illi apud Terentium faciunt) tradere operas mutuas.

Vale.

Florentiae, Idibus Ianuariis MCCCCLXXXVIIII

: V :

Angelus Politianus Tristano Chalco suo s. d.

1 Significas mihi literis tuis decuriam scribarum totam sic delectari Miscellaneis nostris ut inde me quoque, videlicet auctorem, quanto vix incredibile est amore prosequatur. Equidem habeo gratiam studiis meis et vigiliis, in quibus acriter ab ineunte aetate, si minus cum dispendio bonae valetudinis, certe sim[1] periculo maximo versatus. Etenim quamvis ipsa sibi literarum tractatio satis grande praemium sit, adeo scilicet suavis et iucunda, tamen istiusmodi sit accessionibus ut nullum vitae genus esse putem cum literati hominis ocio, dummodo non sterili, conferendum. Nec enim plures Iasoni et Cadmo satu dentium nati sunt hostes quam mihi satu Miscellaneorum nati amici.

2 De Tertulliano quod requiris: Quintus Septimius Florens Tertullianus appellatur, eiusque legi libros, praeter Apologeticum, De pallio, De carnis resurrectione, De corona militis, Ad martyria, De virginibus velandis, De habitu mulierum, De cultu foeminarum, Ad uxorem, Ad Scapulam, De persecutione, Ad Fabium de ex-

gather strength by some lapse of time, and then, at last, expect "an eye for an eye" from me. For now, please allow me free use of your words of praise for a few days, to keep any shrewd observer from saying that you and I, as they do in Terence, "swap favors back and forth."[1]

Florence, January 13, 1489

: V :

Angelo Poliziano to his dear Tristano Calco[1]

You indicate to me in your letter that the entire college of scribes   1
takes so much pleasure in my *Miscellanea* that, as a consequence, they honor me as their author with love almost beyond belief. I in turn owe thanks to my scholarly efforts and sleepless nights, over which I from an early age eagerly spent my time, if not so much to the actual detriment of my health, then certainly at very great risk. And indeed, although the handling of literature is its own sufficiently great reward, given how pleasant and enjoyable it is, nevertheless, the result of bonuses of the sort you offer is that I consider no type of life deserving of comparison with the leisure (provided it is not unproductive leisure) of a literary man. Nor were more enemies born to Jason and to Cadmus by the sowing of teeth than were friends born to me by the sowing of a miscellany.

As for your question about Tertullian, his name is Quintus   2
Septimius Florens Tertullianus, and of his books, I have read (besides the *Apology*) *On the Cloak, On the Resurrection of the Flesh, On the Soldier's Crown, Toward Martyrdom, On the Veiling of Virgins, On Women's Dress, On Feminine Ornament,*[2] *To My Wife, To Scapula, On Persecution, To Fabius on the Encouragement of Chastity, On Patience, On Monogamy, On the Prescriptions of the Heretics, Against Hermogenes,*

hortatione castitatis, De patientia, De monogamia, De praescrip-
tionibus haereticorum, Contra Hermogenem, Adversus Praxeam,
Valentianos, Marcionem, Iudaeos, haereticos omnes. Ipse quorundam, praeter hos, librorum meminit a se compositorum, qui nec
extant. Lactantius, ut in omnibus eruditum doctrinis, ita in elo-
quendo duriorem perhibet. Augustinus lapsum quibusdam locis
miratur, quamvis hominem doctissimum. Cyprianus sua frequenter scripta de illius fontibus irrigavit. Reliqua super eo libellus
Hieronymi Virorum illustrium suppeditabit.

3   Ex Apologetico vero nimium tibi deerat, quod et huic epistolae
totum subnexui. Tu caeteros tamen eius libros cave putes cum
Apologetico conferendos. Tum illud scito volumen esse quod desideras prope immensum. Nam quod ad operam scilicet attinet
meam, libenter equidem de illa tibi verbis eisdem spondeo, quibus
Publio Septimio de civium fortunis Antonius: 'Quid concupiscas,
tu videris; quod concupiveris, certe habebis.'
Vale.
Florentiae, pridie Idus Ianuarias MCCCCLXXXVIIII

: VI :

Angelus Politianus Tristano Chalco suo salutem

1   Scribis Marianum Genazanensem, theologiae consultum, qui sa-
cras istic ad populum contiones habet, tanta esse omnium admiratione apud vos ut eorum facile fidem quae de ipso in Miscellaneis
praedicavimus absolverit, iri ad hunc, plenis undique viis, allici le-

Against Praxeas, Against the Valentinians, Against Marcion, Against the Jews, Against All Heretics. He himself, besides these, makes mention of several books he composed but which are not extant. Lactantius regarded him as learned in all fields but, at the same time, as somewhat rough-going as a stylist. Augustine was surprised that he made slips on certain points, even though he was extremely learned. Cyprian frequently watered his own writings by drawing on Tertullian. Jerome's treatise *On Famous Men* will give you everything else about him.

From your copy of the *Apology*, however, too much was missing, 3 all of which I have attached directly to this letter. Nevertheless, do not dare think that his other works are comparable to the *Apology.* Next, be aware that the volume you want to have is practically gigantic. Naturally, as far as my services are concerned, I make my own pledge about them in the same words Antony used with Publius Septimius regarding the citizens' estates: "Decide for yourself what you want; whatever you want, you shall have it, of course."[3]

Farewell.

Florence, January 12, 1489

: VI :

Angelo Poliziano to his dear Tristano Calco

You write that Mariano of Genazzano,[1] expert in theology, who is 1 giving public addresses to religious congregations, enjoys such great admiration on the part of everyone in your city that he easily has redeemed the pledge I earlier made about him in my *Miscellanea.*[2] You write that everyone flocks to him, filling the streets in all directions, that they are attracted by the charm of his words, are

pore verborum, suspendi sententiarum gravitate, flecti omneis orationis impetu et viribus.

2 Fatebor quid mihi usu venerit cum primum hic apud nos contionari coepit. Accessi ut audirem, sic quomodo alios consueveram, explorabundus et pene (ut verum dicam) contemptim. Sed ut habitum vidi hominis et statum, quasique indolem quandam in oculis et vultu minime vulgarem, coepi aliquid expectare iam quod essem probaturus. Ecce tibi igitur, praefari incipit. Arrigo iam tum aures. Canora vox, verba electa,[1] grandes sententiae. Denique agnosco incisa, video membra, sentio circunductum, capior numero. Iam partiri pergit. Attendo. Nihil impeditum, nihil inane, nihil ibi quod caudam traheret. Texit deinde argumentorum nexus: illaqueor. Retexit: expedior. Inserit alicubi narratiunculas: ducor. Modulatur carmen: teneor. Iocatur nonnihil: rideo. Premit urgetque vires:[2] do manus. Tentat affectus mitiores: statim mihi per os lacrymae. Clamat iratus: terreor ac venisse iam nollem. Denique, pro re ipsa quam tractat, et figuras variat, et vocis flexus, et ubique actionem gestu commendat. Mihi vero etiam (ut fatear) crescere in ipso pulpito, nec supra sui modo sed omnino supra hominis mensuram, saepe est visus. Ac dum sic omnia quasi singula contemplor, cessit miraculo iudicium.

3 Putabam fore tamen ut, consumpta postmodum novitate, minus in dies caperet. Caeterum contra accidit. Idem enim postridie quasi alius audiebatur, sed illo ipso melior qui pridie visus est[3] optimus. Nec tu illud corpusculum contempseris. Invictum, infatiga-

held in place by the solidity of his sentences, are guided by the force and power of his oratory.

I shall admit what happened to me when he first began to give public lectures here in our city. I approached in order to hear, just as had been my habit with others, out of curiosity and, frankly, almost with contempt. But when I saw the young man's bearing and posture and a certain quality in his eyes and face that was not common in the least, I already began to anticipate what I was about to confirm. Look, therefore, for he is starting to speak. I then prick up my ears: a musical voice, choice words, expansive sentences. I notice *commata*, I perceive *cola*, I am aware of his period, I am captivated by his rhythm.[3] Now he proceeds to the division of his arguments. I listen carefully: nothing cumbersome, nothing unimportant, nothing there as a ridiculous appendage. He then weaves a net of arguments: I am snared. He unweaves: I am freed. Here and there he inserts little stories: I am led along. He switches to poetry: I am riveted. He jokes a little: I laugh. He presses and exerts his power: I surrender. He touches gentler feelings: tears stream down my face at once. He cries out in anger: I am petrified, and now I would rather not have come. In short, he varies his figures of speech and vocal inflection in accord with the subject matter at hand and, throughout, enhances his delivery with gesture. To tell the truth, he often seemed to me to grow, there in the pulpit, not only beyond his own dimensions, but entirely beyond those of a human being. And as I thus contemplated everything, essentially detail by detail, judgment bowed before the miraculous. 2

All the same, I thought that, once the novelty wore off, he would captivate me less and less each day. But the opposite happened, for the next day he sounded like a different person, but better than the very one who had seemed perfect the day before. Nor would you scoff at his diminutive body. It is invincible, tireless — with the result that he seems to renew his strength from 3

bile est, ut non aliunde magis reparare vires quam de laboribus ipsis videatur. Quis inde autem tantum vocis, tantum spiritus, tantum virium ac laterum speraret?

4   Adde quod et rusticatus quandoque sum domique cum ipso familiarius egi. Et quidem nihil vidi placidius, nihil tamen etiam cautius. Non eius absterret severitas, non item corrumpit facilitas. Alii, cum se magistros ecclesiarum profitentur, credunt sibi ius esse in homines vitae et necis. Itaque sic intemperanter potestate abutuntur ut nunquam supercilium, nunquam paedagogi vultum et verba illa tetrica deponant.

5   Hic autem noster sic modum tenere didicit ut in ipso tantum pulpito censuram exerceat; cum descendit invicem, civilitas excipiat. Quare sic a me, sic a Pico item Mirandula meo (bone Deus, quo viro!) frequenter aditur,[4] ut nullo magis quam sermone illius et consuetudine tristitiam literati[5] laboris discutiamus. Nam Laurentius ipse Medices, elegans ingeniorum spectator, quantum homini tribuat non modo substructo protinus insigni cenobio ostendit, sed multo etiam magis assiduitate quadam cultuque, sic ut unam cum illo ambulatiunculam omnibus ferme vitae urbanae discursibus anteponat.

6   Itaque te quoque hortor inspicias hominem, si potes, et explores, etiam de proximo. Laudabis et hic Politiani tui iudicium. Nec illi molestus unquam venies; nescit offendi. Non enim is est qui lucem refugiat et oculos, puto, quia bona conscientia testibus omnino gaudet, quamvis utique non desideret.

Vale.

xi Calendas[6] *Apriles* MCCCCLXXXVIIII

no other source than work itself. Who could have expected from him so big a voice, such lung-power, or so much strength and endurance?

In addition, I occasionally have spent time in his intimate company, both in the countryside and at home. And indeed, I have never seen anything so agreeable and, at the same time, so prudent. His strictness is not off-putting, nor, by the same token, does his easy-goingness corrupt. Others, when they proclaim themselves teachers of their congregations, believe that they have control of life and death over people. As a result, they abuse their power so intemperately that they never set aside their scowl, never set aside their schoolmaster's face and their horrible words. 4

Our man, however, has learned to respect limits in such a way that he practices censure only in the pulpit; when, in turn, he steps down, ordinary politeness takes over. He is, therefore, so frequently approached by me and, likewise, by Pico della Mirandola (dear God, what a man!) that we dispel the melancholy of literary endeavor by no one's conversation and company more than his. Indeed, Lorenzo de' Medici himself, a refined observer of natural talent, demonstrates how much he values this person not only by the fine monastery he immmediately began to build, but even more by a kind of constant attention, even to the point that he prefers one stroll with him to practically any of the hustle and bustle of city life. 5

Thus I urge you too, if you can, to observe and get to know the man, also from close by. In this too you will praise the judgment of your Poliziano. Nor will he ever be sorry to see you: he does not know how to be annoyed. For he is not the sort to flee the light and people's eyes. This is, I suppose, because a clear conscience is altogether glad to have a witness, even though it would not feel in the least an absence thereof. 6

Farewell.

March 22, 1489[4]

: VII :

Angelus Politianus Antonio Pizamano[1] s. d.

1 Quid esse hoc dicam, vir doctissime, quod illo ipso tempore quo vos Ioanni Pico Mirandulae, me praesente, tu Grimanusque, non iam tuus potius quam meus, quanquam mentito nomine, quanquam dissimulata patria, quanquam sub mille involucris, exhibuistis, non alium prius aut libentius sermonem quam de vobis ipsis, licet alio revocantibus ac propemodum resistentibus, iniecimus? An non, obsecro, vos surda et ignara quaedam naturae consentientis ratio non modo personam detrahere illam vobis intempestivam, sed etiam exprobare fucum falsarum illiusmodi apud amicos imaginum videbatur? Adeon' autem vos tum fuisse ferreos, adeon' (quaeso) in illo male, mehercules, lepido proposito pertinaces ut cum de utroque vestrum tam ardenter uterque nostrum sic a vobis, quasi certe non a vobis, quaerebamus, et cum apud vos de vobis ipsis, ut apud alios, tam ex animo tamque amanter loquebamur, duritiem tamen, aut obstinationem potius latendi fallendique nos, eandem semper retinueritis? O, si non ita induxissetis animum, qui complexus et quanta illa nostra extitissent gaudia! Quem diem nobis incivili illo, ne dixerim crudeli, commento, quem fortasse etiam vobis invidistis! Etenim ego ne postea quidem laetitiam indicii toto persensi pectore, cum sub articulo uno temporis mihi vos pene prius abstulistis quam obtuleratis. Nam, etsi animus omnino inclinabat eodem, vix tamen credere audebam vos

: VII :

Angelo Poliziano to Antonio Pizzamano[1]

What, most learned man, can I possibly call the fact that, at the   1
very same time that, in my presence, you and Grimani,[2] no longer
yours instead of mine, although under an assumed name, although
with your identity concealed, although under a thousand covers,
presented yourself to Giovanni Pico della Mirandola, we introduced no topic of conversation sooner or more willingly than that
of yourselves, even as you called our attention elsewhere and almost tried to stop us? Or did—please tell me—a kind of deaf and
unconscious assessment of our like-minded nature not seem not
only to strip you of your ill-timed mask but also to reproach the
deceptiveness of disguises of that sort among friends. Was it right
for you then to have been so hard-hearted, so relentless, I ask, in a
plan that was, for heaven's sake, hardly amusing, with the result
that when each of us so eagerly asked you (as if, of course, not
you) about each of you, and when in your presence and in that
of others we spoke so sincerely and lovingly about yourselves,
you nevertheless clung unswervingly to the same callousness—or
rather, obstinacy—of concealing yourselves and deceiving us? Had
you not persuaded yourselves to act so, O what hugs there would
have been, and how great would have been our rejoicing! What a
day you begrudged us—and perhaps even yourselves—by that unkind, not to say cruel, design? As a matter of fact, not even after-
wards did I fully feel, heart and soul, joy over the disclosure, when
in a single instant you took yourselves away from me almost before
you had revealed yourselves to me. For even if my mind was inclined altogether in the same direction, all the same, I scarcely
dared believe that you genuinely were who in fact you were, nor,
indeed, did I think either that I could have been fooled before or

esse, bona fide, qui videlicet eratis (nec enim vel ab eis me antea potuisse vel tum quoque non iterum posse falli existimabam qui se nuper fefellisse confitebantur), ut ne illud quidem tantillum voluptatis liberum sincerumque mihi et ab omni vacuum suspitione reliqueritis. Ut enim pisces atque aves, decepti semel, caeteros etiam cibos, illi hamatos, hae viscatos credunt, sic ab impostura nuper vestra quod etiam merum sincerumque fuit esse id omne tamen dilutum mihi atque incrustatum penitus videbatur.

2   Fecit istuc ipsum olim in me Picus, verum longe ille mitius, nam cum me rusticantem temporarius versipellis adivisset, ac sibi ludos pautisper de amico cepisset, et de se quid sentirem callide, quasi alienus, explorasset, mox tamen, ubi lusit satis, ultro se mihi ridens patefecit, ut omni prorsus erepta nube frui iam liberrime suavissime iuvenis praesentia, dulcissimoque colloquio licuerit et veras audire et reddere voces.

3   Vos, contra, immodici, nisi me fortuna revertentem vestra ipsorum causa rure in urbem pene dixerim fugientibus in ipso[2] limine obiecisset, taciti (quod adhuc abominor), taciti ambo et ignorati mihi, tum pro Venetis Vicentini, pro Pizamanis et Grimanis nescioqui Porticenses discesseratis. Sed enim querelae conticescant, serae iam et nihil profuturae, licitumque amicis fuerit ludere aliquando ex suo commodo amicos, sicuti carissimos homines etiam interdum numina solent, quod viri quidam sapientissimi prodiderunt.

4   Venio nunc ad epistolas tuas elegantissimas, quas mihi et Pico Lactantius noster diligentissimus reddidit, hoc est, utranque

that, by the same token, I could not be being fooled again by those who were revealing that they had just fooled me, with the result that you did not even leave me that modicum of pleasure unfettered, unimpaired and free of all suspicion. Just as fish and birds, after they have been tricked once, believe other food to be, in the first case, hooked, and in the second, limed, so after your recent deception, even what was pure and genuine seemed to me diluted and encrusted.[3]

Pico once did this very thing to me, but to a far milder degree. 2 For though he had come to me in the country, his appearance temporarily transformed, and had gotten himself a few laughs at his friend's expense, and, as if someone else, cunningly had probed what I thought about him, nevertheless, he soon, having had his fill of fun, revealed himself to me voluntarily, laughing, so that, with every cloud of doubt dispelled, it was then possible to enjoy, entirely unreservedly, this most agreeable young man's presence and most delightful conversation, "both to hear and to return true voices."[4]

You, by contrast, without restraint (had chance not thrown me, 3 returning—for your sake, no less—from the country to the city, in the way of what I might almost call fugitives, there at the doorway), silent (which I still find reprehensible), silent both of you and unrecognized by me, had then departed, Vicenzans rather than Venetians, "Porticenzi" rather than Pizzamani and Grimani. But let my complaining, too late now and pointless, fall silent. And let friends be permitted to make occasional sport of friends at their own convenience, just as deities tend to do now and then to the mortals dearest to them—something, indeed, that certain very wise men have recorded.

I come now to your extremely elegant letters, which our dear 4 friend Lattanzio dutifully delivered to me and to Pico, that is to say, both to both, for in this category, what is given to one is clearly given to both. And indeed, perhaps for this very reason,

utrique. Nam quod in hoc genere alteri datur, utrique profecto datur. Et quidem videris in eis mihi vel ob hoc ipsum nervos omneis tuae contendisse humanitatis, ut quod peccaveras antea te nobis coram diffingens, nunc absens eundem refingens pulcherrima vicissitudine redimeres. Etenim sic in literis ipsis amor humanitasque tua et suavitas ingenii nativa quaedam vivit, spirat, exhibetque se ut non (quod solitum est) in atramento, sed in penitissimis praecordiis intinxisse nobis scriptorium calamum videaris. Ita, quod ait Syracosius poeta, si quid nos antea momordisti, nunc innoxium repetita etiam utilitate reddidisti.

5   Nam quod breviores fuerint epistolae, dolemus quidem, sed eas arte longissimas, hoc est a capite crebro repetentes, facere didicimus.[3] Sunt autem adhuc apud me literae quoque aliae tuae, neque non simul et Grimani, quas abhinc annos ferme decem dedistis ad me, nec illae profecto indignae quae tanquam semina iacerent, adulescentes qui quidem forent ad hanc uberrimam frugem perventuri. Nempe igitur sicuti amatores munuscula suae quisque Veneris diligenter servant (anellum puta, catellam, sudariolum, violam quoque, nonnunquam rosam, flosculum), sic ego tuas illas et item Grimani literas, amoris veri gratissima pignora, non modo paulo incuriosius non habeo, sed et sub oculos crebro revoco, nunc mihi ipse, nunc amicis recitans, atque ita memoriam redintegrans, ita affectus renovans, ita consuetudinem mihi vestram quam saepissime asciscens. Quare abs te iure quodam meo postulo ne istud ad me scribendi officium omittas, cuius fructum tanti faciam. Sed cum tibi a studiis gravioribus ocium suppetit, ocium illud in me potissimmum transferas, operamque mihi aliquam, saltem vacui temporis, impertias. Debes hoc amori meo, debes certe humanitati tuae.

6   Dominicum vero Grimanum laetor equidem legationis honorificentissime perfungi munere. Cupio tamen eum salvum quam

you seem to me in them to exert every muscle of your humanity in order to redeem your offense by a beautiful inversion, reshaping from a distance the very you that, back then, you were un-shaping before our eyes. In fact, there in the letter, your love and humanity and a kind of innate pleasantness of disposition so live, breathe, and make themselves visible that you seem to us to have dipped your pen not, as is customary, in ink but, rather, in the deepest recesses of your heart. And so, as the poet from Syracuse says, "If you took something of a bite out of me before, you have made it harmless, with even its usefulness back."

We are, of course, sorry that the letters were, as you say, rather 5 brief, but we have learned to make them very long by repeatedly rereading from the beginning. Moreover, I still have here other letters of yours as well, and of Grimani too, which you, as the sort of young men who were going to reach this most bountiful maturity, sent me almost ten years ago and which were not at all unworthy to lie planted like seeds. Naturally, just as lovers carefully preserve the presents each receives from his Venus (for instance, a ring, a chain, a handkerchief, even a violet, sometimes a rose, a floret), so do I not only keep, not at all indifferently, those letters of yours and, likewise, those of Grimani, most welcome pledges of true love, but I often bring them back out to look at, reading them aloud, now to myself, now to friends, thus restoring my memory, thus refreshing my feelings, thus claiming your friendship for myself as often as possible. I ask you, therefore, by a kind of right I have, not to abandon the task of writing me, the fruit of which I value so highly. But when you have any freedom from more important pursuits, transfer that freedom especially to me, and assign to me at least some measure of the activity of your free time. You owe this to my love, and you clearly owe it to your own humanity.

For my part, I am delighted that Domenico Grimani is dis- 6 charging the office of his embassy with the greatest distinction. Nevertheless, I hope that you welcome him back safe and sound as

primum recipias, ne diutius a Musis ferietur, et ut aucto multis pro merito laudibus ob rem publicam bene gestam non tuo modo sed meo quoque nomine gratuleris, salutes, amplectarisque reducem, tum qua poteris significatione unum me quoque illi inter longa prosequentium officia repraesentes.

7   De codice autem nihil te equidem hortabor. Errarem potius si causam tibi meam commendandam putarem. Tantum dixerim vehementer me illum desiderare, qui lectus a me libenter, custoditus diligenter, etiam deinde fideliter remittetur.

8   Ioannes Picus Mirandula, quasi Roscius quidam literarii theatri, respondebit, arbitror, et ipse ad tuas literas, quas videlicet gratanter accepit. Te cordi et Grimanum, mecum simul, infixos habet, et quidem trabali clavo. Laudat utrunque ubique quacunque occasione, nec occasio illi tamen unquam deest.

9   Sed et Laurentio Medici tuas ego ad me literas recitavi, fabulamque illam simulati[4] nominis ridenti narravi totam. Castigavit tamen ille me verbis, quod cognitos deinde non etiam invitos in aedes suas adduxeram, ut veteris caelaturae vasa gemmasque, quando id vos cupere dixeratis, pro arbitrio spectaretis. Negavi me parem duobus. Nam ne Hercules quidem duos,[5] quod est in proverbio. Verum amat ille vos; favet proposito doctrinaeque isti, vir unus ad omnia magna et honesta natus, educatus, exercitatus, nec minore a vobis (ni fallor) studio visendus, quam illa ipsa caelamina, quae prius appetita, dein tamen oblata, continuo refugistis. Vale.

soon as possible, lest he vacation too long from the Muses, and so that you may congratulate him (not only in your own name, but also in mine) upon his return, deservedly bolstered by abundant praise for his fine management of public affairs, and so that you may embrace him, and, finally, so that you may, by whatever intimation you can, remind him of me alone, among the extensive services of those doing him honor.

On the subject of the book, I myself shall put no pressure on you. I would instead be remiss if I thought you had to take charge of my case. Let me say simply that I really would like to have it, and that, once it has been read by me with pleasure and carefully guarded, it would then faithfully be sent back. 7

Giovanni Pico della Mirandola, like a kind of Roscius[5] of the literary stage, will himself also reply, I think, to your letter, which, of course, he received with joy. He has you and Grimani, together with me, fastened to his heart—with a spike,[6] no less. He praises each of you everywhere, at every opportunity, nor does he ever lack an opportunity. 8

But I read your letter to me to Lorenzo de' Medici as well, and I told him the whole story, while he laughed, of your faked identity. He then gave me a speech of reproach, because, once you were recognized, I did not conduct you both, even unwilling, to his house to look to your hearts' content at his vases and gems, products of ancient engraving, since you had said you wanted this. I said that I was no match for two. "Against two, not even Hercules," as the proverb goes.[7] But he loves you both, supports your way of life and your learning—he, the one man born, raised, trained for all things great and glorious, and who ought to be visited by you, unless I am mistaken, with no less enthusiasm than that with which you suddenly fled those very *objets d'art*, first sought, then even placed in your path. 9

Farewell.

: VIII :

Angelus Politianus Francisco Casae suo s. d.

1 Accepi epistolam tuam qua mihi significas allatum istuc esse de machinula automato quae sit nuper a Laurentio quodam Florentino constructa, in qua siderum cursus cum caeli ratione congruens explicetur, aisque te cupere ut, quoniam famae fides derogetur, ego ad te de ea scribam, si quid comperti habeam. Geram tibi morem, et quamvis longo intervallo id opus, ruri agens, haud aspexi, tamen eius vel quae forma sit, vel ratio, vel usus, quantum consequi memoria potero, breviter exponam. Quae si tibi explicatio paulo videatur obscurior, non nostrae omnino orationi, sed ipsius etiam rei, qua de¹ agitur, subtilitate atque adeo novitati velim attribuas.

2 Columella est quadrata, quae pyramidos modo in acutum desinens fastigiatur, altitudinis fere trium cubitum. Supra eam pro capitello planus orbis est aheneus, auro et coloribus distinctus, et in cuius altera parte omnis siderum errantium cursus explicetur, cuius est dimensio cubitali brevior, rotulisque intrinsecus denticulatis agitur, circulo immobili, summum complectente marginem, quatuor et viginti horarum spatiis distincto. Intraque eum in summo versatili orbe, signa duodecim suis discernuntur gradibus. Interius orbiculi octo, pari ferme inter se magnitudine, visuntur.

: VIII :

Angelo Poliziano to his dear Francesco della Casa[1]

I have received your letter in which you indicate that news has 1
reached you there about the self-propelled device which recently
was constructed by a certain Florentine named Lorenzo,[2] in which
the movements of the stars, in accord with the logic of the skies, is
revealed. And you say that, since faith in the report is being undermined, you want me to write you on the subject if I have any
reliable information. I shall oblige you, and although, having been
in the country, I have not laid eyes on the mechanism in some
time, I nevertheless shall briefly set forth, as best as I can remember, its structure, principle, and function. Should this explanation
seem to you somewhat obscure, please blame this not entirely on
my powers of expression but also on the sophistication and novelty of precisely the thing under consideration.[3]

    There is a small square pillar, roughly four-and-a-half feet high, 2
which, tapering to a point, is topped in the manner of a pyramid.
Above it, in place of a capital, is a flat bronze disc, marked out in
gold and colors, and on one side of which each path of the planets
is laid out. It is less than a foot-and-a-half in diameter, and it is
moved within by gears, while a stationary band, marked with
twenty-four hourly intervals, embraces the outer edge. Inside this,
on the surface of the rotating disc, the twelve zodiacal signs are divided according to the proper degrees. On the interior, eight miniature discs, roughly equal in size, are visible. Of these, two occupy
the central point, so that a lower one, slightly larger, represents the
sun, and an upper one, the moon. A radius extending from the
sun to the band is able simultaneously to indicate, on the latter,
hours, while on the zodiac, months, days, and the number of degrees, and what they call the true and medial movement of the

Ex iis duo medium obtinent punctum, alter scilicet alteri infixus sic ut inferior maiusculus Solem, superior Lunam repraesentet. A Sole radius ad circulum pertingens, in ipso quidem horas, in signifero vero, menseis, dies, graduumque numerum, verumque et medium (quod aiunt) Solis motum pariter indicet. A Luna item stilus prodit, ipsius horarum index, quae scilicet inferius in limbo ipso maioris orbiculi designantur, perque lunaris epicyclii transiens centrum, signiferumque contigens, medium sui sideris declarat motum, alteri item indidem exoriens, lunarisque centrum corporis, hoc est epicyclii oram, secans, verum eius locum manifestat. Quo fit ut tarditas celeritasque, et motus cursusque omnis, et coitus item pleniluniaque visantur. Circum hos orbiculi sex, quorum unus, quem Draconis caput caudamque vocant, Solis pariter Lunaeque defectus insinuat. Reliqui planetis attributi, quorum a singulis binae eminent cuspides, motuum indices, perinde atque in Luna ostendimus. Sed ei retro quoque gradiuntur, quod nequaquam in Luna usu venit, utpote cuius in contrarium feratur epiciclios. Ita et coniunctionum et recessuum et latitudinum ratio in singulis manifesta. Est praeterea limbus alius, signiferi instar, sex illos quos dixi planetarum orbiculos superne secans, unde et orientium gradus signorum et dierum spatia, hoc est quota Sol hora exoriator, apparet. A quibus singuli planetae orbiculis deferuntur, ei vicissim, interdiu quidem ad orientem, noctu vero ad occasum, commeant. Contra, orbis ipse amplissimus, noctu ad orientem, interdiu ad occidentem, quatuor et viginti horarum spatio, planetas torquet.

3   Quae scilicet omnia cum caelo congruere ipso et ratio convincit et peritissimus quisque consentit. Nec est quod mireris incredibilia haec videri permultis, quippe (ut est apud quendam) tarda solet magnis rebus inesse fides. Vix ipsi, inquam, oculis credimus, cum

sun. A pointer likewise extends from the moon as an indicator of the lunar hours, which in fact are designated below on the circumference of the larger miniature disc; passing through the center of the lunar epicycle and touching the zodiac, it announces the medial point in the movement of the planet. Another, likewise rising from the same place, and intersecting the center of the lunar body (i.e., the rim of the epicycle), makes its true location plain. The result is that slowness and speed, motion and each orbit, along with the conjunctions and the times of the full moon, are visible. Surrounding these are six miniature discs, one of which, known as "the tail and head of the Dragon," tells us about solar eclipses, as well as lunar ones. The rest are assigned to the planets; from each one of these protrude twin needles, indicators of their movements, just as I described for the moon. But these also exhibit retrograde motion, which does not happen at all in the case of the moon, inasmuch as its epicycle goes in the opposite direction. Likewise is the system of conjunctions, reversals, and transverses made clear for each. There is, in addition, another band, the size of that of the zodiac, intersecting the aforementioned six miniature discs of the planets on top, from which the gradient movement of the constellations and the intervals of the day (i.e., the time of sunrise) may be seen. The discs by which the individual planets are conveyed move back and forth, toward east in the daytime, and toward west at night. By contrast, the very large disc bends the planets toward the east at night, toward the west in the daytime, in twenty-four-hour intervals.

Reason demonstrates — and every expert concurs — that all of 3 this is in agreement with the heavens themselves. Nor is there any reason for you to be surprised that a great many people find all this hard to believe, since, as is written somewhere, "In important matters, belief is slow to come."[4] I too, I tell you, scarcely believed my eyes, though I watched it every day. As a matter of fact, back when I read that Archimedes of Syracuse had once constructed

haec cottidie intueamur. Atque adeo cum legerem aliquando tale quiddam fabricatum Archimedem Syracusanum, vacillabat etiam in tanto auctore fides, quam plane hic noster absolvit.

4   Et ipso quidem opere laus omnis inferior est, neque enim aliter laudari pro dignitate potest, nisi ut omnem illi laudem esse imparem fateamur. Ipsum certe artificem dubium est morumne et probitatis, candorisque et sanctitatis, an ingenii magis causa admiremur, sic ut et caelitus demissum et in caelo ipso caelum didicisse existimemus.

Vale.

Faesulis, vi Idus Augustas MCCCCLXXXIIII

: IX :

Angelus Politianus Philippo Posco s. d.

1   Gratum fecisti, quod epistolam, quod versiculos misisti. Quaeris quid sentiam. Breve faciam. Recti sunt, festivi, arguti, pleni sensibus et aculeis. Dicerem consummatos, nisi non cum saeculo hoc illos, sed cum vetustate committerem.

2   Quod autem rogas cur ego has particulas 'quodquod' et 'adque' per 'd' potius quam per 't' literas notem, facile responsum. Ac ne te aut circunduci aut etiam falli putes, pauculos testes, neque eos tibi non domesticos, citabo. Est in atrio Capitolino, ad sinistram, opinor, aenei Herculis haud ita pridem inventi, marmur[1] quoddam, vetustis ac iam pene exoletis incisum versiculis, quorum initium est, 'Hercules invicte.' In eo hoc quoque legitur: 'administrandum quodannis.' Adstipulatur etiam huic scripturae ille codex antiquissimus Vergilianus, qui istic in intima palatina bibliotheca adservatur, maiusculis characteribus exaratus, de quo paucula mecum re-

something of this kind, my belief, even in the case of such a master, wavered—belief which this man of ours has now freed from doubt.

Indeed, all praise is inferior to the actual invention, nor can it 4 be praised as it deserves in any way other than by confessing that any praise is unequal to it. Certainly it is hard to say whether we should admire the engineer for his moral integrity and spotless piety, or more for his ingenuity, so that we may suppose him both to be heaven-sent and to have learned the heavens in heaven itself.

Farewell.

Fiesole, August 8, 1484

: IX :

Angelo Poliziano to Filippo Posco

You did me a favor by sending your letter, your epigrams. You ask 1 my opinion. I shall be brief. They are correct, entertaining, clever, full of conceits and barbs. I would say they were perfect, were I not comparing them with antiquity rather than with our era.

As for your question about why I spell the indeclinable words 2 *quodquod* and *adque* with a *d* instead of a *t*, the answer is simple. And to keep you from thinking that you have been misled or deceived, I shall present witnesses, ones who are no strangers to you. In the Capitoline palace, to the left (I believe) of the bronze Hercules discovered not so long ago, there is a certain marble inscribed with ancient verses, now almost entirely worn away, which begin, *Hercules invicte*. There one also reads, *administrandum quodannis*. Also supporting this spelling is that very ancient Vergilian codex,[1] conserved there deep within the palace library, written in capital letters, from which you may review with me a few bits just from

cognas licet ex Bucolicis modo et Georgicis, ne totum tibi sit volumen explicandum. 'Pocula,' inquit, 'bina novo spumante lacte quodannis.' Et paulo post, 'Ut Baccho Cererique tibi sic vota quodannis.' Et rursum, 'Degenerare tamen ni vis humana quodannis.' Item, 'Nanque omne quodannis terque quaterque solum scindendum.' Sed et illud 'adque' pari ratione notatur. Neque te moveat quod in ponte illo Anienis a Narse constructo deprehendas aliter, 'Atque interruptum continuatur iter,' nisi si illi inerudito saeculo standum putas. Ego Quintilianum sequi malim, qui in primo de oratoria institutione libro velut frigidam eludit quae sit a multis servata differentia, ut 'ad' cum esset praepositio, 'd' literam, cum autem coniunctio, 't' acciperet. Itaque veteris adhuc scripturae vestigia in eodem invenias Vergilio, ut 'Adque humiles habitare casas,' 'Ad mihi sese offert ultro,' 'Adque iterum ad Troiam,' 'Adque aere Menalcha,' 'Adque solo proceras erigit alnos,' 'Adque utinam ex vobis unus,' 'Adque adversos detinet hostis,' et mille alia, ut minore etiam quam sum pollicitus me pomerio circumscribam.

3   Quaerit insuper de nobis Lollius noster cur idem in verbo 'adgredior' servemus, ducitque eum (ni fallor) cum consuetudinis vis, tum Prisciani auctoritas, sed ego a consuetudine hac prava ad rectam vetustatem provoco. Inspice (si est ocium) librum eundem. Ita, opinor, inveneris: 'Adgredere, o magnos aderit iam tempus honores,' et item, 'Adgressi, nam saepe senex spe carminis ambos luserat.' Neque mihi sane hoc quidem loco non imbecilla etiam (adsit venia dicto) ac vacillans Prisciani videatur auctoritas, quippe qui etiam censeat errore magis scriptorum quam ratione factum ut 'adfatur,' 'adludo,' 'adrideo,' 'adnitor,' 'adsumo' 'd' retineant. Quis enim putet etiam in nomismatibus[2] ipsis Caesaribus consecratis id mendum admissum, in quibus cum alia ad eundem modum, tum certe 'adlocutio' 'd' litera notatur, nunquam 'l'.

the *Eclogues* and *Georgics*, to avoid your having to leaf through the entire volume. It reads, *Pocula bina novo spumantia lacte quodannis*, and a little later, *Ut Baccho Cererique tibi sic vota quodannis*, and again, *Nanque omne quodannis terque quaterque solum scindendum.*[2] So too *adque* is observed in equal measure. Nor should the fact that you discover otherwise on the bridge over the Aniene built by Narses[3] (*Atque interruptum continuatur iter*) influence you, unless you think we should stand on that uneducated age. I would rather follow Quintilian, who, in the first book of his *Institutio oratoria*, scorns as pedantic the distinction that makes *ad* take the letter *d* when it is a preposition, but *t* when it is a conjunction.[4] Thus you can find enduring evidence of this ancient spelling in the same Vergil, such as *adque humiles habitare casas, ad mihi sese offert ultro, adque iterum ad Troiam, adque aere Menalca, adque solo proceras erigit alnos, adque utinam ex vobis unus, adque adversos detinet hostis,*[5] and a thousand other instances, to restrict myself within even tighter limits that I promised.

In addition, our friend Lollio asks me why I observe the same   3 practice in the verb *adgredior*. Unless I am mistaken, both force of habit and the authority of Priscian are guiding him. But I shall call him forth from wandering habits to the straight and narrow of antiquity! Take a look, if you have time, at the same book. You will find this, I believe: *Adgredere, o magnos, aderit iam tempus, honores.*[6] And likewise: *Adgressi, nam saepe senex spe carminis ambos luserat.*[7] Nor does the authority of Priscian, in this very passage, fail to strike me as (pardon what I say) entirely feeble and wavering, given that he too supposes that it is more a result of writers' error than for good reason that *adfatur, adludo, adrideo, adnitor, adsumo* are made to retain the *d*. Who, indeed, would suppose that this "mistake" had been allowed even on medals dedicated to the Caesars themselves, on which, besides other words in the same fashion, certainly *adlocutio* is spelled with the letter *d*, never with an *l*.

4   Sed vos nimium belli homines ac faceti plane me luditis, qui domi Pomponium habeatis, hominem totius antiquitatis omnisque adeo literaturae consultissimum. Itaque ego ineptus etiam Athenas noctuam.

5   Sed iam vale, nostrasque Lollio occupationes excusas, ad quem scilicet nullas huic quidem tabellario literas dederim. Vale.

: X :

Angelus Politianus Ioanni Gottio Ragusino s. d.

1   Cum per hos quadragesimae proximos dies ennarrandis populo sacris literis essem occupatus, pellegi tamen libros carminum tuorum, quos mihi tu pro singulari humanitate tua multoque inter nos amore dedicaveras. Ei me scilicet cum voluptate maxima, tum maiore prorsus admiratione affecerunt. Nam quem non, obsecro, suavitas illa tanta, lepor elegantiaque versiculorum, tot aculei, sales, argutiae, tanta eruditio, tanta varietas, tantae ubique veneres gratiaeque delectent? Quis non attonitus audiat hominem ab Illyrio, mercimoniis (ut inquit Plautus) emundis vendundisque occupatum, florentibus adhuc annis, tantos in omni poetice fecisse progressus, ut non solum cum suae aetatis hominibus, sed cum ipsa plane antiquitate conferri possit?

2   Persequer nimirum singula, mi Ioannes, quae ego in tuis poematis audacter contra veteres statura deprehenderim, ni metuam

But you excessively cute and clever people clearly are making 4
fun of me, since at home you have Pomponio, an expert on antiquity in its entirety, and likewise, on all literature. I thus look the
fool, "bringing an owl even to Athens."[8]

But now, goodbye, and make the excuse of my responsibilities 5
to Lollio, since, obviously, I have given this courier no letter for
him.

Farewell.

: X :

Angelo Poliziano to Ivan Gučetić of Dubrovnik[1]

Although I have been busy expounding holy scripture to the pop- 1
ulace in these past few days of Lent, I nevertheless have finished
reading the books of your poems which, in keeping with your unmatched humanity and our reciprocal love, you had dedicated to
me. Needless to say, they provoked in me, on the one hand, enormous pleasure, and on the other, even greater admiration. Whom,
pray tell, would so much melodiousness, elegance and sophistication of verse, so many barbs, witticisms, plays on words, so much
learning, so much variation, such great and ubiquitous charms and
attractions not delight? Who would not be stunned to hear that a
man from Illyria, employed "in buying and selling merchandise"
(as Plautus says),[2] has made, while still in the flower of his youth,
such great strides in each poetic art, to the point that he may be
compared not only with people of his own times, but unquestionably with antiquity itself?

I would of course review one-by-one the things in your poetry 2
which I perceive are ready to stand boldly against the ancients, my
dear Ivan, were I not afraid of seeming either to indulge more than

ne aut plus paulo indulgere amori aut assentatiuncula aliqua videar te velle demereri. Sed plane ita sentio: esse hos libellos ita examussim perfectos atque ad summum absolutos ut ne ab Livore quidem iure valeant reprehendi. Debet autem tibi hoc nostrum (qualecunque est) saeculum, quod tu videlicet par veteribus in hoc saltem laudis genere reddidisti. Equidem gratias tibi ago immortaleis, utpote quem tu tuis illustrando carminibus immortalitate donaveris. Ita enim mihi persuadeo: tam lepida ista poemata, tam venusta, tamque ornata et pulchra, omnem esse iniuriam temporum superatura.

Vale.[1]

: XI :

Angelus Politianus Roberto Salviato suo s. d.

1   Beatus es gratiae, mi Roberte, quem sic docti certatim laudant ut tum denique docti credantur cum te maxime laudaverint. Prodigiosus honor, sed tuis meritis non indebitus. Facit enim sedulitas erga hunc ordinem tua non ut ineptus aut adulator qui laudet, sed ut impius aut ingratus habeatur qui non laudet, adeo quippe doctorum studioso favetur ut in ipsum ne invido quicquam liceat. Quare ne, quaeso, morum talium poeniteat, quibus ad splendorem nominis plus multo proficitur quam triumphis. Nunquam enim vestigia gloriae obliteratur ab hominum doctorum impressa, non ingenio dixerim, sed animo.

Vale.

a little in love or to want, by some piece of flattery, to win your favor. But this is what I really think: these books have been so precisely squared and brought to finished perfection that not even by Spite itself can they justifiably be criticized. This age of ours (however one characterizes it) is in your debt for having placed it, at least in this category of achievement, on a par with ages past. For my part, I give you my undying thanks as one on whom, by lending him the luster of your poetry, you have bestowed immortality. For I readily convince myself that those poems of yours, so elegant, so charming, and so richly adorned and beautiful, are going to survive every harmful effect of time.

Farewell.[3]

: XI :

Angelo Poliziano to his dear Roberto Salviati[1]

You are richly regarded, my dear Roberto, given that the learned   1
so compete in your praises that those who praise you most are themselves thought learned as a consequence. A mighty honor— but not unearned. For the result of your attention to this class of persons is not that whoever praises you is considered a silly flatterer but that whoever fails to praise you is regarded as disrespectful or ungrateful. Indeed, such support is given to anyone devoted to the learned that not even an envious man is allowed to say anything against him. Please, therefore, do not regret the sort of lifestyle by which far more is gained for the brilliance of your name than is by way of military success. For the footprints of glory, when pressed not into the minds, I would say, but into the hearts of learned persons, are never erased.

Farewell.

: XII :

Angelus Politianus Andreae Magnanimo suo Bononiensi s. d.

1 Neque desidiae meae neque occupationum culpa omnino est, licet harum quoque nonnulla sit, quod ad epistolam superiorem non rescripsi hactenus, sed tuae potius facilitatis, notae iam sic omnibus ut ob eam protinus et ego licere in te mihi omnia existimaverim, qui si nomen hoc humani retinere studes, quod usu pene iam fecisti tuum, nec irasci silentio nostro potes ullo pacto, nec debes.

2 Quod Miscellaneis nostris ita faves ut Atticis quoque Noctibus eas compares, equidem vellem minus vulgo humanus habereris, ut non ex ingenio tuo, semper ad officium parato scribi talia, sed ex operis ipsius merito crederetur. Tu perge nihilominus ornare isto pacto me, vel immerentem. Non minus enim plerunque delectat falsa quam vera laus, sicuti gratius accidit fere quod dono datur, quam quod ex debito.

Vale.

Florentiae, xvii Kalendas Februarias MCCCCLXXXVIIII

: XIII :

Angelus Politianus Andreae Magnanimo suo s. d.

1 Efflagitari scribis istic ab iis qui libros excudunt formis Herodianum meum (meum enim iure appello, quem quasi Latinitate

: XII :

Angelo Poliziano to his dear Andrea Magnani[1] of Bologna

The fault for the fact that I have not replied before now to your   1
last letter belongs neither to my laziness nor to my responsibilities
(though of these too there is no shortage) but, rather, to your
good nature, now so notorious that, because of it, I supposed I
could get away with any offense against you, who, if you are anxious to retain this reputation for kindness, a designation which,
over time, you practically have made your own, cannot and should
not be angry at my silence in any way.

As for the fact that you so applaud my *Miscellanea* that you even   2
compare them to the *Attic Nights*,[2] well, I would have preferred for
your reputation for kindness to have been less widespread, so that
such things would be thought to have been written as a result not
of your cleverness, always ready for dutiful service, but of the merit
of the work itself. Nevertheless, keep embellishing me in this way,
even if I do not deserve it. Very often, praise is no less enjoyable if
false than if true, given that what is given as a gift is almost a more
welcome arrival than what is paid as due.

Farewell.

Florence, January 16, 1489

: XIII :

Angelo Poliziano to his dear Andrea Magnani

You write that there is great demand on the part of local printers   1
for my Herodian.[1] (I have every right to call him "mine," since I in

donaverim). Tum rogas codicem tibi ipsum tuum remittam aliquando nostra (quod illos cupere ais) manu emendatum. Remitto,
sed (ut verum fatear) leniter potius quam severe castigatum, sic
autem ut nostra errata plura in eo quam librarii deprehendas.

2   Crediderim tamen stilo ipsi certe meo, hoc est interpretis, plus
aliquanto veniae deberi quam auctoris, quoniam meliuscule re-
spondent fere quae scribas, ubi sit liber quasi cursus, quam quae
vertas, ubi nihil extra praescriptum. Accedit et illud, quod hoc
mihi munus interpretandi quasi levioris operae fuit, utpote qui
diebus pauculis dictaverim sic deambulans. Itaque tantum abest ut
mihi inde laudem petam, ut etiam abunde pulchrum fore putem si
vitavero graviorem culpam. Quare cum amicis reliquis, tum tibi in
primis omnem huius operis defensionem non remitto solum, sed
etiam prope interdico, vosque integros ad alia reservo, quae post
edentur.

3   Sed quanquam plurimi sunt apud vos qui mihi etiam plus nimio favent, unus tamen es tu, Andrea Magnanime, cognomento
isto tuo gentilicio dignissime, quem equidem faciam plurimi, cum
quod, ex bonis ortus, et opibus flores et honoribus, tum vel
maxime quod ingenio es elegantissimo, moribus suavissimus, gratia pene quadam (quicquid agis, quicquid loqueris, immo etiam si
nihil agis nihilque loqueris) singulari, ac vultu denique ipso (quod
dicitur) homines devincis. Itaque nihil quenquam metuo ubi tu
mihi studeas. Nunquam enim male de Politiano sentiet qui placere
eum Magnanimo intelleget.

4   Unum tantum est quod a te nunc contendo. Cures, pro reliqua
in nostris rebus diligentia, ut quam minimum quasi degenerent ab

essence have granted him Latin rights.[2]) Then you ask me to send you, eventually, a copy of your own, corrected in my own hand, which is what you say those people want. I am sending it, but to tell the truth, it has been corrected rather more gently than sternly, simply to ensure that, in it, you encounter more of my own mistakes than scribal errors.

I would expect, however, that rather more leniency should certainly be shown to my style here, i.e., to the style of a translator, than is shown to the style of an author, since whatever you write (with free rein) turns out somewhat better than what you translate, limited by the original. In addition, this task of translating was a rather casual undertaking for me, as is evident from the fact that I dictated what you have over two or three days, while taking walks. It is, therefore, so far from my mind to ask for praise for this that I even think that it will be quite lovely enough simply to have avoided any serious criticism. Thus I not only absolve but even almost forbid my other friends and you especially from defending this work at all, and I keep you fresh for what will be published next. 2

But although there are many among you who support me even beyond excess, you, Andrea Magnani, most deserving of that family name of yours,[3] are the one I value most highly, you who not only, coming from a fine background, now abound in resources and high responsibilities, but who also, to the greatest degree possible, are endowed with a most cultivated intellect, the most charming of temperaments, and an elegance which, whatever you do, whatever you say — nay, even if you do nothing and say nothing — is nearly unmatched; finally, as they say, you win people's hearts with your smile. I fear no one at all, therefore, as long as you are on my side. No one who realizes that Magnani likes Poliziano will ever have a bad thought about the latter. 3

There is only one demand I now make of you: in accord with your carefulness elsewhere on my behalf, see to it that the volumes 4

285

origine quae mox volumina formabuntur, utque ne illae ipsae quidem adnotatiunculae omittantur, quas marginibus adscripsimus. Inter eas vero etiam locos (puto) tris quatuorve ad summum reperies ubi fuit excusatione utendum corrupti apud Graecos exemplaris. Ad haec vero facile procuranda obeundaque magis idoneum habere magisque ex usu tuo neminem possis quam Alexandrum Sartium, civem tuum, literatum hominem, nostrique studiosum, tum (quod ego in hac re primum puto) neutiquam in amici negocio dormitantem.

Vale.

In Rusculo Faesulano, pridie Nonas Maias MCCCCLXXXXIII

which soon will be set and printed degenerate (so to speak) as little as possible from the original, so that not even the tiny glosses I wrote into the margins are omitted. Among these you will find, I think, at most, three or four instances in which I had to make the excuse of corrupt readings in the Greek. But to look easily into and resolve all this, you could have no one more suitable or more useful to you than Alessandro Sarti,[4] your fellow citizen, a man of literary learning, devoted to me and, most importantly in my opinion, never the least bit sluggish in taking care of something for a friend.

Farewell.

In the country house at Fiesole, May 6, 1493

APPENDIX

The following letter appears in preface to Poliziano's letter on the death of Lorenzo de' Medici (here, Letter 4.2) in the edition published in Bologna not long after the event (on which see the Note to the Text).

Pamphilus ad Lectorem

Cum ante diem octavum Kalendarum Sextilis acutissimi ingenii et utriusque linguae litteratissimi Angeli Politiani epistola mihi quaedam demonstrata de obitu divi Laurentii Medicis fuisset ab exactissimis viris Andrea Magnanimo et Alexandro Sartio Bononiensibus, fuit ea quidem mihi quam gratissima ac longe iucundissima perlegenti. Neque potui maiori affici gaudio ex acumine atque stili robore. Est enim undique magis repleta varietate, ornata salibus, pluribus depicta clausulis quam viderim nusquam antea. Cogitavi ego, ut qui me tantopere delectarant, afficerem eosdem, aliquo munere refrigerii, quo mihi frequentius recondita patefaciant, qualiacumque illi Politiani amantissimi quotidie habeant et in eorum versentur manibus. Curavi igitur eam impressoribus tradere, ut et alii quoque Phoebicolae ea perfruantur voluptate mea opera, quam ego gnavia atque diligentia Felsineorum perceperam ex animo.
Vale.

Panfilo[1] to the Reader

When on July 25 a certain letter on the death of the divine Lorenzo de' Medici by Angelo Poliziano, a man of penetrating intellect and extraordinarily learning in both languages, was shown to me by those most conscientious men of Bologna, Andrea Magnani and Alessandro Sarti, it was for me, as I read through it,

an entirely welcome source of immense pleasure. Nor, as a consequence of its perceptiveness and the robustness of its style, could I have been affected by any greater feeling of joy. For everywhere you turned, it was more filled with variation, more graced with wit, embroidered with more rhythm than I have ever seen before. I began to consider how I myself might, by some product of my leisure, affect those same men who had caused me so much delight, in order that they might share with me more often whatever secret treasures they have and handle from their beloved Poliziano. I thus saw to it that the letter was handed over to the printers, so that other Apollonians might also enjoy through my efforts the pleasure I experienced so deeply through the care and attention of men from Bologna.

Farewell.

Note on the Text

❦❧❦

Fata Epistolarum

As noted in the Introduction, on May 23, 1494, Poliziano wrote a letter to Piero de' Medici, announcing completion of "el libro delle Epistole," including "una epistola a Voi proprio per proemio di tutto el libro."[1] Poliziano died in late September of the same year, before publication of the planned edition could be realized. Then, in July 1498, the Venetian press of Aldo Manuzio yielded *Omnia opera Angeli Politiani et alia quaedam lectu digna*, beginning with twelve *epistolarum libri* containing a total of 251 letters by Poliziano and others. In a prefatory letter to the entire volume, Manuzio advises the reader who may note infelicities in the texts therein to keep in mind that they were prepared for publication not by Poliziano himself, but by his friends, chiefly Alessandro Sarti of Bologna (*scito non esse haec edita ab ipso, sed ab amicis, et praecipue ab Alexandro Sartio Bononiensi*). Scholars regularly, and surely rightly, imagine Poliziano's student Pietro Crinito (Del Riccio Baldi) to figure among the "friends," though the common assertion that Sarti and Crinito "edited" the *Epistolarum libri* overstates Manuzio's clarity: as Poliziano's eighteenth-century biographer Friedrich Otto Mencke had observed with greater care, the Aldine preface simply does not tell us who did what to which texts among the volume's contents, and when.[2]

In 1943 Augusto Campana announced that "the time now seems ripe for an edition of the correspondence of Angelo Poliziano," but he set the bar high, calling for an integration of the Aldine corpus with all other known letters, including those written in the vernacular.[3] Faultless on its own terms, Campana's prospectus has left us, more than half a century later, still without any

modern edition; he also tacitly avoids the question of the letters'
Nachleben, which depended overwhelmingly on the published collection. Far more important, however, is the literary status of the
collection *as a collection*; i.e., if Poliziano assembled the letters in a
purposeful way, as of course we must assume, then dispersing the
Aldine letters among other surviving letters restores their identity
as letters but risks losing something else.

On this last subject, however, Campana expresses, in passing,
anxiety about the extent to which the Aldine presents the same
corpus assembled by Poliziano himself in 1493. As Campana
notes, Léon Dorez had earlier detected several likely posthumous
modifications, including the fascinating substitution of the name
of Pico della Mirandola's murderer with that of Crinito.[4] There
can, in fact, be no question that the collection was modified, given
that the final book in the Aldine contains letters written after
Poliziano's death. More recently, Mario Martelli has made an emphatic case for being skeptical about the contents and organization
of the entire Aldine corpus (though at least some of his arguments
depend on the overly generous assumption that confusion in the
sequence of the letters cannot be Poliziano's own doing), ending
his study by calling for an edition that, wherever possible, undoes
the damage done to Poliziano's intentions by his editors—salutary
advice which, however, seems likely to prove as paralyzing as
Campana's.[5]

In fact, preoccupation with the (admittedly dark) path that
connects Poliziano's 1493 letter to the 1498 Aldine distracts us
from what may be a more interesting story: the relationship between the corpus Poliziano left behind and the texts of the original letters as sent. Preparation of the present edition has included
collation of manuscript collections of Poliziano's letters that enable
us to reconstruct some of those original texts. Again and again,
those reconstructions reveal that the Aldine provides revised texts,
not only of the letters Poliziano wrote, but also of those he re-

ceived from others. Some of those revisions (including a number of omissions) alter the original's sense, but the overwhelming majority are stylistic, including variants in wording and word-order that are far too frequent to be attributable to scribal caprice. In the great majority of cases, the Aldine's differences represent improvements (however small), either by general criteria or by those delineated elsewhere by Poliziano himself. (It should be noted at once that the apparatus of the present edition reports only a fraction of these variants, usually only when they would affect the text's English translation.)

Who is responsible for these modifications? One could argue that Crinito, at least, was competent to make some of them. But the sheer extent of the changes, many of them maniacally minute, force us, in the opinion of the present editor, to recognize the hand of the master. Particularly poignant in this regard are Poliziano's most careful modifications, which occur not only in his own letters, but also of those of his closest friends. Pico della Mirandola, for example, enjoyed a thoroughgoing purge of infelicities.

While this factor does not obviate the concerns raised above, it does substantially raise the stakes for the Aldine, which remains our chief witness, however problematic, to an ensemble of letters that was Poliziano's not only in terms of selection and arrangement, but also (and emphatically) in terms of language, even in the case of letters Poliziano himself had not originally written. In other words, the Aldine provides our best (if imperfect) picture, not of a diverse archive of letters, but of a thematic and stylistic unity (not unlike the *Miscellanea*) to be counted among Poliziano's very last literary works.

Sources of the Text

For the reasons just given, the principal aim of the present edition is to represent the text given by the posthumous Aldine edition of

Poliziano's collected works, which begins with the letters, divided into twelve books, for which they are the *editio princeps*:

Ald   *Omnia opera Angeli Politiani et alia quaedam lectu digna.*
                   Venice, 1498. (Venetiis in aedibus Aldi Romani
                   mense Iulio MIID.)

Very rare and minor divergences among surviving copies of the edition are presumably the result of corrections of the plates during printing; the basis of the present edition is the the facsimile (Rome, Bibliopola, n. d. [1968]) from which recent scholars largely have worked.

Autograph copies of letters by Poliziano survive, but none for a letter that figures in the Aldine corpus. However, Ida Maïer, *Les manuscrits d'Ange Politien* (Geneva, 1965), lists five manuscripts that collect assorted letters by and to Poliziano (and others), all of which include letters also found in *Ald*, along with others. All have been collated with the first four books of *Ald* in preparation for the present edition.

Two of these (Torino, Biblioteca Nazionale, Ms. I.III.13$^{1-2}$ and Firenze, Biblioteca Medicea Laurentiana, Ms. Strozz. CVI) are virtually identical to the matching texts in *Ald*, the order of which they closely follow, though they also include other material. It has not yet been possible to determine whether they descend from an immediate ancestor of *Ald* or from *Ald* itself, though, at present, the latter seems more likely. They are not reported in the following notes.

The remaining three are listed below after the *sigla* employed in the present edition and followed by the dates assigned to them by Maïer, along with a list of the letters in the present volume they contain. (In several instances, a listed letter actually appears twice in the same manuscript; in such cases, readings are reported in the Notes below with the appropriate *siglum* followed by 1 or 2, according to the order in which the reported text appears.)

M   Firenze, Biblioteca Medicea Laurenziana, Ms. Plut.
XC sup. 37. Fifteenth century. A note on f. IV
records that the ms. is in the hand of Jacopo
Modesti da Prato, one of Poliziano's students.
Includes Letters 1.3, 8, 9, 12, 13, 14; 2.13; 3.7, 17, 18,
19; 4.2, 6, 7.

R   Firenze, Biblioteca Riccardiana, Ms. Ricc. 974. Late
fifteenth century. Includes Letters 1.4, 6, 9, 10, 11, 12,
13, 14, 15, 16, 17, 18; 2.6, 10; 3.1, 4, 6, 7, 8, 9, 11, 15, 16,
23, 24; 4.6, 7, 8, 9, 10.

V   Roma, Biblioteca Apostolica Vaticana, Ms. Capp. 235.
Sixteenth century. Includes Letters 1.1, 2, 3, 4, 5, 8,
9, 10, 11, 12, 14, 20, 21, 22; 2.2, 4, 10, 11, 13, 14, 15; 3.1,
4, 6, 8, 9, 11, 12, 13, 15, 17, 18, 19, 20, 21, 22, 24; 4.2, 4,
5, 6, 7, 10, 11, 12.

To these may be added the following, hitherto uncatalogued and
apparently unknown:

P   Philadelphia, University of Pennsylvania, Rare Book
and Manuscript Library, IC.P7599.514d. Eighteen
(last blank) manuscript leaves, paper, containing
seventeen letters and two orations, bound between
two printed books, the first of which is an edition of
Poliziano's Letters (*Epistolae lepidissimae*, ed. Pierre
Gillis, printed by Theodore Martens, Antwerp,
1510). A reader's note indicates that the manuscript
leaves were copied before 1511. Includes, for this
volume, Letters 1.9, 23; 2.5, 7; 3.14, 23.

M R and V often offer texts markedly different from those
found in *Ald* and can only descend from copies of the letters that
precede their final redaction for publication; the same appears to
be the case for P. While they await further research, it may be said
that they are independent — i.e., none descends from any of the
others.

Some of the letters in *Ald* also appear in manuscript and early printed copies of the works of Poliziano's correspondents. Of these, the following have been collated with *Ald*:

GFPico   Giovanni Pico della Mirandola, *Opera omnia*. Ed. Gianfrancesco Pico della Mirandola. Bologna, 1496. Includes Letters 1.3, 5, 8.

Leoniceno   Niccolò Leoniceno, *Plinii ac plurium aliorum auctorum qui de simplicibus medicaminibus scripserunt errores.* . . Ferrara, 1492. Includes Letters 2.6 and 7.

L   Lucca, Biblioteca Statale, Cod. 1415. Fifteenth century. An extensive collection of the letters of Ermolao Barbaro. It has not been consulted directly but is reported here on the basis of Ermolao Barbaro, *Epistolae, orationes et carmina*, ed. Vittore Branca (Firenze, 1943). Contains Letters 1.9, 12, 14.

The present edition also incorporates several readings from the following:

1492   An extremely rare printed pamphlet containing Letter 4.2 (on the death of Lorenzo) published in Bologna, by Francesco de' Benedetti, on July 25, 1492,[6] from which several manuscript copies of this single letter apparently descend. James Hankins kindly collated a copy in the Houghton Library of Harvard University (Inc 6151.9) against my text; he has also provided the text of its prefatory letter, included here in an Appendix. I subsequently inspected the copy in the Biblioteca Corsiniana in Rome (52.E.30).

Letter 4.3 appears among the prefatory material of Poliziano's translation of Herodian (Rome, 1493), though the text there is virtually identical to that of the *Epistolarum libri*. It is not reported here.

Editorial Criteria

Wherever possible, the manuscripts have been used to correct errors in *Ald*. Beyond this, their variants are useful first and foremost for the reconstruction of earlier versions of the text, including, of course, that of the letters as they actually were sent to their addressees. This is not the scope of the present edition. However, it was felt that a selection of these variants merited reporting here, for two reasons. First, they often provide very useful additional information about the contexts of individual letters, especially their dates, often lacking in *Ald*. Second, they offer an intriguing portrait of Poliziano at work.

As a general rule-of-thumb, meaningful variants have been reported when they would materially affect the English translation of the text. This largely obscures the fact that the bulk of the revisions consisted of very minor linguistic *pentimenti*, though the editor has included a few of these that seemed especially interesting. But wherever *Ald* omits whole phrases or passages found in the manuscripts, these invariably have been reported below (and translated in the Notes to the Translation). The result is that, with the present edition, the interested reader can reconstruct, to the extent made possible by the manuscripts, the content and the bulk of the form of the original letters.

Note, however, that *Ald* almost invariably regularizes the letters' salutations to the formula *author* (nominative) *addressee* (dative) *suo* (sometimes omitted) *s[alutem] d[icit]*, but that such changes have been recorded here only when especially conspicuous, especially since, for *M R V*, the salutations are fully reported in Maïer's catalogue.

Numerous minor errors in *Ald* have been corrected without comment. Emendations proposed by two editors subsequent to Manuzio and adopted here are reported as follows:

Asc	*Omnium Angeli Politiani operum . . . tomus prior.* Ed. Josse Bade (Badius Ascensius). Paris, 1519 (first published 1512).
Episc	*Angeli Politiani Opera, quae quidem extitere hactenus, omnia . . .* Ed. Nicolaus Episcopius. Basle, 1553. Facsimile Torino, 1971.

Where the name of an ancient author appears after a reading in the notes, the reference is to the text given by most or all modern editors.

Latin Orthography

Poliziano was famously opinionated about the correct (i.e., ancient) spelling of Latin; best known is his championing (first in *Miscellanea* I. 77) of the spelling *Vergilius* (against *Virgilius*), but he expressed his views on lesser controversies, and his own practice demonstrates still more preferences not always shared by his contemporaries. The orthography of *Ald* is consistent with Poliziano's normal practices elsewhere; it is also consistent enough internally (i.e., between Poliziano's own letters and those of others, though there are occasional variations) to suggest that he regularized the collection in manuscript and that his editors avoided undoing his choices. It is a testament to Poliziano's linguistic acumen that his usage seldom departs from that sanctioned by the rigorously classical *Oxford Latin Dictionary*, which the ITRL has adopted as its standard.

Few of the instances in which Poliziano is, instead, at variance with the *OLD* are likely to give the modern reader much trouble, and it has seemed unwise to regularize these wholesale in the present edition, given the importance that Poliziano attached to such matters, and given that *Ald*'s importance in this regard was recognized already by Ascensius, who in a prefatory letter makes a

point of his decision to respect many of *Ald*'s peculiarities. The present edition offers the following compromise between the interests of readability and a desire to provide a reasonably accurate picture of Poliziano's Latin: in accordance with the general practice of the ITRL, *v* has been substituted throughout for consonantal *u*; relatively minor and isolated divergences from classical orthography have been made to conform with the *OLD* without comment; clear and consistent preferences, however, have largely been preserved. These last are summarized for the reader's convenience below:

Ald often shows an *n* before a consonant where modern reconstructions of classical Latin have instead an *m*. Thus, *Ald* almost invariably prefers *-nqu-* to the combination *-mqu-* when it is not the result of the ordinary use of the enclitic conjunction *-que*, e.g., *nanque* (for *namque*), *quanquam* (for *quamquam*), *quenquam* (for *quemquam*), *tanquam* (for *tamquam*), *unquam* and *nunquam* (for *umquam* and *numquam*), *utrunque* (for *utrumque*), *-cunque* (for *–cumque*), etc.). Likewise, *duntaxat* (for *dumtaxat*) appears throughout. Other combinations of *m/n* with a following consonant are treated more erratically. In most cases, the present edition preserves the orthography of *Ald*; abbreviations by suspension are expanded according to *Ald*'s preferred spelling.

Other invariable or almost invariable preferences (some sanctioned though not preferred as *lemmata* by the *OLD*) that have been preserved in the present edition but which may surprise the classically-trained reader are as follows: *caeteri* (for *ceteri*), *epistola* (for *epistula*), *foemina* (for *femina*), *litera* (for *littera*), *pene* (for *paene*). (Other instances in which *Ald* prefers *ae* or *oe* where the *OLD* prefers a single *e*, however, usually have been made to conform with the latter, in-

cluding *Ald*'s consistent use of *coep-* as the perfect stem of *capio*.)

Likewise preserved are *ocium* and *negocium* (for *otium* and *negotium*) and *suspitio* (for *suspicio*), regarding which *Ald*'s preferences are emphatic; however, other substitutions of *-ci-* for *-ti-* and *vice versa* (many of which vary for the same word within *Ald* and among the manuscripts) have been made to conform with the OLD.

Somewhat less consistently, *Ald* prefers *benivolus* to *benevolus* and *monimentum* to *monumentum*, but in each case, both are found and have been left as they appear.

The diphthong *oe* occasionally appears in place of the more classical *ae* (e.g., *coelum*, *poenitet*, *moeror*) and has been left intact.

Ald frequently employs the early Latin ending *-eis* (later written *-is*, then mostly supplanted by *-es*) for the nominative and accusative plurals in the third declension. These have been preserved.

Poliziano expressly defends (in Letter 5.3) *adulescens* (against *adolescens*), *intellego* (against *intelligo*), and *toties / quoties* (against *totiens / quotiens*); here his preferences are genuinely classical, and in the very rare cases in which the rejected forms appear in *Ald*, these have been adjusted without comment.

By contrast, *adque* (for *atque*) appears only once (Letter 1.16.2) in the first four books of *Ald* (though several times in the manuscripts) outside of its explicit defense in Letter 4.9.2; the evidence suggests that the preference was early and, perhaps, especially felt when writing members of Leto's Roman Academy; there may too have been an eventual adjustment to the more familiar form by Poliziano and/or his editors during preparation of the letters for publication. In this edition, *adque* is preserved when it appears in *Ald* and noted below when it appears in the manuscripts.

Greek

The manuscripts invariably either omit or hopelessly mangle Poliziano's Greek, leaving *Ald* as the only useful witness (and thus the only text reported here, except where the manuscripts are the only source). *Ald* in turn shows a few obvious spelling errors and very frequent confusion about diacritical marks. The present edition largely corrects these without comment except where it has seemed likely that a variant spelling is Poliziano's own.

The epigram in Letter 1.7.2 re-appears later in *Ald* with the other poems of the *Liber epigrammatum graecorum* (LEG); two minor differences are recorded in the notes. The poem now also appears, with commentary, in the edition of the *LEG* of Filippomaria Pontani (Rome, 2002).

Dates

The manuscripts and, for the letters they do not contain, content and context, reveal frequent errors in the letters' dates in *Ald*, where they are always given according to the ancient Roman calendar of days and months and with years that follow the ordinary calendar rather than the Florentine one (by which the new year began on March 25). The regularization of more idiosyncratic practice in the original letters seems to have been the principal culprit, and a number of corrections and emendations are proposed by the present edition, with details in the notes.

Miscellaneous

Punctuation and capitalization have been modernized without comment. The division of the text into paragraphs, with numbers to facilitate reference, is the editor's own. Most abbreviations have been expanded, except for the *s[alutem] (p[lurimam]) d[icit]* of the salutations.

NOTES

1. Isidoro Del Lungo, ed., *Prose volgari inedite e poesie latine e greche edite e inedite di Angelo Ambrogini Poliziano* (Florence, 1867), p. 85.

2. Friedrich Otto Mencke, *Historia vitae et in literas meritorum Angeli Politiani* (Leipzig, 1736), pp. 513-14.

3. Augusto Campana, "Per il carteggio del Poliziano," *La Rinascita* 6 (1943): 437-72. Echoed by Alessandro Perosa, "Contributi e proposte per la pubblicazione delle opere latine del Poliziano," in *Il Poliziano e il suo tempo* (Firenze, 1957), pp. 89-100, reprinted in Alessandro Perosa, *Studi di filologia umanistica I: Angelo Poliziano* (Rome, 2000), pp. 3-15.

4. Léon Dorez, "La mort de Pic de la Mirandole et l'édition aldine des oeuvres d'Ange Politien (1494-1498)," *Giornale storico della letteratura italiana* 32 (1898): 360-4.

5. Mario Martelli, *Angelo Poliziano: Storia e metastoria* (Lecce, 1995), pp. 205-65. Martelli proposes, among other things, extensive reorganization of the letters of books two and three.

6. IGI (*Indice generale degli incunaboli delle biblioteche d'Italia* [Rome, 1943-81]), no. 7957. See also Alessandro Perosa, *Mostra del Poliziano nella Biblioteca Medicea Laurenziana, Manoscritti, libri rari, autografi e documenti (Firenze, Sept. 23 - Nov. 30, 1954): Catalogo* (Florence, 1955), p. 181 (no. 267).

Notes to the Text

☙❧

BOOK I

LETTER II

1. *V adds* vobis

2. urbis huius *Ald* : vestris *V*

3. Eustathius *Ald* : Constantinus *V*

4. nostro *Ald* : vestro *V*

5. pulcherrimum *Ald* : *V omits*

6. Martem . . . praecipue *is my emendation* : Martem Romani originis auctorem Martem Caesariani potissimum colebant milites orbis terrarum victores Martem praecipuus *Ald V*

7. quae *is my emendation* : quod *Ald V*

8. Ethrusca *V* : Etrhusca *Ald*

9. nostris *Ald* : vestris *V*

10. civibus nostris tibique *Ald* : tuis civibus tibique potissimum *V*

11. qui . . . asciveritis *Ald* : *V omits*

LETTER III

1. et alios *Ald M* : reliquos *V GFPico*

2. amici hominis *Ald* : alienas *M GFPico* amicitias *V*

3. *V adds* ut censorem. *M GFPico add* non adeo mihi bellus videor ut censorem vel negligem vel accusem.

4. metuam . . . Suffenus *Ald V* : ne sim, ut inquit ille, Suffenus timeam. Nimirum omnes fallimur, nec videmus manticam quae in tergo est. *M GFPico*

5. *M GFPico add* tam multo praesertim studio, tam ex animo efflagitanti. Quod si is essem a quo in eiusmodi [cuiusmodi *M*] re tibi gratia referri

303

posset, non tacerem Graecum illud, Lisippum Apellis et Apellem Lisippi alterna opera vicissim uti solitum.

6. *M adds* et quotiens Laurentium Medicem cui sylvam tuam dubiam cum vestro qui laudatur Virgilio palmam facis nuncupasti videris, totiens me ei tuis verbis intelligat esse deditissimum. Iterum vale. Quarto Idus Martias 1483.

LETTER IV

1. quique . . . frontis *Ald R* : qui severe a me haud rugosae frontis homine *V*

2. provocatum *Ald R* : provocantem *V*

3. nihil offendi *Ald* : non offendi nihil *R V*

4. Sed . . . voluntatem *Ald* : In illis non iudicium tibi sed voluntatem *R V*

5. n⟨a⟩evus esset *Ald* : aliquis nevus *R* : aliquis nevus inesset *V* : aiebat interim decentiorem faciem esse in qua aliquis naevus fuisset *(Seneca, Contr. 2.12.2)*

6. senecio *Asc* : seneno *Ald R V*

7. *V adds* ut est apud Horatium

8. Vale *Ald* : Sytham Manuelemque et Albericum ac siqui praeterea apud te sunt . . . [*sic*] iube, queso, salvere meis verbis. *V* : Scytham Manuellemque et Alberinum ac siqui propterea sunt [*a very corrupt Greek word follows, probably* ἀνώνυμοι *vel sim.*] iube, quaeso, salvere meis verbis. Laurentius iunior delitiae nostrae legit epistolam tuam. Agnovit humanitatem. Multa ut rescriberem iniunxit. Tuus plane est totus. Sed [*the rest of this sentence is an indecipherable series of Greek and Roman letters, all probably transcribing Greek in the exemplar*]. Vale, atque indicem Graecorum codicum quos recens emeris mitte ad nos, quaeso, hisque adde comitem (si potes) Manuellis epistolam. *R*

LETTER V

1. non *Ald* : haud *V GFPico*

2. genus *Episc* : generis *Ald V GFPico* : Id genus *is good Latin, but Pico may have written* id generis, *which is not, on mistaken analogy with expressions like* id temporis.

3. singulatim *V GFPico* : sigilatim *Ald*

4. semper . . . versatus *Ald* : antea pre omnibus abhorrerem ab huiusmodi institutis *V*

5. *V GFPico add* Indicem grecorum librorum qui mecum hic diversantur [*i.e.*, deversantur] cum Manuelis epistula quod tue litere postulant ad te mitto. Indicem tuorum itidem desidero. Laurentio iuniori meo nomine salutem dicito, ad quem scripturus eram, sed pudor deterruit ne videar hominem literis compellare.

LETTER VI

1. *R adds* Delitiae nostrae iunior Laurentius Medices in oculis te gerit, amat, miratur, emulari etiam cupit. Iubet se tibi commendem dicamque ipsius plurimam salutem. Tu nos ama, ut facis.

LETTER VII

1. τά γε *Ald* : τάδε LEG

2. πυρκαϊῆ *Ald* : πυρκαϊᾷ LEG

LETTER VIII

1. quanquam *Ald V GFPico* : verum *M*

2. nostram *Ald V GFPico* : vestram *M*

3. cinnus *Ald M V* : cignus *GFPico*

4. genuina *Ald V GFPico* : propria *M*

5. iniuria *Ald GFPico* : malitia *M* : iniuria materia *V*

6. *M V GFPico add* Ego quidem ut te ipsum ita tua omnia amo atque desidero, tum eo magis quod te mihi exemplar proposui ad quod effingar [*V corrects to* effingam], etsi is es quem ut sequi omnes debent ita consequi pauci possunt.

7. *M adds* Idibus Iul. 1481 Mirandula.

Letter ix

1. Nec . . . saepe *Ald* P R $V^{1,2}$: *M omits*

2. M R V^2 *add* Venetiis : *R* V^2 *continue* Idibus Septembris [Septenbribus V^2] 1484

Letter x

1. Hermolao Barbaro Patritio Veneto responsum V^2

2. sibi R $V^{1,2}$: *Ald omits*

3. R $V^{1,2}$ *add* ego

4. R V^2 *add* Adque [Atque V^2] haec hactenus. Tu quaeso non gravere [ne gravare V^2] cum tibi otium [ocium V^2] contingit scribere ad nos aliquando. Quidquid [Quicquid V^2] enim abs te proficiscetur, id apud me monumentum [monimentum V^2] aere perennius.

5. R *adds* Florentiae : V^2 *adds* Flor. Nonis Non. [*sic*] 1484

Letter xi

1. trichas *Ald V* : chrichas *R* : *The h should be retained (also at 2.13), since P. likely thought the Latin word was derived from the Greek* θρίξ, *pl.* τρίχες, *"hair," as did Du Bois. Cf. Egidio Forcellini, Lexicon totius Latinitatis (many editions), s. v. tricae.*

2. V *adds* Non. Ian. Flor. 1488

Letter xii

1. Si . . . Quamquam *Ald M R V* : Ut ferramenta oleo, sic amicitiae officiis extersae non contrahunt aeruginem, contrahunt neglectae, verbum popularius quam verius. Sortiuntur inclinationes et segmenta mundi terram, et alius coeli positus atque vultus divisa rebus omnibus ingenia distribuit, ut surdis etiam brutisque rerum amicitiae et inimicitiae suae constent inde. Affectus quoque caecos et quae Graeci propria et anaetiologeta vocant huc ferimus accepta. Hinc et simpathiae et antipathiae tota et sola ratio. Sentit hanc vim et homo, sed *L*

2. istaec siderum *Ald M R V* : ista coeli *L*

3. Huiusque *Ald* : Huius *L* : Uniusque *M R V*

4. iunxit *Ald M R V* : vinxit *L*

5. Nihil . . . excutitur *Ald L M V* : *R omits*

6. quandocunque . . . referre *Ald M R V* : quandoque referam *L*

7. *L adds* Mirandulam nostrum iubeo salvere. Mediolani, vii Cal. Febr. MCCCCLXXXVIII. *M adds* Mirandulam nostrum et decus et lumen salvere iubeto [*corrected to* iubeo]. Mediolani. Klis. Febr. MCCCCLXXXVIII. *R adds* Mirandulam nostrum et decus et lumen salvere iube. Mediolani. *V adds* Mirandulam nostrum et decus et lumen salvere iubeo. Mediolani. Klis. Febr. 1494.

LETTER XIII

1. *M R add* Patriarche Aquileiensi : *M continues* Oratori Veneto

2. magnificisque *Ald* : magnisque *M R*

3. *M adds* Florentiae, vi Id. Mar. 1491.

LETTER XIV

1. Hermolaus Angelo Politiano viro eruditissimo *R* : Hermolaus Barbarus Orator Venetus Patriarcha Aquileiensis Angelo Politiano s. d. *V*

2. ut amico . . . ut *Ald* : quantum amico et benivolo sed quantum Politiano id est *L* : quoniam amico et benivolo sed quia Politiano id est *M R V*

3. *R adds* Romae. *M adds* Romae, pridie Kal. Aprilis 1491. *L V add* Romae, pridie Klas. Apriles MCCCCLXXXXI.

LETTER XV

1. nescioquid . . . sum *is my emendation* : scio quid scripturus sum *Ald* R^2 : scio quid scripturus sim R^1

LETTER XVI

1. super *Ald* : sub *R*

2. atque *Ald* : adque *R*

3. adque *Ald R V* : *see the introductory remarks to these notes.*

4. αὖ *Ald* : εὖ *Apollonius (Loeb)*

5. τισι Νόμοις *is my emendation* : Tisinomis *Ald R* : *Florence, Biblioteca Medicea Laurenziana, Ms. Plut. XXXII 9, P.'s source for the scholia on Apollodorus (2.1010–14, ed. Wendel), has* Νυμφόδωρος ἔν τισι νόμοις *(Nymphodorus, frag. 15 Müller); P. summarizes the scholion in his autograph notes in Paris, Bib. Nat., Ms. Gr. 3069, f. 233v, where he writes* ut Nymphodorus ἔν τισι νόμοις *(Gianvito Resta, "Apollonio Rodio e gli umanisti," in Enrico Livrea and G. Aurelio Privitera, Studi in onore di Anthos Ardizzoni, Rome, 1978, p. 1123). The meaningless transliteration of the title in Ald and R cannot be P.'s doing; I have thus restored this and the following Xenion to the Greek.*

6. ξένιον *is my emendation* : Xenion *Ald* : Xenieti *R*

7. Maias *is my emendation* : Mart. *Ald* : *R omits the date. Ald thus impossibly dates this letter before the preceding one, to which it is a reply. The emendation is one possible solution.*

LETTER XVII

1. *R adds* literarum alumno

LETTER XVIII

1. in *Ald* : erga *R*

2. Demetrius . . . remuneratur. *Ald* : *R omits*

LETTER XIX

1. eos : eo *Ald*

LETTER XX

1. seorsum . . . quibus *Ald* : in quibusdam syllabis quas etiam notasti *V*

2. fecisti *Ald* : proferebas *V*

3. de *Ald* : pro *V*

4. ἀνδροτῆτά τε καὶ *Homer* : ἀνδρότητα καὶ *Ald*

5. haud mora *P.'s printed corrections to the* Miscellanea *(see Notes to the Translation)* : aut mora *Ald* : illico *V*

6. aut cum *Asc (and Vergil)* : autem *Ald V*

7. hoc *V* : hec *Ald*

8. plane *Ald* : sane *V*

LETTER XXI

1. te *V* : *Ald omits*

LETTER XXII

1. Item *Ald* : Iam *V*

2. Quin *Ald* : Cum *V*

LETTER XXIII

1. praescribuntur *P* : perscribuntur *Ald*

2. Februarias *is my emendation* : Ianuarias *Ald* : *This letter cannot have come a year after the preceding, to which it is a reply.*

BOOK II

LETTER II

1. laterculorum aut calcis *Ald* : et laterculorum et calcis *V*

2. Vale *Ald* : Bonon. xi Kl. Febr. 1490 *V*

LETTER IV

1. quem . . . mutaverat *Ald* : cum eum . . . mutavisset *V*

2. mihi . . . addidit *Ald* : quantum bonae spei proposuit *V*

3. et indoctorum . . . fugarentur *Ald* : *V omits*

4. *V adds* aliquem

LETTER V

1. commendari *Ald* : laudari *P*

2. invidiae . . . occaecati *Ald* : invidia ac livore onerati *P*

3. iam *Ald* : *P omits*

4. delectant *Ald* : oblectant *P*

5. *P adds* sed

LETTER VI

1. inscitiam *Ald R* : ignorantiam *Leoniceno*

2. maxime *R Leoniceno (and Pliny)* : *Ald omits*

3. quae . . . elegantia *Ald Leoniceno* : quae est in tuis literis elegantia *R*

4. quam *R (and Ovid)* : qua *Ald Leoniceno*

5. Graeci *Ald Leoniceno* : *R omits*

6. ocimi *is my emendation* : ocymi *Ald R Leoniceno*

7. *Leoniceno adds* Florentiae, die iii Ianuarii MCCCCLXXXXI.

LETTER VII

1. capessendam *P* : capescendam *Ald Leoniceno*

2. deprehendere *Ald P* : reprehendere *Leoniceno*

3. magis *Ald P* : *Leoniceno omits*

4. quae . . . appellatur *Ald Leoniceno* : *P omits*

5. quoniam *Ald Leoniceno* : *P omits*

6. pati *Ald Leoniceno* : *P omits*

7. tunc *Ald Leoniceno* : *P omits*

8. *P adds* in

9. et Plinius ipse *Ald Leoniceno* : Plinius *P*

10. aliquando *Ald Leoniceno* : *P omits*

11. aliquanto *is my emendation* : aliquando *Ald P* : aliqn. *Leoniceno*

12. ex Serapionis . . . Plinio *Ald Leoniceno* : *P omits*

13. Vale *Ald P* : *Leoniceno adds much more (see note on the translation)*

LETTER X

1. Hieronymo Donato *Ald* : Domino Hieronymo [Ieronimo *R*] Donato Veneto Patritio *R V*

2. affers *Ald* : facis *R V*

3. nostra *Ald (presumably in agreement, as Du Bois notes, with an understood silva; cf. 2.11.2)* : nostro *R V*

4. sed . . . interpretor *Ald R* : *V omits*

5. atque *Ald V* : adque *R*

6. ipse *Ald* : ipsi *R V*

7. nedum *Ald* : ne *R V*

8. cupimus *Ald R* : cupiamus *V*

9. magnete *Ald* : magneti *R V*

LETTER XI

1. MXVD *Martelli* : M·xii·D *Ald* 1485 *V* : *The Aldine date of 1488 cannot be right, since it is impossible that three and a half years separate this letter from Donà's original letter to Pico (2.9) that sparked the triangulated exchange. Martelli (p. 257), who also notes the inconsistency between the date given and the letter's reference to a* quinquennium *since P.'s visit to Venice (1480), emends as indicated, plausibly supposing a misreading of* v *as* ii, *though the error could also spring from a misread arabic numeral somewhere along the way; the date of 1485 is, in any case, confirmed by V.*

LETTER XII

1. comparari *is my emendation* : comparare *Ald*

2. hec *Ald*

LETTER XIII

1. elegantia *Ald V* : indulcentia *M*

2. *See note on 1.11.1.*

3. legatur *Ald V* : *M omits*

4. ergo *Ald V* : ego *M*

5. quam *Ald M* : *V omits*

6. facias *V M* : faciat *Ald*

7. cogito *Ald V* : agito *M*

LETTER XV

1. flatus *Ald* : proflatus *V*

2. sacerdotia *Ald* : sacerdotii *V*

BOOK III

LETTER I

1. *R adds* a laudato viro

2. *V R add* te

LETTER II

1. poterant *Asc* : poterat *Ald*

LETTER III

1. condicto *Asc* : condito *Ald*

2. excogitari *Asc* : excogitare *Ald*

LETTER IV

1. *R V add* Preceptori Ducis Urbinatis

2. *Ald adds* enim

3. lassare *Ald* : laxare *R V*

4. *V adds* inter amicos

5. superstitiosam probationem *Ald* : superstitionem *R* : superstitiosam ac curatam probationem *V*

6. est est . . . amicitiae examen *Ald* : ad manum quo amicum examinem Lidius lapis *R* : est ad manum quo amicum examinem Lydius lapis *V*

7. *V adds* uno tamen excepto Demetrio, communi preceptore nostro, quem equidem audacter cum quovis veterum conmiserim. Is ita amorem erga nos libravit suum ut nescias uter magis ab illo, sed scias tamen utrumque maxime amari.

LETTER VI

1. illex *Ald V* : ille *R*

2. myrothecii *Asc* : mitheci *Ald R V*

3. *V adds* et quam de se promovit expectationem pervertitur

4. seculi *R V* : saeculis *Ald*

5. scatens *Ald V* : sentiens *R*

6. niti *Ald R* : uti *V*

7. is *R V* : his *Ald*

LETTER VII

1. me *M R* : *Ald omits*

2. tibi *M* : *Ald R omit*

LETTER VIII

1. ut eius pene *Ald* : ut eius plane *R* : at enim plane *V*

2. atque *Ald V* : adque *R*

3. *R V add* nunc

LETTER IX

1. *R V add* uni

2. noster *Ald R* : *V omits*

LETTER X

1. quadraginta *is my emendation* : quandringentis *Ald* : *see note to translation*

2. dedit *is my emendation* : iit *Ald*

LETTER XI

1. Pontifici *Ald* : Episcopo $R^{1,2}$ *V*

2. $R^{1,2}$ *V add* Alexandrum

3. dici . . . delectatus *Ald* $R^{1,2}$: visus mihi sum medius fidius cum istis colloqui Musis *V*

4. eam *Ald* $R^{1,2}$: demum *V*

5. Isocrates $R^{1,2}$: Socrates *Ald V*

6. meo infixus cordi *Ald* R^1 : in affixus cordi meo R^2 meo cordi affixus *V*

7. iam pluris *is my emendation* : etiam pluris *Ald* R^1 : pluris etiam R^2 *V*

LETTER XII

1. orbum . . . patrem *is my emendation* : nunquam patrem quam orbum esse *Ald V*

LETTER XIII

1. literarum *Ald* : literatorum *V Asc*

LETTER XIV

1. loquaris *Ald* : *P omits*

2. vero *Ald* : autem *P*

3. conplura *Ald* : plura *P*

LETTER XV

1. Pontifici *Ald V* : Episcopo *R*

2. praecepi *V (and Vergil)* : percepi *Ald R (abbreviated in the latter)*

3. esse crediderunt *Ald* : crediderunt *V* : tradiderunt *R*

4. Quod . . . unus *Ald R* : Quod autem scribis et ipse puto, non continuo peius esse quod variet *V*

5. Quapropter . . . habitus *Ald R* : quapropter nemo unquam suffragiis omnibus habitus est *V*

6. *V adds* ipsum

7. Hunc . . . superstitiosumque *Ald R* : Ciceronem vero Calvus exanguem et tritum, Brutus aut⟨em⟩ fractus [*sic*] et elumbem, alii inflatum et tumentem, nec satis pressum, exultantemque supramodum et superfluentem, alii contra ieiunum atque aridum, quidam parum antiquum, quidam etiam in dicendo viro molliorem, postremo alii frigidum superstitiosumque *V*

8. fortius *R V* : potius *Ald*

9. verum . . . agnosces *Ald* : tum denique cognosces *R* : tunc denique verissimum cognosces *V*

LETTER XVII

1. grates *Ald* : laudes *M* : gratias *V*

2. Pythagorei *Ald* : Pythagorici *M* : *V omits*

3. Orphei *Vergil* : Orphi *Ald M V*

4. languoris *is my emendation* : langoris *Ald M V*

LETTER XVIII

1. *M V add* clarissimo viro

2. *M V add* Mediolani *before* Idibus

3. *V adds* Tuus Iachobus Antiquarius

LETTER XIX

1. propriis *Ald M* : *V omits*

2. obstreperet *V M* : opstreperet *Ald*

3. debeam *M V* : debebam *Ald*

4. cuilibet *Ald* : cuiuslibet *M V*

5. *Ald adds* ut

6. istius *M*

7. Gellius *M V* : Agellius *Ald*

8. publico bono *Ald M* : *V omits*

9. hominem *Ald V* : *M omits*

10. meditabar *M V* : meditabatur *Ald*

11. *M V add* iam

LETTER XX

1. Clarissimo viro D. Angelo Politiano s. *V*[1] : Iacobus Antiquarius clarissimo viro Angelo Politiano s. *V*[2]

LETTER XXI

1. Clarissimo viro Angelo Politiano s. *V*

2. possit *Ald* : potest *V*

3. demonstrasti *Ald* : demonstrabas *V*

4. displicinae *Ald* : discipline *V*

5. delationem *Ald* : delectationem *V*

6. iucundissimi *V* : iucundissima *Ald*

7. molliant *Ald* : emolliant *V*

8. vos *Ald* : nos *V*

9. xvi Calen. Ian. MCCCCLXXXVIIII *Ald* : xii Klas. Ianuarias 1489. Ia. Antiquarius *V*

LETTER XXII

1. me *is my addition* : *Ald V omit*

2. te *V* : *Ald omits*

LETTER XXIII

1. quod *Ald P* : qui *R*

2. inter eas *is my emendation* : interea *Ald P R*

3. enim is sum *Ald P* : in eorum sum numero *R*

LETTER XXIV

1. obsecrationes *R V* : observationes *Ald*

2. assereret *Ald* : asseveraret *R V*

3. probe R V : prope *Ald*

4. ut . . . doctus V : ut autem ego ne doctus *Ald* : ut ego ne aut doctum quidem sum R

5. R V *add* consueverim

6. MCCCCLXXXXI *Ald* : MCCCCLXXXI V : R *omits*

BOOK IV

LETTER I

1. Maias *is my emendation* : Aprilis *Ald* : *Lorenzo died April 8; as Antiquari tells at the beginning of the letter, he received the news April 10 and returned to Milan two days later, writing to P. soon thereafter.*

LETTER II

1. possumus . . . possimus M : possimus et si quid tamen possumus V : possimus et si quid tamen possimus *1492* : possimus *Ald*

2. audivimus *Ald* M : audimus V *1492*

3. vidit autem statim *Ald* V *1492* : M *omits*

4. *so punctuated by Ald* : *1492 punctuates* Venerat, iam : M V *have no punctuation*

5. in M V *1492* : *Ald omits*

6. M V *add* sanctitatem

7. iam *Ald* V *1492* : M *omits*

8. foedaretur M V *1492* : sedaretur *Ald*

9. aliae quae *Asc* : aliaeque *Ald* M V *1492*

10. proprium *Ald* V *1492* : propri(a)e M

LETTER IV

1. veras V : vera *Ald*

LETTER V

1. sim *Ald* : sum cum V

LETTER VI

1. electa *Ald V* : lecta *M R*

2. vires *is my emendation* : veris *Ald M* (*though the scribe of M seems confused*) : viris *V* : *R omits*

3. est *R* : *Ald V omit*

4. aditur *Ald V* : auditur *R*

5. literati *Ald V* : literarii *R*

6. *V adds* Florentiae *before* xi Calendas

LETTER VII

1. *R V add* Veneto Patricio Philosophiae doctori egregio (*R omits* egregio)

2. *R V add* portae

3. didicimus *R V* : dicimus *Ald*

4. simulati *Ald* : dissimulati *R V*

5. duos *Ald* : *R V omit*

LETTER VIII

1. qua de *Asc* : quale *Ald*

LETTER IX

1. marmur *Ald* : marmor *R* : *cf. Quint., Inst. 1.6.23.*

2. nomismatibus *is my emendation* : nomismatis *Ald R*

LETTER X

1. Vale *Ald R* : 1483 et 1484 *V*

Notes to the Translation

꽃॰밌

In preparing the following notes, the editor has made liberal use of the commentary on most of the letters by Francois Du Bois (Franciscus Silvius), occasionally supplemented by briefer remarks by Josse Bade (Jodocus Badius Ascensius), both consulted in a copy of the latter's 1519 edition of Poliziano's collected works in the Berenson Library of the Villa I Tatti in Florence.

The thumbnail identifications of Poliziano's contemporaries are based, where possible, on the incomplete *DBI = Dizionario biografico degli italiani* (Rome, 1960–), supplemented by Mario Emilio Cosenza, *Biographical and Bibliographical Dictionary of the Italian Humanists and the World of Classical Scholarship in Italy, 1300-1800* (2nd ed., Boston, 1962). Both of these have also guided the spelling of proper names in the translation.

An indispensible tool, especially for Poliziano's descriptions of books, has been Silvia Rizzo, *Il lessico filologico degli umanisti* (Rome, 1973).

The timeline that appears as an appendix to Ida Maïer, *Ange Politien: La formation d'un poète humaniste, 1469-1480* (Geneva, 1966), has also been consulted.

Abbreviations of the titles of ancient works are generally those employed by Simon Hornblower and Antony Spawforth, eds., *Oxford Classical Dictionary* (3rd ed. rev., Oxford and New York, 2003), itself abbreviated *OCD*

BOOK I

LETTER I

1. The Cumaean Sibyl wrote her prophecies on palm-leaves, which the wind then scattered through her cave (Vergil, *Aeneid* 3.444ff. and 6.74ff., with the notes of Servius).

2. P. is referring to his influential *Miscellanea* (properly, *Miscellaneorum centuria prima*), a collection of one-hundred mostly philological essays he published in 1489, later included in the Aldine edition of his collected works (and in its successors) and now available (though not widely) in the edition of Hideo Katayama (Tokyo, 1989). At his death P. left unfinished a second installment, unknown until the autograph draft resurfaced in the last century, published with a facsimile in four volumes in 1972 but far easier to find in reduced form as Angelo Poliziano, *Miscellaneorum centuria secunda*, edd. Vittore Branca and Manlio Pastore Stocchi, *editio minor* (Florence, 1978).

3. P. thus begins with the ancient writer who looms largest over Renaissance debates about proper models of Latin style; P. had built his own reputation in part by resisting Cicero's formidable influence. Most of the writers in the ensuing catalogue of alternatives — ranging from the most familiar to the most obscure — may be found fairly easily in the OCD, to which the reader is referred.

4. I.e., Pliny the Younger, who published nine books of letters, here called "orator" for his panegyric on the emperor Trajan.

5. P. is probably thinking of Sidonius, *Epistulae* 1.1.1, where an appeal to Pliny as a model is immediately followed by a reference to the *rotunditas* of Symmachus.

6. The story is told by Quintilian, *Institutio oratoria* 8.1.2.

7. Philostratus, *Dialexeis* 1. See also Plato, *Phaedrus* 267B.

Letter II

1. The ms. adds "by you" (plural), and the appearance of *vos* here and at other points in the letter as it appears in the ms. suggests that Piero was not the original addressee, at least not alone.

2. P. here abruptly abandons the prevailing view that Florence had been founded by the Roman dictator Sulla; for this and the other controversies behind this letter, see Nicolai Rubenstein, "Il Poliziano e la questione delle origini di Firenze," in *Poliziano e il suo tempo* (1957), pp. 101–10. Gaius Julius Caesar Octavianus (the future Augustus), Marcus Antonius

(Mark Antony), and Marcus Aemelius Lepidus formed the so-called Second Triumvirate in 43 BC.

3. A *iugerum* roughly corresponds to two-thirds of an acre. The street plan of central Florence still largely conforms to that of the ancient city that grew on the grid of the original Roman military colony.

4. The work in question is the anonymous *Libri regionum*; the "extremely old copy" is Florence, Biblioteca Medicea Laurenziana, Plut. 29, 32; for the textual confusion that provoked P.'s errors (the work is not by Frontinus; the *Libri regionum* actually assign the foundation to the members of the *First* Triumvirate; the apparent reference to three *imperatores* is the result of corruption of *triumviri*), see Rubenstein, op. cit., pp. 105–6.

5. Vergil, *Eclogues* 1.30ff, on which Servius claims that Amaryllis figures Rome. Lydus (see next note) gives this arcane name as Eros.

6. Philadelphus is the sixth-century Greek writer usually known as Lydus, born in Philadelphia in Lydia (whence his usual name and that used by P.). His discussion of the name of Rome is in his fragmentary *De mensibus* 4.73. The Floralia were a licentious festival celebrated in ancient Rome in late April and early May, notionally in honor of the goddess of flowers, Flora.

7. Lydus, *De mensibus* 4.75. Eustathius, *Dionysius Periegetes* 803.

8. Pliny the Elder, *Natural History* 3.52.

9. Ptolemy, *Geography* 3.1.43. Pliny the Elder, *Natural History* 14.36.

10. Procopius, *De bellis* 7.5.1ff.

11. The "Forerunner" is John the Baptist; the building in question is Florence's famous Baptistery.

12. Hesiod, *Astronomy* frag. 180.

13. Silius Italicus, *Punica* 8.476–7

14. The ms. omits, "in return . . . city."

LETTER III

1. Extremely influential (though controversial) philosopher and adventurer protected by Lorenzo de' Medici; he was P.'s closest friend and associate.

2. The elaborate (and largely untranslatable) erotic and sadomasochistic humor of this sentence depends on personifying Pico's poems as *Amores* (not simply "love-affairs" but also "Cupids"; *Amores* or *Erotes* was Pico's title, as Letter 1.7.1 makes clear) and ultimately turns on two technical terms: the Latin phrase *ad unguem*, "to the point of being ready for the fingernail," which strictly refers to a carpenter's ultimate test of the smoothness of a join but which was used broadly in Latin to describe the successful finish of any work of art (especially poetry), and the symbol of the "skewer" or "dagger" (†), *obeliscus* here instead of the more usual transliterated Greek *obelos*, used in textual criticism since antiquity to mark spurious lines of verse.

3. Pico had instead written, "I am not so sensitive that I would be bothered by someone else's erasures; I do not have such a fine opinion of myself as to ignore or reproach a critic."

4. Suffenus, Catullus tells us (*Carmina* 22; see also 14), was a generally witty fellow who, however, erroneously thought his own poetry excellent. ("There is no one whom you will not detect being a Suffenus in one thing or another," Catullus warns.) In his original letter, Pico had added the poem's often cited summation of its own lesson, "Of course we all are deceived, and no one sees the knapsack he carries on his own back"; Poliziano's omission of this makes the literary reference somewhat more difficult to recognize.

5. Pico had continued, "especially when he is asking you with so much enthusiasm and so earnestly. But if I were the sort of person from whom, in a matter of this kind, repayment of a debt of gratitude could be expected, then I would not fail to mention what the Greeks say: by reciprocal effort, Lysippus was accustomed to make use of Apelles, and Apelles, of Lysippus."

6. One of the mss. adds, "And as often as you see Lorenzo de' Medici, to whom you dedicated your *Sylva* — you give him a prize to share with your

praised Vergil [?] — let him know by your own words that I am utterly devoted to him. Again, farewell. *March 12, 1483*."

LETTER IV

1. Servius on Vergil, *Eclogues* 2.31.

2. The citizens of ancient Rome were divided, according to wealth and political office held, into three "orders": the senatorial order, the highest, followed by the equestrian and plebeian orders. There was in addition an elite hereditary class of patricians.

3. I.e., Ovid (Publius Ovidius Naso), known here through Seneca the Elder, *Controversiae* 2.2.12.

4. P. included a copy of his Latin translation (done in 1479) of the *Manual (Enchiridion)* of Epictetus.

5. See Horace, *Satires* 1.7.19–20.

6. The mss. add, "On my behalf, tell Scytha, Manuel, Alberico, and any other anonymous persons there with you to look after themselves. Lorenzo junior, my joy, read your letter. He recognized your humanity. He told me many things to add in reply. He is utterly yours. But [*here the text is corrupt*]. Farewell, and please send me a list of the Greek books you have bought recently, and add, as a companion, if you can, Manuel's letter."

LETTER V

1. The Epictetan *anechou kai apechou* (Latin, *sustine et abstine*), often translated "bear and forbear," which circulated as an emblem in the Renaissance.

2. Respectively, the schools of Aristotle, of Plato, and of Zeno (founder of Stoicism, so called from the *stoa* or portico in which he lectured).

3. Pico's original instead ended as follows: "As your letter requests, I am sending the list of Greek books which are staying here with me, along with Manuel's letter. I would like a comparable list of yours. Say hello for me to Lorenzo junior, to whom I was going to write, but modesty prevented me, not wanting to seem to accost the fellow by sending a letter. Farewell."

LETTER VI

1. Horace, *Odes* 1.6.11–12.

2. In a painting of the moments before Iphigenia's sacrifice, the Greek artist Timanthes depicted profound grief in the faces of all the bystanders, but veiled the face of the girl's father, Agamemnon, as beyond his powers of representation (Pliny the Elder, *Natural History* 35.75).

3. Homer, *Iliad* 8.282, where Agamemnon praises Teucer for the Trojans he has just slain.

4. Manuel Adramitteno, Cretan friend to both Pico and P., instructed the former in Greek.

5. A mountain near Athens famous for its honey.

6. Homer, *Iliad* 6.236, where Glaucus exchanges his gold armor for the bronze armor of Diomedes.

7. P. apparently is referring to the difference in antiquity between the Greek spoken in Attica (i.e., Athens) and that used in Greek cities in Sicily and Italy; given his use of *graecissare* later in the letter, he probably has in mind Plautus, *Menaechmi* Prol. 11–12.

8. The ms. adds, "My joy, the younger Lorenzo de' Medici, keeps you before his eyes, loves you, admires you, and even wants to emulate you. He instructs me to put in a good word on his behalf and to give you his best regards. Love me, as you are doing."

LETTER VII

1. On this poem, see the commentary in Pontani's edition, pp. 216–221.

LETTER VIII

1. A proverbial expression that probably derives from a joke at Cicero's expense at the theater, recorded by Seneca, *Controversiae* 7.3.9 and Macrobius, *Saturnalia* 2.3.10.

2. Pliny the Younger, *Epistulae* 4.3.5. Modern editors give the addressee as Arrius Antoninus, but some manuscripts have *Hadriano*.

3. Pico had continued, "I love and long for all things yours, as I do regarding your very person, all the more in that I have placed you before

me as a model according to which I may be shaped, even if you are some-one whom, just as all should follow, few can reach."

4. One of the mss. adds, *July 15, 1481, Mirandola.*

LETTER IX

1. P. and Pico had been with Barbaro in Venice in June and July of 1491.

2. The mss. adds, *Venice, September 13, 1484.*

LETTER X

1. Homer, *Iliad* 2.370–74.

2. "Barbarism" is of course a play on Ermolao's surname. P.'s *e barbaria media receptum iri* is in keeping with the letter's military metaphors and may faintly echo the celebrated recovery of the Parthian standards by Augustus in 20 BC (*signis receptis* on Augustan coins and inscriptions). But *barbaria media* probably should also be understood as "half-barbarism," playing on the root meaning of *barbarus* (the word mimics the incomprehensible speech of foreigners, originally non-Greeks) to suggest macaronic (and, more simply, ungrammatical) Latin and Greek.

3. Vergil, *Aeneid* 2.349–50, where Aeneas rallies the youth of Troy in flames.

4. The mss. end instead as follows: "But enough about that. Please do not regard it as too much of a burden to write to us from time to time when you have a moment free. Whatever originates from you is 'a monument more lasting than bronze' [Horace, *Odes* 3.30.1] in my eyes. Farewell. *Florence, November* (?) 5, 1484."

LETTER XI

1. P. may be thinking of *Nicomachean Ethics* 8.5.1, which, however, takes a more guarded view of the matter.

2. Horace, *Ars Poetica* 191–2, describing the only appropriate conditions for the use of a *deus ex machina*.

3. Literally, "Saleable wine has no need of hung ivy." Erasmus, in his *Collectanea adagiorum* (404) of 1500, borrows the proverb from this letter,

explaining that it seems to be of recent coinage and that it refers to the contemporary practice of using ivy (perhaps painted representations thereof) to indicate the presence of a tavern to passersby.

4. Florentine ambassador in the frequent employ of Lorenzo de' Medici.

5. Dioscorides Pedanius, first-century AD author of a pharmacological work Περὶ ὕλης ἰατρικῆς (*On medical material*), on which Barbaro composed a commentary around 1481–2, published posthumously as *In Dioscoridem corollarii* (Venice, 1516).

6. The ms. adds, "*January 5, Florence, 1488.*"

LETTER XII

1. One of the mss. begins very differently: "Like metal tools cleaned with oil, so friendships cleaned with dutiful actions do not attract rust, though they will do so if neglected. This saying is more popular than true. Tendencies and territories divide the face of the earth, and, for all things, each position and face of heaven assigns particular innate qualities, so that even the attractions and repulsions of dumb and unthinking entities in nature are derived from this source. I believe that this is also the source both of invisible influences and of what the Greeks call 'unmotivated properties'; from the same comes the complete rationale for sympathies and antipathies. Human beings experience this force too."

2. The "Herculean knot" binds the two snakes twined around the caduceus (Macrobius, *Saturnalia* 1.19.16); it also referred to a bandaging technique (Pliny the Elder, *Natural History* 28.64); Barbaro notes the former in his gloss on the latter in *Castigationes Plinianae*, vol. 3 (28.21). Barbaro may also have been aware that a Roman bride's girdle was tied in a "Herculean knot."

3. It is perhaps impossible to capture in English Barbaro's delicate wordplay here, which depends on the differences in meaning between *gratias habere* (to feel grateful), *gratias agere* (to express thanks), and *gratias referre* (to repay a favor), subject of a well-known chapter (41) of Lorenzo Valla's *De linguae latinae elegantia*, Barbaro's likely inspiration.

4. The last phrase turns on the ability of *fides* to designate "faith" or "trust" in a general sense as well as financial "credit"; probably Barbaro

also intends a double reading of *professione nominis*, which first depends on the technical use of *nomen* to designate an entry in an account, but which also suggests that the men of Lorenzo's circle have frequent occasion to pronounce the "name" of their benefactor (see 1.9.1, *mihi multus in ore Politianus est*).

5. The mss. add, "I instruct [*or* Do instruct] our friend Mirandola, both grace and glory, to look after himself. *Milan, January 26 [or February 1], 1488.*"

LETTER XIII

1. The mss. add, *Patriarch of Aquileia, Ambassador of Venice.*

2. The ms. adds, *Florence, March 10, 1491.*

LETTER XIV

1. The ms. adds, *Ambassador of Venice, Patriarch of Aquileia.*

2. The mss. add, *Rome, March 31, 1491.*

LETTER XV

1. The original Roman names for July and August. Leto is referring to fragments of an inscription of an ancient Roman calendar known as the *Menologium rusticum Vallense.*

2. Valerius Flaccus, *Argonautica* 5.140ff.

3. With or without my emendation (see Notes to the Text), Leto presumably is referring to the *epistola longa* mentioned in 2.17, not apparently to be identified with any of the letters in the collection.

4. Lorenzo de' Medici's uncle, partner in the Medici bank, papal treasurer, and major patron of Florentine painters.

5. Possibly Fabrizi da Camerino (Fabricius Camers).

LETTER XVI

1. See *Miscellanea* 43.

2. Valerius Maximus, *Argonautica* 5.147–9.

3. Apollonius of Rhodes, *Argonautica* 2.1009–14.

4. Nymphodoros of Amphipolis; on P.'s source, see the note to the text.

5. Apollonius of Rhodes, *Argonautica* 2.377–8.

6. *Orphica, Argonautica* 741; Strabo, *Geography* 12.3.18.

7. Apollonius of Rhodes, *Argonautica* 1.71–4.

LETTER XVII

1. The ms. adds, *Protégé of Letters.*

2. Antonio Petreio, participant in the Roman conspiracy, eventually canon of S. Lorenzo and head of the Laurentian Library.

3. Leto's Latin echoes Martial, *Epigrams* 1, Pref.

4. I.e., he will pay attention to P.'s revision and "polishing" of his compositions, figured very often in Latin by the "file" (*lima*) used by sculptors to finish their works. But Leto probably is making a dirty joke that my English paraphrase only partially captures.

5. A reference to Leto's house on the Quirinal Hill in Rome.

6. Demetrius Chalcondyles, Athenian, professor of Greek in the Florentine Studium.

LETTER XVIII

1. Horace, *Odes* 1.13.18.

LETTER XIX

1. Pico had published his *Heptaplus*, a mystical and allegorical reading of the creation story in Genesis, earlier that year.

2. A close echo of Pliny the Elder's description of Cicero as *extra omnem ingenii aleam positus*, "placed above all risk (*alea*, dice or any other game of chance) of genius" (*Natural History* Pref. 7).

LETTER XX

1. On this letter, and P.'s attempts to correct the criticized verses in the *Miscellanea* after printing, see Guido Pette, "Un verso di Callimaco nella tradizione latina del Poliziano," *Sileno* 7 (1981): pp. 205–17.

2. P. is referring to Homer and Vergil's hypermetric verses, i.e., verses that exceed the limits of dactylic hexameter by at least one syllable.

3. Homer, *Iliad* 24.6.

4. Vergil, *Aeneid* 6.724.

5. Vergil, *Georgics* 4.442.

6. Vergil, *Aeneid* 1.432.

7. *Miscellanea* I 80, where Poliziano translates Callimachus, *Hymn* 5 ("On the Bath of Pallas").

8. Statius, *Thebaid* 10.660.

LETTER XXI

1. Horace, *Satires* 1.4.100.

2. The Aldine instead reads "I was hoping to be able. . ." The omission of *te* is probably an error, but if not, it seeks to make Guarini worry about damaging his *own* reputation, rather than P.'s.

3. Horace, *Ars Poetica* 389.

4. Terence, *Eunuchus* 452–3.

5. Niccolò Leoniceno (on whom see Letter 2.3) and Ludovico Pittorio of Ferrara.

6. *Magnifico* (in Italian) was an honorific epithet in general use; only in later memory did it become particularly attached to Lorenzo "the Magnificent."

BOOK II

LETTER I

1. Filippo Beroaldo the Elder, Bolognese humanist who edited and commented on numerous classical texts, perhaps best known for his work on Apuleius.

LETTER II

1. The Latin juxtaposes *politura* ("polish") and P.'s name; Beroaldo's meaning plays on their similarity.

2. Expression borrowed from Apuleius, *Apologia*, 40.7

3. I.e., P. owes Pico a reciprocal "hello from Beroaldo" (*nomen* as "name"), but doing so will leave B. even deeper in P.'s debt (*nomen* as "debit").

4. The ms. adds, *Bologna, January 22, 1490.*

LETTER III

1. Niccolò Leoniceno taught mathematics, philosophy, and medicine in Ferrara.

2. The precise reference of *barbari* (which in origin designated people beyond the reaches of the Greek-speaking world) is elusive here. Leoniceno and P. will use the word in Letters 6 and 7 to refer to Arab writers on science and medicine; here too he may allude to the preservation of Greek philosophy by Arab scholars, though he may instead mean to conjure the "barbarous" Latin of scholastics, a topos that goes back to Petrarch.

3. Homer, *Iliad* 1.3, adjusted into the present tense. Leoniceno is referring to the saving of lives through medicine.

LETTER IV

1. Valerius Maximus 2.10.8.

2. Plutarch, *Moralia*, 985–992, "Bruta animalia ratione uti" (Loeb vol. 12, pp. 492–533).

3. Pausanius 6.10.2. Glaucus was taken as a boxer to the Olympic Games by his father, who had watched him use his hand as a hammer to refit a plough. Inexperienced and near defeat, Glaucus was led to victory by his father's shouted reminder.

4. Antaeus was a giant, eventually slain by Hercules, who derived his strength from contact with his mother, the Earth.

5. The ms. omits, "and that the battalions . . . leaders."

LETTER V

1. Two figures from Homer's *Iliad*: Thersites, hideously ugly, mocked Agamemnon; wise old Nestor offered the Greeks frequent counsel.

2. Vergil, *Aeneid* 5.754.

3. Vergil, *Aeneid* 1.78–9.

LETTER VI

1. Whatever Leoniceno "dictated" (*dictata* probably indicates a written text but suggests something less than a finished treatise) seems to have been lost. Leoniceno published the present letter from Poliziano, followed by his own reply in the form of a letter (a much longer version than what appears here as Letter 2.7), as *De Plinii et aliorum in medicina erroribus*, first printed in Ferrara, December 18, 1492, a text which prompted wide debate about Pliny's accuracy.

2. Latin name for the influential Persian physician and writer on science and philosophy Ibn Sina (980–1037).

3. The comparative of *antiquus* regularly means "important" in classical Latin, but here P. also means a bit of a joke: "nothing should be *more ancient* than the truth."

4. These and similar aphorisms circulated widely, attributed to Aristotle.

5. Pliny the Elder, *Natural History* 16.145 and 24.81. At the center of the complicated debate that follows here and in the following letter are two Greek botanical terms: κισσός ("ivy," corresponding to the Latin *hedera*) and κίσθος ("rock-rose," a different plant altogether). Pliny notes their similar spelling at 24.81, but already at 16.145 he had himself confused them, borrowing from Theophrastus, *Enquiry into Plants* 6.2.1, a description of the latter, mistaking it for the former. (It is worth noting in passing that the *De Plinii erroribus* makes it clear that Leoniceno correctly read κίσθου in this passage in Theophrastus; thus its corruption into κισσοῦ in the vulgate is not part of the controversy here.) Broadly speaking, Pliny and Poliziano are wrong; Leoniceno is right. But a textual corruption in 24.81 slightly muddies the waters. The passage should end *Sub his maxime nascitur hypocisthis, quam inter herbas dicemus* ("Primarily under these sprouts the *hypocisthis*, which we shall mention among the herbs," as Pliny in fact does at 26.49). P. and Leoniceno both, however, in their copies of the text, read the final phrase as *quam inter hederas diximus* ("which we have mentioned among the ivies"), which would then refer to

what proves to be a nonexistent earlier discussion. P. takes the blind reference as the real source of Leoniceno's objections (this is not true in the *De Plinii erroribus*, but we do not know how Leoniceno made the case in the earlier text; the fact that P. felt the need to recapitulate Leoniceno's arguments suggests they were not entirely clear, at least to P.) and will propose eliminating the problem by marking a full stop after *hypocisthis* and attaching *quam inter herbas diximus* to the beginning of the sentence which begins at 24.82, where it would instead modify *cissos*. P.'s subsequent arguments largely seek to minimize the (correct) impression that Pliny's description at 16.145 cannot be of ivy.

6. Ovid, *Heroides* 3.1: *Quam legis a rapta Briseide littera venit . . .*

7. Ovid, *Heroides* 4.1: *Quam nisi tu dederis caritura est ipsa, salutem, / mittit Amazonio Cressa puella viro.* The double sense of *salus* is virtually untranslatable: Phaedra sends Hippolytus her *salus* ("hello"), but she will lack *salus* ("health") unless he gives her back her *salus* (both senses).

8. Pliny the Elder, *Natural History* 16.145.

9. Theophrastus, *Historia Plantarum* 3.18.6.

10. A play on Pliny's name, Gaius Plinius Caecilius *Secundus*.

11. See note on 1.11.4.

12. P.'s use of *alea* to refer to evaluation (and the fluctuating values it produces) is probably inspired by Pliny the Elder, *Natural History* Pref. 7. Compare Guarini's language in 1.19.2 (where Pliny is the certain source).

13. See note on Letter 3.1. P.'s meaning is, of course, aggressively ethnocentric (vindicating the authority of Greco-Roman science), but note that the English "barbarian" is more strongly pejorative than the Latin; "foreigner" is in some ways a closer translation.

14. The text published by Leoniceno adds, *Florence, January 3, 1491.*

LETTER VII

1. Johannes Serapion (Ibn Sarâbî) "the Younger," Arab author, ca. 1100, of a widely influential pharmacological compendium, translated into Latin in the thirteenth century as the *Liber aggregatus in medicinis simplicibus*, first printed in Venice in 1479, later also known in vernacular translations.

2. Barbaro's *Castigationes Plinianae* would first be printed in 1492–93, in Rome.

3. The list probably was not included in the letter proper and, in any case, is not included in the published correspondence. It doubtless provided the basis for (and may in fact be identical to) Leoniceno's *De Plinii et aliorum in medicina erroribus* (see note on previous letter).

LETTER VIII

1. Giovanni Gioviano Pontano, major humanist of the Aragonese court in Naples.

2. Ferdinando I (Ferrante) of Aragon, King of Naples, died January 25, 1494.

3. An ancient prayer uttered at the beginnings of things.

4. Alfonso II of Aragon, King of Naples for less than a year, abdicating in favor of his son in January 1495.

5. He replaced his father as Duke of Calabria upon the latter's ascent to the throne of Naples; upon his father's abdication he became Ferdinando II (Ferrandino), King of Naples, ruling until his death in October 1496.

6. Federico of Aragon, another son of Ferdinando I, becoming King of Naples upon the death of his nephew, Ferdinando II.

7. City on the easternmost point of Italy's "heel," conquered in 1480 by the Turks under Mehmed II, reconquered by the Aragoneses in the following year.

LETTER IX

1. Girolamo Donà (or Donato), Venetian poet, humanist, and widely active political figure.

2. Line from a lost Greek comedy, known to Donà through its quotation by Cicero, *Letters to Atticus* 4.11.2.

3. The second of P.'s *Silvae*, delivered as the introduction to P.'s 1483 course on the *Works and Days* of Hesiod and immediately printed, available in the *ITRL* in Charles Fantazzi's edition (2004) of the *Silvae*.

4. Theocritus, *Idylls*, 7.44.

5. Theocritus, *Idylls*, 7.37, slightly modified.

LETTER X

1. An echo of Cicero, *Ad familiares*, 7.1.6, where *subinvitare* makes its only appearance in classical Latin, also in reference to writing (and to *amor*, later theme of P.'s letter).

2. P. mingles numerous sources here. The quotation is of Horace, *Odes* 3.4.5–6 (*me ludit amabalis / insania*), though P. possibly is also thinking of the same author's *leuis insania* at *Epistulae* 2.1.118. The image of the poet deluded about his own talent, however, comes not from these passages, though it is frequent in Horace (see *Epistulae* 2.2.105ff., and the *Ars Poetica* generally); P.'s most conspicuous source is instead Catullus 22 (on the bad poet Suffenus, see Pico's letter to P., 1.3), which ends with the Aesopian image of the knapsack (*mantica*; see Phaedrus 4.10), likewise deployed by Horace, *Satires* 2.3.299, and again by Persius, *Satires* 4.24, though neither is referring specifically to poets. The same poem by Persius is, in turn, a possible inspiration for P.'s general theme of self-knowledge, continued from the previous sentence (*mecum congrediar* perhaps paraphrases *in sese . . . descendere* of line 23).

3. P. is quoting Horace, *Odes* 1.18.14–15. But also on his mind is *Letters to Atticus* 13.13.1, where Cicero gives his revision of his own *Academica* a rave review, *nisi forte me communis φιλαυτία decipit*.

4. Homer, *Iliad* 6.236.

5. P. thus represents Donà's *amor non vulgaris* with a pair of homoerotic images. Achilles lends his armor to his beloved Patroclus in Homer, *Iliad* 16.129ff. (P. takes up the question of the lovers' relative ages in *Miscellanea* I, 45.) P.'s source for the *naevus in articulo* (this last word can properly refer to any joint) is Cicero, *De natura deorum*, 1.79, quoting what presumably is a Latin translation of a (now lost) Greek original by Alcaeus, early lyric poet from Lesbos.

6. Hesiod, *Works and Days*, 349–50, though P. may be thinking of Cicero's paraphrase at *De officiis* 1.48.

7. Plautus, *Menaechmi*, 15.

8. In a striking contamination of two elements of the same story (best known in its telling by Ovid, *Metamorphoses* 3.339–510, which exploits the same parallel), P. describes Echo using terms (*regerere*, used of visual reflection, and *refundere*) more obviously suited to Narcissus and his pool. Reference to the myth perpetuates the letter's motif of self-knowledge.

9. The Aesopian fable is given by Phaedrus, *Fabulae*, 1.3. But P. takes his language from the allusion to the story in Horace, *Epistulae* 1.3.19–20.

10. A play on the literal meaning of *picus*, "woodpecker."

11. Plato, *Ion*, 533D-E, where the magnet is a metaphor for the transitivity of inspiration from one person to another.

12. The Greek term continues the echo of Plato's *Ion*. Given the general theme of dependence on the divine, it seems likely that the relatively rare Latin word *depluit* is borrowed from Columella, *De re rustica*, 10.206 (where modern editors prefer to read *defluit*), describing Jupiter's "violent rain into the lap of his mother" (Earth), impregnating her with spring.

13. Language borrowed from Seneca, *Epistulae*, 56.5, the only appearance of *pausarius* in classical literature. It is difficult to capture the double meaning of P.'s *modos dat*, not only "he marks time" but also "he provides the ways" (of praising you).

14. In mythology, a utopian early period of human history, often described in literature; especially influential were Hesiod, *Works and Days*, 109–20, and Ovid, *Metamorphoses* 1.89–112.

15. I.e., like Icarus, son of Daedalus, whose wings of feathers and wax melted when he flew too close to the sun. The story was often told, but P. here closely follows Horace, *Odes* 4.2, which begins "Whoever, Iulus, is eager to emulate Pindar hangs on wings which Daedalean care joined with wax, soon to give his name to a translucent sea." P. borrows directly from line 25, *multa Dircaeum levat aura cycnum* (which in Horace refers to Pindar, not to his imitators or to Icarus). The echo of Horace's paean to Pindar is anticipated by P.'s use of the Greek word for the work of the rhapsode (properly a professional reciter of poetry).

16. Pointed borrowings from Plato, *Phaedrus*, 238D, where Socrates likewise describes himself as νυμφόληπτος (literally, "captured by nymphs") and observes that he is falling into a dithyramb (a kind of song or poem originally in honor of Dionysus). Socrates first attributes his ecstasy to the dialogue's suggestive and sacred surroundings but then immediately transfers the blame to the attractiveness of his interlocutor and returns to his subject-matter: the nature of (pederastic) love.

17. With *furor* P. introduces a third ancient term (after *inspirare* and ἐνθουσιασμός, above) used to describe poetic inspiration. But given the context — an admission of the promiscuity of his admiration — P. almost certainly is directing Donà to Horace, *Satires* 2.3.325, "fierce passions (*furores*) — a thousand for girls, a thousand for boys."

18. P.'s translation of the Greek expression λευκὴ στάθμη.

19. The "Florentine Plato" is Marsilio Ficino.

LETTER XI

1. Hesiod, *Works and Days* 350.

2. A reference to the ancient debate between "Attic" and "Asian" rhetorical styles.

3. Pseudo-Phalaris, *Epistulae* 23.1.5–6.

4. Giuliano de' Medici, killed April 26, 1478, in the cathedral of Florence as part of the so-called "Pazzi Conspiracy," subject of P.'s *Coniurationis commentariolum*, though Donà's *carmen* would seem to suggest not this (prose) work but, rather, some lost work in verse.

5. Theocritus, *Idylls* 9.33–5, modified.

LETTER XII

1. Third-century AD commentator on Aristotle. Donà's Latin translation of his *On the Soul*, complete by January 1491, would be printed in Brescia, September 13, 1495.

2. Donà was in Milan April 1489 to June 1490 (officially he was Venetian ambassador until March 1, 1490).

3. The beginning of the second book of Alexander's *On the Soul*.

LETTER XIII

1. "Fescennine verses" were bawdy songs performed at Roman weddings. *Bacchanalia* (properly, the Latin name for Greek mysteries of Dionysus, famously suppressed as licentious by Roman authorities in 186 BC) may be hyper-classicism on P.'s part for "Carnival."

2. This last phrase is borrowed from Horace, *Satires* 1.9.21 (*demitto auriculas*), where it is used of a donkey resentful of the load on its back. See also Erasmus, *Adagia* 4.6.100.

3. Referring to the practice of placing a ring in the animal's nose, by which to lead it. See Erasmus, *Adagia* 2.1.19.

4. P. was an ordained priest and (from 1486) canon.

5. P.'s variation on Scipio's *dictum* about leisure, preserved (through Cato) by Cicero, *De officiis* 3.1.

6. P. borrows *quam oculatissimo loco*, "in the most conspicuous place possible," from Pliny the Elder, *Natural History* 34.24, where it describes the Roman Senate's instructions for the placement (the site chosen is the speaker's platform in the Forum) of a statue in honor of Gnaeus Octavius, murdered while on an embassy.

7. I.e., P. will tear at Ermolao's clothes to impede his departure.

8. Niccolò Seratico, Milanese humanist.

9. P. completed his translation of the *Problemata* by August 1478, as we learn from a letter appended to the text in the Aldine edition of P.'s *Opera omnia*.

10. Domenico Grimani, major Venetian political figure, likewise well-known for his formidable collection of books and artwork.

11. Echoing ancient technologies of erasure (i.e., not necessarily his own) familiar as *topoi* of classical literature, P. means that he is thinking of erasing the whole thing (with a sponge) if Donà confirms the duplication, thus avoiding the work of revision (with a file).

12. Jacopo Antiquari, literary and political figure from Perugia and close friend of Poliziano and of other humanists, and Jacopo Gherardi of Volterra, humanist, churchman, and diplomat.

LETTER XIV

1. This is Donà's meaning, though his wording is awkward, as is the connection to the previous idea. The final image is from Cicero, *De officiis* 3.77, who gives a rustic proverb according to which an honest person is one "worthy of a game of finger-flashing in the dark" (*dignum . . . quicum in tenebris mices*), where *micare* refers to a game (*mor[r]a* in Italian) by which one guesses the sum of the fingers held up by oneself and one's opponent. Donà's *dimicare* might reflect ignorance of this technical meaning, but it is more likely that he is simply trying to vary or render more generally applicable the language of his source.

2. Pindar, *Pythian Odes* 1.85–7.

3. Literally, "to whom it will seem rather soiled," or better, "in whose eyes it will become rather soiled."

LETTER XV

1. I.e., Letter 2.14.

2. I.e., Poliziano.

3. Giorgio Merula, humanist, originally from Alessandria, active in Venice and, from 1485, in Milan. Francesco (sometimes given as Gianfrancesco) Dal Pozzo or Puteolano, humanist and major figure in the early printing of classical literature.

BOOK III

LETTER I

1. Callimachus Experiens, adopted name of Filippo Buonaccorsi, humanist, member of Leto's Roman Academy, who fled Italy for Poland over the alleged plot against Paul II in 1468, of which he was accused of being the mastermind.

2. Achilles, replying to a speech by Odysseus seeking to persuade him to set aside his anger and return to the war (Homer, *Iliad* 9.312–13).

3. See Plautus, *Pseudolus* 945. Erasmus (*Adagia* 3.6.27) identifies *obtrudere palpum* as proverbial for deception, though his attribution of the expres-

sion to the calming of restless horses by the hand-clapping of their trainers is certainly incorrect.

4. P.'s meaning turns on a line from a lost play by the early Roman poet Naevius, several times quoted by Cicero (*Tusculan Disputations* 4.67; *Letters to His Friends* 5.12.7, 15.6.1; see also Seneca, *Letters* 102.16), in which Hector says, "I am pleased to be celebrated by you, father, that is, by a celebrated man" (*Laetus sum laudari me abs te, pater, a laudato viro*).

5. From "marketable" on, P. uses the language of slavery; here he alludes to the impossibility under ancient law for slaves to own property in their own right.

LETTER II

1. Direct reference to Horace, *Ars Poetica* 343, the most famous contribution to the long debate about the relative merits of the *dulce* and the *utile* in poetry.

2. See Letter 2.9.4, note 3.

3. Quotation of Horace, *Ars Poetica* 143: *ex fumo dare lucem.*

4. Vergil, *Aeneid* 6.487–8.

LETTER III

1. Humanist from Padua who moved to Urbino to become tutor of the son of Duke Federico da Montefeltro.

2. Isocrates, *To Demonicus*, 1.

3. Presumably Odasio's translation of an essay from Plutarch's *Moralia*, "On Envy and Hate."

LETTER IV

1. The mss. add, "Tutor to the Duke of Urbino."

2. See Letter 1.12.1, note 2.

3. *Oculeus totus* is borrowed from Apuleius, *Metamorphoses* 2.23, which likewise mentions Lynceus, an Argonaut of legendary eyesight. Momos criticized Hephaestus' design of the human body for not providing windows in its chest through which its true thoughts might be visible

(Lucian, *Hermotimus* 20). Epicurus here is known through Seneca, *Letters* 7.12.

4. The mss. are slightly different: "For I have, ready at hand, a touchstone [*lapis Lydius*] with which to test a friend."

5. Seneca, *Letters* 9.6, quoting the Stoic philosopher Hecaton of Rhodes, who offers this non-medical *amatorium*: "If you want to be loved, love."

6. The Greek verb derives from the word for stork, the chicks of which bird were celebrated for piously nurturing their parents. One of the mss. here continues, "an exception having been made, however, for Demetrius [Chalcondyles], our common tutor, whom I would of course match with absolutely any of the ancients. He so balances his love toward us that you cannot tell which is loved more by him, but all the same you know that each of us is loved as much as one can be."

LETTER V

1. Pietro Contarini was a Venetian nobleman, poet, and historian.

LETTER VI

1. See Catullus 1.1.

2. The conjunction of *austerus* and *dulcis* is properly an intentional oxymoron, though P. is invoking both words' extended meanings as descriptions of agreeable style.

3. See Cicero, *Letters to Atticus* 2.1.1.

4. See Cicero, *De finibus* 3.7.

5. Plutarch, *Life of Demosthenes* 2.

6. See Cicero, *Letters to His Brother Quintus* 1.1.3.

7. The ms. adds, "and overturns the expectation of himself he first put forth."

8. Reference to Q. Fabius Maximus Verrucosus (this last name literally means "warty"), who famously saved the Roman state by delaying pitched battle with Hannibal and hence was called Cunctator (the "delayer").

9. Federico da Montefeltro had been Duke of Urbino until his death in 1482.

10. See Juvenal, *Satires* 4.89–90.

11. Guidobaldo da Montefeltro, son of Federico.

12. P. probably simply means that he would need a longer letter, though Bade proposes that *longiore subsellio* refers instead to the size of the audience. The phrase is based on Cicero, *Letters to His Friends* 3.9.2, regarding which, however, the precise meaning of *longi subselli* is debated.

13. Plautus, *Pseudolus* 608.

14. Expression borrowed from Plautus, *Bacchides* 247.

15. Ovid, *Fasti* 5.410, of the dying centaur Chiron, cared for by his pupil Achilles.

16. Language borrowed from Vergil, *Eclogues* 1.23.

LETTER VII

1. Venetian humanist best known as the author of an official history of Venice.

2. I.e., Sallust (C. Sallustius Crispus), who has Catiline describe healthy friendship as a coincidence of desires and dislikes (*Bellum Catilinae* 20.4).

3. Martial, *Epigrams* 3.5.11–12.

LETTER IX

1. Giovanni Lorenzi was secretary to the Venetian cardinal Marco Barbo and, later, papal secretary and Vatican librarian (1485–92); he translated several works from Greek.

LETTER X

1. Marco Lucido (or Lucio) Fazini, known as Phosphorus, Roman humanist.

2. Tuscan humanist with close ties to the Medici, active in Rome.

3. Pliny (*Natural History* 35.36.85; see also Valerius Maximus 8.12 ext. 3) relates that the Greek painter Apelles had thus reproached a cobbler

who, having first criticized his depiction of a figure's shoes, proceeded to comment on the rendering of the legs.

4. For the meaning of *papyros et chartas* here, see Rizzo, p. 26. The precise reference of the metaphor used by Phosphorus, who is complaining not about ornament but about particular kinds of scholarship, is elusive. Du Bois notes that *encaustum atramentum* is the ink used by printers; Phosphorus would thus allude to printed (i.e., woodcut) decorations; *encausticas tabellas* would either be free association from this ("encaustic paintings," though these properly have nothing to do with the practice in question) or else mean simply "prints." (Note that, given the subsequent mention of Calderini and Valla, the "four hundred" of the Aldine cannot be right.) In any case, the general sense seems to be that the authors of forty years before, with the exception of Valla and Calderini, darkened rather than illuminated their subjects.

5. Influential humanist and teacher active in Rome; Poliziano's posthumous attacks on his scholarship in the *Miscellanea* drew disapproval.

6. Crassus (making an exception of Antonius), in Cicero, *De oratore* 1.172.

7. Cicero, *Sen.* 13 (which, however, observes that we cannot all be Scipiones or Maximi) and *De officiis* 1.118.

8. For this last, "republican" view, see Leonardo Bruni, *History of the Florentine People* 1.38.

9. All figures associated with prophecy. Hammon was an oracular Egyptian deity whom the Greeks and Romans associated with Zeus/Jupiter. Roman prophecy was largely dependent on the Etruscans and their methods.

10. Phosphorus is adapting Martial ventriloquizing Rome celebrating Trajan: "Come nobles of the Parthians and chiefs of the Seres, come Thracians, Sarmatians, Getae, Britons: I can show you a Caesar" (*Epigrams* 12.8.8–10).

LETTER XI

1. The ms. has instead, "When I read this letter, it seemed to me—so help me!—that I was conversing with those Muses of yours."

2. Theocritus, *Idylls* 7.37.

3. Isocrates (the Aldine and the ms. have "Socrates," but this is unlikely to be P.'s own mistake), *Busiris*. Libanius, *Enc.* 4 (Foerster 8.243). Lucian, *The Fly* (*Muscae laudatio*). P. knows of this lost work by Favorinus from Gellius, *Noctes Atticae* 17.12; the *febris quartana* was so called because the fever recurred every "fourth" (as the Romans counted; we would say "third") day and generally indicates malaria.

4. Martial, *Epigrams* 9.48.3.

5. Cicero, *De senectute* 85.

6. Plutarch, *Life of Demetrius* 11.3.

7. P. aptly defines the crucial but difficult word *humanitas* (embracing a range of qualities distinct to human beings) with a pair of important Greek terms: *philanthropia*, kind and generous feeling toward other people, and *paideia*, properly the education of children but used by Greek writers to designate intellectual culture more generally (compare the Latin *doctrina*, though its meaning is narrower). His source is Gellius, *Noctes Atticae* 13.17, who, however, restricts the proper meaning of *humanitas* to *paideia*.

8. Literally, "with a beam-nail," a proverbial expression for fixity.

9. See Quintilian, *Institutio oratoria* 12.9.18, attributing the phrase to a farmer's preparation for every contingency. See also Erasmus, *Adagia* 3.1.34.

10. The strap (often wrongly imagined as a girdle) of Venus first appears in Homer, *Iliad* 14.214–21. For the image, P. also depends on Libanius; see *Miscellanea* 11.

LETTER XII

1. Cicero, *De finibus* 1.7, reports that the Roman satirist Lucilius quipped that he wrote not for erudite Romans but for Tarentines, Consentines, and Sicilians (probably in reference to the corruption of their Latin by Greek). In the same passage he announces that he, by contrast, is ready to be read even by Persius, alluding to verses by Lucilius from which he quotes at *De oratore* 2.25, "I'm not interested in Persius as a reader: I

want Laelius Decimus" (i.e., Lucilius wants a less erudite critic). On the learning of this Gaius Persius, about whom nothing else is known, see *Brutus* 99.

2. I.e., out of what I earned (as "interest") on my friendship with Alessandro I have created another friendship (and thus more "capital"). Pliny the Elder, *Natural History* Pref. 23.

3. In assent or submission.

4. The Hernici were a people that occupied the part of Latium that includes modern Segni, seat of Phosphorus' bishopric. Vergil (7.683–4) notes their rocky habitat, and Servius reports that their name was derived from a Sabine word for "rocks."

5. In antiquity, the *curia* was the meeting-place of the Roman senate; in post-classical Latin it often means "court," including, of course, the papal one, probably meant here. But the classicizing phrase *curiae et fori* also suggests a fairly generic meaning (see Seneca, *Letters* 77.17, where the conjunction of *curia* and *forum* is metonymic for "politics" by naming its two principal arenas).

6. Cicero, *Letters to His Friends* 2.12.2; *Pro Plancio* 66.

7. Juvenal, *Satires* 2.167, of Rome, but to ironic purpose: this is Juvenal's vicious satire of various kinds of homosexual practices in Rome, and the assertion (in which the precise meaning of *homines* is tricky) is applied to the corruption of foreign hostages.

8. If this were Juvenal, then *quadam* would modify an understood *satira*, but since Juvenal does not say anything much like this, we presumably should understand that Phosphorus is quoting Alessandro (perhaps *in quadam epistula*), who would be the reference of *eius*.

9. Samarobriva is the ancient name of Amiens and was the capital of one of the Belgic tribes. Batavia is ancient Holland. Probably Phosphorus' ethnic reference is ancient rather than modern—i.e., he has chosen two peoples from the fringes of ancient Roman civilization and means something like "unless bellicose barbarians entertain you." But a more contemporary reference to Burgundy is also possible.

10. After his defeat by Caesar's forces at Pharsalus, Pompey fled to Egypt but was stabbed and beheaded.

LETTER XIII

1. Ancient proverb attributed to Pythagoras. See Erasmus, *Adagia* 1.1.1.

2. See Suetonius, *Life of Terence* 3.

3. See Persius, *Satires* 4.52.

4. Publilius Syrus, *Sententiae* (ed. Meyer) A56: *Amici mores noveris non oderis.*

LETTER XIV

1. According to his *Life*, Aesop was presented for sale after one slave who said he could do "anything" and another who said he could do "everything"; Aesop reported in turn that he could do "nothing," since that was all that was left.

2. Macrobius, *Saturnalia* 3.16.4 (quoting from a lost part of Cicero's *De fato*), where Scipio is warned about inviting too many people to share for dinner the rare catch of an *acipenser*.

3. Phosphorus is alluding to the potential ambiguity produced by Latin indirect discourse here, which puts both subject (you) and object (them) into the same grammatical case.

4. P.'s eventual target in the controversy over imitation of Cicero; see Letters 8.16 and 17.

LETTER XV

1. Vergil, *Aeneid* 6.103–4. *Facies* here means "form" or "kind," but P. intends a second layer of meaning: there are no new "faces" among his detractors.

2. Horace, *Ars Poetica* 50, discussing neologism; "belted Cethegi" stand for "men of old."

3. In the midst of apparent modesty, P. is baiting his critics: *sciolus* ("smatterer," diminutive of *scius*) is extremely rare in ancient literature (though common in Renaissance invective) and thus might seem a *por-*

tentum, but it is used by no less an authority than Jerome, in his own letters.

4. See Quintilian, *Institutio oratoria* 12.10.69.

5. I.e., his style is overworked. Plutarch, *Life of Demosthenes* 8.3, where, however, the complaint is made by Pytheas.

6. Drawn from Tacitus, *Dialogus de oratoribus* 18 (where, however, the first criticism listed by P. is instead Cicero's about Calvus) and Quintilian, *Institutio oratoria* 12.10.12–14 (though P. garbles the sense of 12.10.14).

7. Adaptation of Ovid, *Remedia amoris* 389–91.

Letter xvii

1. Humanist who corresponded with scholars and monarchs throughout Europe. P. met her while in Venice with Pico in the summer of 1491. For an extended discussion of this letter (and of other correspondence between P. and Fedele), see Lisa Jardine, "*O Decus Italiae Virgo*, or the Myth of the Learned Lady in the Renaissance," *The Historical Journal* 28.4 (1985): pp. 799–819.

2. Vergil, *Aeneid* 11.508–9, addressed to the warrior Camilla by Turnus.

3. The Pythia gave Apollo's oracular response at Delphi. Aspasia, mistress of Pericles and teacher of rhetoric, conversed with Socrates, who reports an oration of hers in Plato's *Menexenus*. Socrates names a certain Diotima as the source of his theory of love in Plato's *Symposium*.

4. Poets whose works survive in varying degrees, from a few verses of the riddler Cleobulina to the extensive fragments of Corinna and Sappho. P. had included several of the same names in his *Nutricia*.

5. The erudition of Cornelia was legendary; on her eloquence, as well that of Laelia, see Cicero, *Brutus* 211; on Hortensia's, Valerius Maximus 8.3.3 and Appian, *Civil Wars* 4.32–4.

6. Vergil, *Aeneid* 1.493, of the Amazon queen Penthesilea.

7. See Vergil, *Georgics* 2.488–9.

8. Vergil, *Eclogues* 4.55–7.

LETTER XVIII

1. Political figure and friend of humanists, born in Perugia but active in Milan.

2. I.e., Calderini.

3. The *centurio primi pili* was the senior centurion of a Roman legion; despite the substitution of *homo*, Antiquari's point is probably related to his reference to P. as a *centurio* at the letter's end: P. attacks Calderini because he wants his position.

4. Antiquari is referring to ancient representations of Opportunity (*Occasio* in Latin, *Kairos* in Greek) as a youth whose hair fell down over his face but who was bald behind, since one can grab opportunity as it approaches but not once it has passed; see *Disticha Catonis* 2.26 (used as a teaching text in Renaissance grammar classes) and Phaedrus, *Fabulae* 5.8.

5. In other words, having established yourself as the head of a division of one hundred soldiers (a *centuria*, punning on P.'s designation of his hundred-item *Miscellanea* by the same term), you should now advance to a higher rank and thus to a broader command: since *legatus* and *imperator* can designate the commanders of one or more legions (theoretically composed of 1000 soldiers), Antiquari is implying (somewhat playfully) that P.'s sequel should be on a commensurate scale.

6. The mss. add *Milan* before the date.

LETTER XIX

1. Among their duties, the Roman censors placed a mark beside the names of any citizen they considered guilty of immoral conduct; among the legal consequences was the loss of the right to vote. For *censoria virgula*, see Quintilian, *Institutio oratoria* 1.4.3.

2. Juvenal, *Satires* 13.141, where the precise reference of the (probably proverbial) phrase is controversial. Juvenal contrasts his thus-designated addressee with "us common fowl, hatched from ill-starred eggs." Given the phrase *si dis placet*, it seems likely that P., like others, connects the passage in Juvenal to the white hen that gave an omen to Livia, wife of Augustus, the descendents of which were kept as sacred by subsequent emperors.

3. Horace, *Epistulae* 2.1.55ff. Dossennus (line 173, where P. probably read *Dossennius* in place of *sit Dossennus*), "Hunchback," refers to Plautus, not to another poet so-named, though P. was neither the first nor the last to assume otherwise.

4. Gellius, *Noctes Atticae* 12.2.

5. Quintilian, *Institutio oratoria* 10.1.125ff. Black and white pebbles were sometimes used for jurors' votes and to mark lucky and unlucky days on calendars.

6. Ptolemy acknowledges the otherwise unknown Marinus of Tyre as a source of his own *Geography* but criticizes his mistakes (1.6ff.). Strabo frequently observes the errors and superficiality of Eratosthenes. Galen's diatribe against Thessalus is in *On the Therapeutic Method*, 1.4 (ed. Kühn, pp. 252ff.). Cicero's most extended comments on Hermagoras are in *De inventione*, 1.8.

7. The departure about which Plato complains (*Symposium* 180A) regards the relative ages of the lovers Achilles and Patroclus, object of P.'s own attention in *Miscellanea I*, 45. Aeschylus is judged a superior dramatist to his rival Euripides in Aristophanes' comedy *Frogs*.

8. This is P.'s probable meaning, taking *decuriatus* as genitive of *decuriatus, -ûs*, to be understood as synonymous with *decuria* and referring to the official rosters of judges.

LETTER XX

1. Du Bois glosses *vehellas* (spelling it *vehelas*) as *invectivas*; Bade, as *invectiones*. The form suggests a diminutive version of the sort of verbal attack described by the verb *invehere*.

2. *Repungere* here suggests writing; compare *pungere*.

3. The general reference is to Orpheus and his bewitching music; the conjunction of *simulacrum* and *harmonia* plays on the *simul-* of the former (though it actually derives from *simulo*) to suggest assembly; *simulacrum* here is thus the visual counterpart to (oral) harmony.

4. Tristano Calco, recipient of Letters 4.5 and 6.

LETTER XXI

1. Given the following *barbarice*, Antiquari is clearly thinking of Donatus, *Ars maior* 3.1 ("De barbarismo"), where the misspelling of *disciplina* as *displicina* figures among the examples. Antiquari may also intend wordplay in the resemblance of *displicina* to *displicere* ("to displease"): "nuisances rather than sciences."

2. See Letter 2.10.3.

3. Antiquari refers here to the technicalities of ancient Roman voting.

4. The ms. instead gives the date as December 21, 1489.

LETTER XXII

1. Plato, *Phaedrus* 231d.

LETTER XXIII

1. Bernardo Ricci, orator and poet from Messina.

2. Exclaimed by horse-dung to real apples during a flood, in a late addition (expunged by modern editors) to the circulating corpus of fables attributed to Aesop. Poggio Bracciolini presented similar short tales in his *Facetiae*.

LETTER XXIV

1. P. alludes to the motto inscribed over the entrance to the Temple of Apollo at Delphi — *Gnothi seauton*, "Know yourself" — and in particular to its adoption by Socrates, who claimed to know himself to the extent that he was aware of his own ignorance.

2. Aristotle, *Metaphysics* 2.1 993b; P.'s contempt here is probably directed at scholastic Aristotelians.

BOOK IV

LETTER I

1. Famous doctor and astrologer from Spoleto; he was professor of medicine at Pisa and Lorenzo's personal physician. See Letter 4.2.20.

LETTER 11

1. This famous letter receives extended commentary (with, however, characteristic hostility to P.) in Peter Godman, *From Poliziano to Machiavelli: Florentine Humanism in the High Renaissance* (Princeton, 1998), pp. 3–30.

2. Vergil, *Aeneid* 2.10.

3. *Senior*, as Du Bois observes, literally translates the Greek *presbuteros*; he thus assumes that P. uses the term as a loose synonym for "priest." The word may also echo Lorenzo's reference to the priest as the Lord himself, since *Dominus* is *Signore* in Italian. But P.'s first meaning, here and below (*ne seniori suo foret minus obsequens*) is probably the literal one: Lorenzo, despite his position, but in keeping with the humility and politeness emphasized throughout P.'s account, defers to the older man.

4. *Experientissimus* here is usually taken to mean "expert" and *ut quidem visum est* as "or so he seemed"; P.'s meaning would thus be essentially the same here as when, later in the letter, he calls Pier Leoni *excellentissimus* (*ita enim habebatur*) *medicus*. Neither translation, however, is true to the Latin. P. is instead anticipating the following *inexpertum* and means that Lazzaro is "very experimental," i.e., ready to try many possible therapies. Maestro Lazzaro of Pavia was the personal physician of the Duke of Milan.

5. I.e., a lotion, but P.'s use of a Greek term is probably significant to Lorenzo's reaction, since the latter's mirth (*hilare*) may be in part over P.'s word-choice, which he recognizes as much as the mere sound of his voice. P. may even be playing on this with *agnita voce*—i.e., Lorenzo not only recognized P.'s "voice" (*vox*) but also his erudite "word" (also *vox*).

6. This line is often quoted out of context. It is, first and foremost, a joke: Lorenzo wishes that he had lived to see the (impossible) perfection of their library, i.e., forever.

7. Girolamo Savonarola, Dominican preacher whose fiery sermons and calls for reform galvanized an ever-growing following until his execution in 1498.

8. The mss. add, "sanctity."

9. P. presumably means "any Medici."

10. P. is referring, of course, to the famous dome, designed by Filippo Brunelleschi, of Santa Maria del Fiore, Florence's cathedral. For *testudo* as "dome," see Letter 1.16.1.

11. I.e., because the Medici family coat of arms consisted of a shield to which were attached balls.

12. The cage was behind the Palazzo Vecchio (where the street is still called the Via dei Leoni). Since the lion was a symbol of Florence, the incident is here reported as a portent of civil strife in the absence of Medici rule.

13. I.e., like St. Elmo's fire, usually seen at sea. P.'s *Castores* (the phenomenon was associated with Castor and Pollux in antiquity), underscored by the fact that the flames are "twin" (*geminae*), gives the omen a classical ring.

14. There were other reports that Pierleone was thrown down the well by the Medici as punishment for his failure to cure Lorenzo, and in this regard, P.'s *sponte* seems shrill, although, properly speaking, the word is a regular feature of ancient reports of prodigies.

Letter iii

1. Humanist from Faenza of whom little else is known.

2. Otherwise unknown.

3. Cicero uses *Politia* as a Latin transliteration of Πολιτεία ("Republic"), the title of Plato's famous dialogue. Beyond the play on P.'s name (the main point here), Carmento probably means no more than that the *Miscellanea* are P.'s own *magnum opus*.

Letter iv

1. Terence, *Phormio* 267.

Letter v

1. Humanist from Milan.

2. These last two are actually alternate titles for the same work.

3. Cicero, *Philippics* 5.33.

LETTER VI

1. Popular Augustinian preacher with whom Savonarola early competed for an audience; protégé of Lorenzo de' Medici.

2. *Miscellanea,* Preface.

3. *Incisum* and *membrum* are Latin terms for the Greek *comma* and *colon,* the building-blocks of periodic structure in ancient rhetorical theory; *numerus* is the attendant use of rhythmical endings in prose.

4. One ms. specifies *Florence* as the place of composition.

LETTER VII

1. The mss. add "Venetian Patrician and Distinguished Doctor of Philosophy." Pizzamano was particularly known as a scholar of Aquinas.

2. Domenico Grimani, major Venetian humanist and political figure.

3. Echo of Horace, *Satires* 1.3.56.

4. Vergil, *Aeneid* 1.409, of Aeneas and Venus.

5. Celebrated actor of ancient Rome and friend of Cicero, who defended him in the speech *Pro Roscio comoedo.*

6. See Letter 3.11.2, note 57.

7. The expression first appears in Plato, *Phaedo* 89C.

LETTER VIII

1. Florentine whom the Medici employed as a trusted agent and ambasssador.

2. Lorenzo della Volpaia, founder of a dynasty of famous clockmakers and manufacturers of scientific instruments.

3. The following tentative translation has been aided by a modern reconstruction of Lorenzo della Volpaia's 1510 planetary clock by Alberto Gorla, Giuseppe Brusa, Emmanuel Poulle, and the Istituto Statale D'Arte di Firenze, for the Istituto e Museo di Storia della Scienza in Florence (Inv. 3817).

4. Ovid, *Heroides* 17.130.

LETTER IX

1. P. means the late-antique ms., sometimes called the Vergilius Romanus, that is now Biblioteca Apostolica Vaticana, Vat. lat. 3867.

2. Vergil, *Eclogues* 5.67; 5.79; *Georgics* 2.398–9.

3. Persarmenian eunuch who recaptured and governed Italy for Justinian in the sixth-century AD.

4. Quintilian, *Institutio oratoria* 1.7.5.

5. Vergil, *Eclogues* 2.29; 3.66; 4.36; 5.90; 6.63; 10.35; 10.45.

6. Vergil, *Eclogues* 4.48.

7. Vergil, *Eclogues* 6.18.

8. Like our "carrying coals to Newcastle"; Athena's owl was the symbol of her namesake city.

LETTER X

1. Celebrated in his day for works in Latin, Greek, and Croatian (of which, however, only a single Latin poem survives) and still famous for the villa and garden (with arboretum) he built outside Dubrovnik.

2. Plautus, *Amphitryon* 1–2.

3. One ms. adds, oddly, "1483 and 1484" (perhaps reflecting confusion over a Florentine date?).

LETTER XI

1. Florentine friend of Pico della Mirandola.

LETTER XII

1. Teacher and translator to whom P. dedicated his own translation of Herodian (on which see the following letter).

2. Of Aulus Gellius.

LETTER XIII

1. I.e., P.'s Latin translation of Herodian's *History of the Empire after Marcus*, first published in July of 1493, in Rome.

2. P. means, of course, that he has translated Herodian into Latin, but he employs a Roman legal category (that of *Latinitas* or the *ius Latii*) as a metaphor.

3. A play on the Latin form of his surname, *Magnanimus*.

4. Alessandro Sarti of Bologna was, among other things, partly responsible for the posthumous Aldine edition of P.'s *Opera omnia* in which the *Epistularum libri* appear.

APPENDIX

1. Alessandro Perosa, *Mostra del Poliziano nella Biblioteca Medicea Laurenziana, Manoscritti, libri rari, autografi e documenti* (Firenze, Sept. 23–Nov. 30, 1954): *Catalogo* (Florence, 1955), p. 181 (no. 267), proposes identifying "Pamphilus" as Panfilo Sasso, poet from Modena.

Bibliography

Branca, Vittore. *Poliziano e l'umanesimo della parola.* Turin, 1983.

Grafton, Anthony. "Angelo Poliziano and the Reorientation of Philology." In *Joseph Scaliger: A Study in the History of Classical Scholarship.* Vol. 1: *Textual Criticism and Exegesis.* Oxford, 1983.

Greene, Thomas M. "Poliziano: The Past Dismembered." In *The Light in Troy: Imitation and Discovery in Renaissance Poetry.* New Haven, 1982.

Greswell, W. Parr. *Memoirs of Angelus Politianus, Joannes Picus of Mirandola,* 2nd ed. Manchester, 1805. Contains numerous translations from Poliziano's letters.

McLaughlin, Martin L. "The Dispute Between Poliziano and Cortesi." In *Literary Imitation in the Italian Renaissance: The Theory and Practice of Literary Imitation in Italy from Dante to Bembo.* Oxford, 1995.

Mencke, Friedrich Otto. *Historia vitae et in literas meritorum Angeli Politiani.* Leipzig, 1736. A vast compilation of biographical data.

Picotti, Giovanni Battista. "Tra il Poeta ed il Lauro: Pagina della vita in Agnolo Poliziano." *Giornale storico della letteratura italiana,* 65 (1915): 263–303 and 66 (1915): 52–104. Reprinted in Piccotti's *Ricerche umanistiche,* (Florence, 1955).

Pontani, Filippomaria, ed. *Angeli Politiani Liber Epigrammatum graecorum.* Rome, 2002. With a commentary on the poem in 1.7.

Roscoe, William. *Life of Lorenzo de' Medici, Called the Magnificent.* London, 1796. Often reprinted, though eventually in an abridged form. Much of Roscoe's recreation of Poliziano and his circle is based on his correspondence.

Index

꙳ᔕꙮꙴ

Numbers in italics refer to letters written by or to the person listed. Authors appear here only when letters refer to them by name.

Publication of this volume has been made possible by

The Myron and Sheila Gilmore Publication Fund at I Tatti
The Robert Lehman Endowment Fund
The Jean-François Malle Scholarly Programs and Publications Fund
The Andrew W. Mellon Scholarly Publications Fund
The Craig and Barbara Smyth Fund
for Scholarly Programs and Publications
The Lila Wallace–Reader's Digest Endowment Fund
The Malcolm Wiener Fund for Scholarly Programs and Publications